D0075020

PUERTO RICO'S STATEHOOD MOVEMENT

Recent Titles in
Contributions in Political Science
Series Editor: Bernard K. Johnpoll

PUERTO RICO'S STATEHOOD MOVEMENT

Edgardo Meléndez

Contributions in Political Science, Number 220

GREENWOOD PRESS

NEW YORK · WESTPORT, CONNECTICUT · LONDON

Library of Congress Cataloging-in-Publication Data

Meléndez, Edgardo.
  Puerto Rico's statehood movement / Edgardo Meléndez.
    p. cm.—(Contributions in political science, ISSN 0147-1066
  ; no. 220)
    Bibliography: p.
    Includes index.
    ISBN 0-313-26131-8 (lib. bdg. : alk. paper)
    1. Puerto Rico—Politics and government—1898–1952. 2. Puerto
Rico—Politics and government—1952– 3. Statehood (American
politics) 4. Political participation—Puerto Rico. 5. Political
parties—Puerto Rico. I. Title. II. Series.
JL1056.M45 1988
324.27295—dc19   88-10249

British Library Cataloguing in Publication Data is available.

Library of Congress Catalog Card Number: 88-10249
ISBN: 0-313-26131-8
ISSN: 0147-1066

First published in 1988

Greenwood Press, Inc.
88 Post Road West, Westport, Connecticut 06881

Printed in the United States of America

The paper used in this book complies with the
Permanent Paper Standard issued by the National
Information Standards Organization (Z39.48-1984).

10 9 8 7 6 5 4 3 2 1

Copyright Acknowledgments

The author and publisher are grateful to the following for permission
to use previously copyrighted material in this book:

Parts of chapters two and three appeared in "La estadidad como proyecto
historico: Del anexionismo decimonónico al proyecto republicano en
Puerto Rico," *Homines* 8, no. 1 (July 1984 - January 1985).

An earlier version of chapter four appeared in "La crisis del movimiento
anexionista en Puerto Rico, 1924–1952," *Revista de Ciencias Sociales* 26,
no. 1–2 (1987).

An earlier version of chapter five appeared in "The Social Basis of
Postwar Annexationism in Puerto Rico and the Emergence of the New
Progressive Party, 1952–1968," *Homines* 11, no. 1–2 (March 1987–
February 1988).

Contents

Abbreviations

CEREP Centro de Estudios de la Realidad Puertorriqueña—Center for the Study of Puerto Rican Reality

CPE51 Ciudadanos Pro-Estado 51—Citizens for the 51st State

EDA Economic Development Agency

FLT Federación Libre de Trabajadores—Free Federation of Workers

MPI-PSP Movimiento Pro-Independencia–Partido Socialista Puertorriqueño—Pro-Independence Movement-Puerto Rican Socialist Party

PEP Partido Estadista Puertorriqueño—Puerto Rican Statehood Party

PER Partido Estadista Republicano—Republican Statehood Party

PIP Partido Independentista Puertorriqueño—Puerto Rican Independence Party

PNP Partido Nuevo Progresista—New Progressive Party

PPD Partido Popular Democrático—Popular Democratic Party

PR Partido Republicano—Republican Party

PRP Partido de Renovación Puertorriqueña—Puerto Rican Renovation Party

PS Partido Socialista—Socialist Party

PUR Partido Unión Republicana—Republican Union Party

PURP Partido Unión Republicana Progresista—Progressive Republican Union Party

PURR Partido Unión Republicana Reformista—Reformist Republican Union Party

Sch. Pub. Admin., UPR School of Public Administration, University of
   Puerto Rico

SPR-PRC Sección Puerto Rico–Partido Revolucionario Cubano—Section Puerto
   Rico–Cuban Revolutionary Party

Acknowledgments

Like many other books these days, this one began as a dissertation thesis. My greatest debt goes to Irving L. Markovitz and Frank Bonilla, who read the somewhat long and hard-to-read text (the first draft was presented in a terrible dot-matrix print) with extreme patience and understanding; their comments were always a positive contribution to this study. Larry Goldbaum did the initial editing, a great task by any account. Several other people read parts of the manuscript and provided critical and very helpful comments. I am extremely grateful to Edwin Meléndez, Aaron G. Ramos, Jim Gerassi, Pedro Cabán, A. G. Quintero-Rivera, Félix Ojeda, Milton Pabón, Arturo Torrecilla, Rogelio Escudero, and Jorge Benítez, among others, for their comments. The people of the *Colección Puertorriqueña* of the University of Puerto Rico General Library, where most of the research was done, were extremely cooperative with my work, particularly Ms. Myriam Felicié. This study would not have been possible without the moral and material support given to me by Ligia Vélez and Edwin Meléndez, Sr., my parents. To them, and to Patricia Cristina Meléndez, my dearest daughter, who had to stand my many hours of work, this book is dedicated.

PUERTO RICO'S STATEHOOD MOVEMENT

CHAPTER ONE

Introduction

Creemos que la sutil ruta surcada en los mares de nuestra política insular por la idea anexionista no ha sido estudiada con suficiente rigor histórico. Unos cuantos fetiches bien intencionados, otros cuantos mitos profundamente sentidos, y algunas vanidades simpáticamente aplaudidas han hecho perder de vista algunos aspectos importantes de la historia de esa idea, que solo ha sido considerada como ruta preconcebida del imperialista astuto.
— Antonio Rivera, *El Laborantismo* (1943)

[I believe that the subtle route ploughed in the seas of our insular politics by the annexationist idea has not been studied with sufficient historical rigor. Several well-minded fetiches, several other profoundly held myths, and some sympathetically applauded vanities have made us lose sight of some important aspects of the history of this idea that has been considered as a preconceived path only by the astute imperialist. (author's translation)]

Proannexationist forces in Puerto Rico have increased their electoral strength since the creation of the Commonwealth in the early 1950s. Moreover, the demand for making the island the fifty-first state of the United States has gained wider acceptance; a pro-statehood party, the *Partido Neuvo* Progresista (PNP— New Progressive Party) gained control of the government in 1968, 1976, and

1980. This book will evaluate the statehood movement in Puerto Rico, the social forces that historically have conformed its politics, and the nature of its program.

HISTORICAL BACKGROUND

Since the latter part of the nineteenth century, when the island was under Spanish domination, some sectors in Puerto Rico have sought the annexation of the island to the United States. The principal advocates of annexation were found among those groups seeking independence and autonomy from Spain. Under the presence of the United States, the annexationist forces organized the Republican Party, the most important expression of pro-statehood sentiment in the first six decades of this century. The Republican Party was active in the government from 1900 to 1904, but was later overshadowed by the Union Party. In 1924 the most conservative sectors within the Republican and the Union parties formed an electoral alliance known as the Alianza (Alliance), winning the elections that year and again in 1928. In 1932 the Republican factions were united once again in the Republican Union Party; together they joined the Socialist Party in forming the Coalición, an electoral coalition that won the elections in 1932 and 1936. However, in the 1940s the Republicans lost electoral support as the emergent Popular Democratic Party (PPD) gained dominance of Puerto Rican politics. In the 1950s the Partido Estadista Republicano (PER—Republican Statehood Party) became the main opposition party to the PPD, with increasing support. In 1968 the PNP won the elections, becoming the first statehood party to win a majority of votes. Since the victory of the PNP in 1968, and increasingly since 1976, the statehood movement has become a major political force in the island, and statehood has become a crucial issue in the relations between Puerto Rico and the United States.

There are several important distinctions between the contemporary statehood movement and that movement prior to the creation of the PNP that must be made to understand the historical significance of recent developments. First, in contrast to past statehood organizations, under the PNP the statehood movement has become a mass movement with a broad, multiclass basis of support. The Republican Party, in the first decades of this century, was representative of the commercial, financial, and sugar-producing sectors of the local bourgeoisie. The middle classes also supported it; and up to 1915, when the Socialist Party was formed, it received the support of a sector of the working class that favored annexation. But the creation of the Socialist Party divided the support for annexation along class lines, and even under the Coalition, statehood could not become a viable political alternative. On the contrary, the PNP has drawn its support from different social groups and classes, making it a strong and viable political movement.

Second, the statehood movement has evolved from an ideologically conservative, socially pro–status quo position to a more "reformist," even neo-

"populist" one. During the first decades of the 1900s, the statehood issue was given an idealistic aura by its middle-class leadership, who tried to adapt Puerto Rican institutions and values to the more "advanced" American ones. But the crisis of the sugar industry and the rise of the PPD in the 1940s augmented the influence and control of the sugar bourgeoisie over the movement and its ideology, giving it a conservative, if not reactionary, character. The success of the PNP signifies the rise to dominance in the movement of an industrial bourgeoisie in alliance with new middle classes. In order to broaden the basis of support for statehood, they have presented a program and ideology more tuned to the interests of other classes and groups and stripping the statehood issue of the conservative guise it acquired during the 1940s and 1950s.

Finally, the contemporary statehood movement is led by a more dynamic leadership whose program calls for achieving statehood in the short run; in previous decades, statehood was seen as a goal to be achieved only in the long run. The political program of the PNP under Carlos Romero Barceló is that of *estadidad ahora* (statehood now). The emergence of this "immediatist" statehood program has to be understood within the framework of the recent changes in the economic and political structures in Puerto Rico, mainly the process of further economic and political integration of the island to the United States after the 1950s. Furthermore, after the 1970s some sectors within the U.S. government and society believed statehood to be an "alternative" to solve the "Puerto Rican problem."

EXPLAINING THE STATEHOOD MOVEMENT

The statehood movement is one of the most important phenomena in the political history of twentieth-century Puerto Rico. It has been also, until recently, one of the least studied phenomena, despite the fact that a pro-statehood party has been so crucial in Puerto Rican politics for the past two decades. The statehood movement was generally studied as part of a historical-political narrative (mostly centered on the issue of political status), within the framework of political development, or simply as educational propaganda.[1] These studies treat the statehood movement superficially, focusing on mere fragments of its program and ideology, its leadership, and its political maneuvers. It is only recently that the statehood movement has been studied from a broader historical and social scientific perspective.[2]

Out of the studies that have dealt with this subject we can extract several explanatory approaches. One of the most accepted explanations sees the contemporary statehood movement resulting from the "modernization" of Puerto Rico and the growth of the middle class. As argued by Henry Wells, this middle class, "strongly committed to the attainment of possessions, comfort and convenience, economic and physical security, quality education, and other modern welfare values," has emerged as a consequence of the modernization program implemented under the Commonwealth by the PPD. According to Wells, the middle class has turned against the PPD and its Commonwealth status because there "seemed to be a feeling on their part that they were more likely to accumulate welfare values under statehood than under Commonwealth status."[3]

Like that explanation, but more explicit in its argument, is the approach that sees the statehood movement as a movement of a middle class assimilated to American culture and without any sense of national identity. Under such analysis, it is argued that the absence of a national identity is the result of cultural imperialism and the lack of a national bourgeoisie. The contemporary statehood movement becomes predominantly a cultural phenomenon, largely determined by the assimilation of Puerto Ricans, particularly by the economic elites. As has been stated, "annexation to the colonial power will not be the cause of Puerto Rican assimilation but one of its own effects."[4]

Another explanation relates the statehood movement to the politics of social classes and their conflicts. In his examination of class politics in twentieth-century Puerto Rico, A. G. Quintero-Rivera sees the Republican Party as a representative of the "intermediary petty bourgeoisie and an emergent anti-national bourgeoisie." He states that the "anti-national" bourgeoisie comprises intermediaries for American capital (managers, partners), sugar plantation owners, and commercial sectors linked to American interests; the petty bourgeoisie, mostly its professional ranks, wanted the modernization of Puerto Rico to follow the American model. With regard to the contemporary statehood movement, Quintero-Rivera characterizes it as the political movement of the "new middlemen" of American capital in Puerto Rico. According to his argument, from the kind of industrialization that Puerto Rico experienced and from the penetration and dominant position of American capital in the economy there has emerged a sector linked to American capital (the new middlemen) that sees statehood as being in its best interest.[5] At the same time, as the program of industrialization became capital intensive in the 1960s, an urban sector of economically marginal population emerged; this population has been attracted to statehood either because of the lack of attention given to them by the PPD or because of the welfare benefits given to them by the U.S. government and considered to be secure only in statehood. According to this argument, support from this sector comes in the form either of a "protest vote" against the PPD or from the opportunistic political behavior of the urban marginals.[6]

Another analysis within this framework is that presented by Aarón G. Ramos.[7] Ramos divides the evolution of annexationism in twentieth-century Puerto Rico into two major periods: the old Republican annexationist politics from the beginning of the century to the forties, and the new brand that emerged in the post–World War II period. Ramos further divides the first historical period into two phases. In the first one, characterized by José Celso Barbosa's idealistic and popular brand of annexationism, sectors of the bourgeoisie and the middle classes joined to present a program of capitalist transformation and republican ideals. The second phase, opened by Barbosa's death in 1921, inaugurated a period of political realism in which, under the conservative leadership of the sugar bourgeoisie and facing strong opposition to statehood in the metropolis, the Republicans argued for a gradualist strategy for annexation. The modern statehood movement also is characterized by two major phases: a transitional period represented by the PER, and the ascendancy of the populist politics of the PNP. The PER's politics were characterized by the struggle between the old conservative Republican leadership and the new groups produced by post-war capitalism—the industrial elite and the new middle classes, who espoused a more reformist and "populist" brand of politics. Under the leadership of the industrial bourgeoisie, the PNP presented a program for annexation based on a "consensus capitalism" linking the interests of the popular masses to those of the industrial elite. Under the leadership of Carlos Romero Barceló, the annexationist program acquired a populist tone; statehood became defined as the resolution of social inequality in the island by integration to the American welfare state as another minority ethnic group struggling for equality within the federation.

Another approach in explaining the statehood movement is that of "class/economy integration," argued by Frank Bonilla and Ricardo Campos. According to Bonilla and Campos, the industrialization of Puerto Rico after the 1950s has propelled the integration of the island's economy to the United States, turning it into an "enclave or regional economy of the American economy." Bonilla and Campos have argued that the regional character of the Puerto Rican economy was based on the determination of the prices of capital, labor, and commodities by the market mechanisms and political structure of the United States. Along with the process of economic integration there has been a process of absorption of the "local class formations . . . within the larger U.S. system of class relations."[8] This includes the absorption of the Puerto Rican bourgeoisie into the U.S. bourgeoisie, with the concomitant consequences in terms of economic organization and class interests. Bonilla and Campos argue that the differences between the Puerto Rican bourgeoisie and sectors of U.S. capital "take the form of intra-class conflict. . . . Their organization and movement is not that of a social class with its own interests; their interests respond to the reproduction of the mode of production as a whole. For this reason, the Puerto Rican capitalists merely tag along as an overseas appendage of the U.S. bourgeoisie." They conclude that as a result of this economic integration and social absorption, the Puerto Rican bourgeoisie supports statehood.[9] In more recent articles, Bonilla and Campos have used the theory of circuit flows of capital, labor, and commodities between the United States and Puerto Rico to explain the integration of Puerto Rico to the U.S. economy. This leads to a reassessment of the Puerto Rican bourgeoisie and its relation to the question of annexation: "The Puerto Rican business class, unequally allied in a network of interests with their U.S. counterparts, steadfastly opposes independence. Faced with the sharpening economic and social crisis of recent decades, this sector increasingly views annexation as the path to economic salvation.''[10]

STATEHOOD AND THE MIDDLE CLASS

As a point of departure for this book, some comments are required regarding these explanatory approaches. First of all, I disagree with the proposition that the contemporary statehood movement is merely an urban, middle-class movement, in terms of either its social basis or its ideology. As stated earlier, one of the main characteristics of the contemporary statehood movement is its multiclass basis of support. Studies of the 1968 elections have shown that support for the PNP was neither all middle class nor all urban. According to one statistical study of the metropolitan area of San Juan, the lowest level of support for the PNP came from the ''middle socio-economic sectors,'' while most of the support for the party in this area came from the ''upper'' and ''lower and middle lower socio-economic groups.''[11] In another study of that election it was found that even though the electoral support for the PNP was mainly urban, the rural areas followed the pattern of increased support for the party.[12]

Also, the notion that the statehood movement is a middle-class phenomenon does not take into account the ideological changes that have taken place within the movement and fails to explain its historical evolution. Statehood in Puerto Rico has always been supported by the middle classes; but it has also been supported by the bourgeoisie. And during the 1940s and 1950s, when the politics and ideology of statehood were dominated by the sugar bourgeoisie, the movement's program and ideology were far from representing the ''modern welfare values'' that Wells argues for; they were in fact closer to a reactionary position in the true sense of the word (defending past values and realities). The change in the program and ideology from the PER of the 1950s and early 1960s to the PNP after 1967 was due not only to the rise of a ''new'' middle class but also to the preponderant position achieved in the movement by the local industrial bourgeoisie, as exemplified by Luis Ferré. In fact, it was Ferré and his group who headed the transition from the reactionary PER to the PNP, and this change was in no way related to the search for ''modern welfare values'' by the middle class but rather to social and political conflicts in Puerto Rico at the time. Furthermore, this notion makes no account of the support given by sectors of the working class and marginals to statehood throughout the century; and it has been these sectors more than the middle classes that have seen in statehood the basis for the attainment of modern welfare values through the presence of the American state in Puerto Rico.

STATEHOOD AND NATIONAL IDENTITY

Even when we agree that the issue of national identity is a factor to be considered in explaining the statehood movement, it is necessary to include in such analysis the economic and political structures that have influenced its development. To regard the statehood movement as a derivation of a cultural phenomenon (assimilation), in isolation of other factors, detracts from our ability to understand it. Furthermore, this notion of the contemporary statehood movement as responding to the assimilation of the population may be misleading; for example, the ideology of the movement has backed down from making cultural assimilation a prerequisite for statehood: hence the development of the concept of *estadidad jíbara* (Creole statehood). The notion that Puerto Ricans could maintain and secure their identity and culture under statehood was developed during the 1930s and 1940s. Since then no major political or ideological figure within the movement has posited cultural assimilation as a prerequisite for the attainment of statehood. Assimilation was an issue during the first decades of U.S. domination in Puerto Rico. The defense of cultural assimilation, as proposed early in the century by the Republicans, was seen as a mechanism to further the economic, social, and political integration of Puerto Rico to the United States. But even then the Republican Party could espouse the concept of *la patria regional* (the regional fatherland), based on the notion of "independence within the federation," which was to provide the local dominant classes power over local cultural affairs as well as local political and economic structures.

The issue of national identity should be studied in relation to its economic, social, and political contents and consequences. In Puerto Rico, politics has always been status politics, and this means that different social classes and groups put forward different economic, social, and political programs around this issue; this in turn provides for different interpretations of what is national identity.[13] To try to understand statehood as the politics of cultural assimilation (or independence as the politics of national identity) is to misunderstand the issue completely. Assimilation has not been the policy of statehooders since the 1930s, and it would be wrong to explain the support for statehood in Puerto Rico on the basis of the degree of cultural assimilation of the population. For example, it would be incorrect to argue that the Puerto Rican population has been assimilated during the past two decades, in spite of a very strong annexationist movement. After all, the concept of Creole statehood emerges from the fact that there has been no cultural assimilation of the population; and it even argues that the population's national identity would be protected under statehood. Moreover, if we relate annexationism to assimilation, how do we explain the crisis of annexationism during the 1940s (the "deassimilation" of the population) and its rise during the 1960s (the "reassimilation" of the population)? How do we explain the transformation of nineteenth-century Orthodox Autonomists (who were not annexationists) into the core of the Republican Party after the U.S. invasion? How do we explain the origins of Puerto Rican annexationism at all? Furthermore, how do we explain the coexistence during the 1920s and 1930s of independence side by side with statehood as the major political alternatives in the Republican platform? Finally, how can we explain the use of concepts like "regional fatherland" or "Creole statehood" within statehood programs? Certainly the use of cultural factors to explain the statehood movement in Puerto Rico will not do. The politics and programs of statehood can only be understood by examining how social classes and groups organize themselves to advance their interests; the nature and form of their conflict; and how they are influenced by existing social, economic, and political structures.

STATEHOOD AND SOCIOPOLITICAL CONFLICT

The last assertion introduces us to the third approach to Puerto Rican annexationism, which studies the statehood movement within the framework of social and political conflict between social classes and groups. This approach has provided the best analyses for the understanding of the statehood movement and its historical evolution.[14] Nevertheless, some of its propositions need to be redefined, including the one dealing with the characterization of the Puerto Rican bourgeoisie. For example, it has been argued that during the first decades of this century there was no "national bourgeoisie" in Puerto Rico; also, the bourgeoisie of the same period has been characterized as an "anti-national" bourgeoisie. Likewise, the contemporary local bourgeoisie has been characterized as "dependent-intermediary" or as "new middlemen" of U.S. capital.[15] The general problem posed here is trying to explain the absence of a national state in Puerto Rico; the answer given is that because there is no national bourgeoisie, the Puerto Rican bourgeoisie has always favored annexation. While this may be correct, the characterization of the Puerto Rican bourgeoisie and its relation to annexationism needs to be reassessed.

Some sectors of the Puerto Rican bourgeoisie that are linked directly to American capital favor annexation, but other sectors that are not linked directly to American capital also favor annexation. The Puerto Rican bourgeoisie's support for statehood is not necessarily based on a direct link to U.S. capital; rather, they support statehood because they believe that only the presence of U.S. capital and state in Puerto Rico can assure the preservation of capitalism on the island. That is why the Puerto Rican bourgeoisie has always supported some kind of relationship with the United States, including statehood. Historically, the Puerto Rican bourgeoisie as a whole has been in favor of annexation. But the bourgeoisie's support for statehood is not absolute. As noted before, during the 1920s and 1930s the Republican Party, with the sugar bourgeoisie in a preponderant position in the party, espoused independence as an alternative if statehood was not granted. Furthermore, to say that the Puerto Rican bourgeoisie is "anti-national" or that there is "no national bourgeoisie" may obscure the fact that there is a Puerto Rican or local bourgeoisie, and that it has largely favored annexation. This is precisely the question to answer.

This is the problem facing those characterizations of the contemporary Puerto Rican bourgeoisie as "intermediary" or "new middlemen." For example, the transition from an "anti-national" bourgeoisie to the "new middlemen" (in

Quintero-Rivera's term) is never fully explained. Moreover, the use of these characterizations to explain the bourgeoisie's annexationist postures is limited. Most sectors of American capital in Puerto Rico are there because of the benefits they receive from the Commonwealth, benefits that probably will no longer exist in statehood. Their local representatives (the new middlemen) probably know that. Furthermore, using the rise of the "intermediary" or "new middlemen" bourgeoisie to explain the contemporary statehood movement fails to provide a complete understanding of their relationship in two ways. First, since the U.S. invasion and the penetration of American capital into Puerto Rico, there have been intermediaries or middlemen for U.S. capital on the island. While the nature of U.S. capital has changed over time, the intermediaries' function has remained the same. So there's really nothing new about middlemen in Puerto Rico. Second, while sectors of these intermediaries have supported statehood in varying degrees, it would be historically inaccurate to cast them as the main social force behind the rise of contemporary annexationism. As will be shown, the main social force behind the formation of the PNP, in terms of leadership and program, came not from the intermediaries but from the local industrial bourgeoisie. Though the role of the intermediaries increased under Romero's leadership of the PNP, the position of this local bourgeoisie is still crucial in understanding contemporary statehood politics.

Another important issue in the study of Puerto Rican annexationism is the increasing support the urban and rural poor have given the statehood party during the past two decades. But it is inadequate to try to understand this support as merely a protest vote against the PPD or as transient opportunistic behavior on their part. Rather, their support stems from the economic constraints imposed on them by the economic instability of the Commonwealth and by their increased dependence on governmental subsidies. Most of these funds come from the federal government, because of the inability of the Commonwealth government to finance itself; so it has been the statehood movement that has attracted the support of these sectors.

STATEHOOD AND INTEGRATION

The study of the annexationist movement would be incomplete without examining how local, social, economic, and political structures, and their continuous process of integration to those structures in the United States, have influenced the political process in Puerto Rico. This has been a major contribution by the class/economy integration approach. But the main concern of this approach is the nature of capitalism in Puerto Rico, rather than Puerto Rican politics per se. This imposes a high level of abstraction on the analysis that requires certain forms of mediation to the concrete study of politics. As Gregor McLennan has argued, "the different levels and modalities of being are accommodated in science at different levels of abstraction . . . long term outcomes must square with more particular mechanisms. These lower-level phenomena (class struggle, politics, historical 'accidents,' individual careers) have conditions of existence that mediate the broader process expressed at a higher level of abstraction."[16] This is related to the issue raised earlier of how to characterize the Puerto Rican bourgeoisie. Broad generalizations about this class as a whole ("anti-national," "intermediaries," "appendages") are inadequate to explain the socioeconomic and political particularities in the development of this class and how they became historically linked to American capital.

Some clarifications are necessary regarding the relationship between integration and annexationism in Puerto Rico. Puerto Rico's integration to the United States cannot explain the whole of annexationism, for example, how it originated; annexationist tendencies preceded the integration to the United States. Proannexationist sentiment flourished as a reaction to Spanish colonialism on the island. Under U.S. hegemony the socioeconomic and political structures undergoing integration to the United States have determined the evolution and development of annexationism. In the same way, integration is not the result merely of abstract structures but of the behavior of social classes and groups organized politically. Both state and economic integration of Puerto Rico to the United States was possible because of the support given to that process by local classes and groups. This is the context, for example, in which to understand the Republican Party of the first decades of this century. Economic integration has varied in form in different periods but it has always been related to the expansion of capitalism in Puerto Rico under the hegemony of U.S. capital. This process has been accompanied by the integration of the colonial government to the American state.

STATE AND POLITICS IN PUERTO RICO

From 1898 to 1952 the island was subject to a direct colonial administration, whereby the metropolitan state directly administered the colony; it also limited the political space available to the local classes. The Commonwealth, on the other hand, although it has not altered the colonial nature of the state structure in Puerto Rico, provided the local dominant groups autonomy for the administration of local affairs. But instead of moving away from the metropolitan state, the colonial state in Puerto Rico has moved further in. Beginning with the formation of the colonial government in 1900 under the Foraker Act, the granting of U.S. citizenship to the Puerto Ricans in 1917, the transfer of federal relief programs to the island during the 1930s, and increasingly after the foundation of the Commonwealth, the institutions of the American state have been extended to the colony. Under the Commonwealth the demarcations between the colonial and the metropolitan state have been increasingly obliterated. At the same time that the Commonwealth provided a power structure within reach of local groups for the administration of the colony, the American state has increased its presence and intervention in the island. But as before, the locus of power remains in the metropolis; this is why local groups are so prone to be involved with the power structures of the metropolis, as colonial power brokers.

It is important to consider the institutional presence of the American state in Puerto Rico. The state is no abstract entity; it comprises apparatuses or institutions that carry out certain tasks required for the maintenance and reproduction of that society and of the state itself. In Puerto Rico the state is represented by the institutions and apparatuses of both the American state and of the colonial state (the Commonwealth since 1952). Economic integration of Puerto Rico has been accompanied by integration of the local state structures to the American state since the beginning of U.S. domination in Puerto Rico.[17] This integration increased after the formation of the Commonwealth, and manifests itself in different forms, such as the increase in federal funds to Puerto Rico after the 1960s. One consequence of this has been the increased ties between the American state and those Puerto Ricans who benefit from these transfers: those who depend on them for subsistence, and those whose jobs or profits depend on federal funds. The contemporary statehood movement is the direct beneficiary of this increased identification of the population with the American state.

Because of the colonial nature of Puerto Rico's political structure, politics in the island have historically revolved around the issue of the political status. In the twentieth century, status politics in Puerto Rico necessarily concerns the presence of the American state on the island. This is nowhere felt more strongly than in the statehood movement, which required the U.S. presence to become a relevant political movement. During the nineteenth century Cuba had a far stronger annexationist tendency than Puerto Rico, in both places linked to the independence movements. But after the Spanish-American War, Cuba's stronger nationalist movement was able to contain Cuban annexationism and obtain independence for Cuba, while Puerto Rico, with a far weaker nationalism, became a U.S. colony and annexationism became an important political movement. The annexationist program and ideology in Puerto Rico have been directly linked to the institutional presence of the American state in the island. During the first two decades of U.S. domination, the statehood program revolved around the issue of the application of the U.S. Constitution to Puerto Rico and the economic, political, and ideological Americanization of the island. After the 1920s the issue became statehood as an alternative to colonialism and the equality of U.S. citizenship for Puerto Ricans. After the 1960s statehood was linked to the transfer of the U.S. welfare structure to Puerto Rico.

The evolution of the statehood movement cannot be understood from the perspective of status politics. If it is true that in one way or another the traditional political forms (autonomy, independence, and annexation) have been at the center of political conflict since the nineteenth century, it is also true that these are political recipients with different contents in different historical periods. The status issue is not an autonomous sphere, unchangeable in time and space. Status politics reflects the debate around the form of the state in Puerto Rico. As such, it represents the alliances and programs of social classes in specific structural and historical conditions. This is what differentiates, for example, the autonomist politics and program of the nineteenth century from those of the PPD in the 1940s or the 1980s. The same applies to the annexationist politics and programs of the twentieth century. These cannot be understood merely as an ideological phenomenon existing independently of social forces. From the idealist annexationism of the nineteenth century, to the Republican project of the early decades of the twentieth century, to the crisis of Republicanism in the forties and the redemptionist and statehood-as-equality programs of the PNP, annexationism in Puerto Rico has reflected the major changes within Puerto Rican society.

This book deals with the evolution of the statehood movement in Puerto Rico, from the nineteenth century to the present. Chapter 2 examines the politics and society of nineteenth-century Puerto Rico and the origins of annexationism during this period. Chapter 3 addresses the organization of the statehood movement under American domination during the first three decades of the twentieth century. Chapter 4 will examine the crisis of Republicanism and the statehood program during the 1930s and 1940s. Chapter 5 deals with the transformation of the statehood movement in the postwar period, from the formation of the Republican Statehood Party in the early 1950s to the creation of the New Progressive Party in 1968. Chapters 6 and 7 deal with the evolution of the PNP, the growth of the statehood movement during this period, and the social forces leading and supporting this movement. Chapter 6 will examine the politics and government of the PNP under Luis Ferré. Chapter 7 analyzes the PNP statehood program and government under Romero Barceló, the PNP rupture of 1984 and the formation of the Partido de Renovación Puertorriqueña, and the aftermath of the 1984 elections.

NOTES

1. The first two categories include the indispensable multivolume work of Reece B. Bothwell, ed., *Puerto Rico: Cien años de lucha política*, 4 vols. (Río Piedras: Editorial Universitaria, 1979); Bolívar Pagán, *Historia de los partidos políticos puertorriqueños*, 2 vols. (San Juan: M. Pareja, 1972); Carmen Ramos de Santiago, *El gobierno de Puerto Rico* (Río Piedras: Editorial Universitaria, 1970); Robert W. Anderson, *Gobierno y partidos políticos en Puerto Rico* (Madrid: Editorial Tecnos, 1970). A strictly partisan view is presented by Wilfredo Figueroa Díaz, *El movimiento estadista en Puerto Rico* (Hato Rey: Editorial Cultural, 1979).

2. Aarón G. Ramos, "The Development of Annexationist Politics in Twentieth Century Puerto Rico," in Adalberto López, ed., *The Puerto Ricans* (Cambridge, Mass.: Schenkman, 1980), pp. 257–72; Ilya Villar Martínez y Haroldo Dilla Alfonso, "Las tendencias anexionistas en el proceso político puertorriqueño," *El Caribe Contemporáneo* no. 6 (June 1982), pp.70–91; Luis Martínez Fernández, *El Partido Nuevo Progresista* (Río Piedras: Editorial Edil, 1986); and Mariano Negrón Portillo, "El liderato anexionista antes y después del cambio de soberanía," *Revista del Colegio de Abogados de Puerto Rico* (October 1972), pp. 369–91.

3. Henry Wells, *The Modernization of Puerto Rico* (Cambridge: Harvard University Press, 1969), p. 333. Also within this approach are: Gordon Lewis, *Puerto Rico: Power and Freedom in the Caribbean* (New York: Monthly Review Press, 1974), p. 344; and Kenneth Farr, *Personalism and Party Politics: Institutionalization of the Popular Democratic Party of Puerto Rico* (Hato Rey: Inter-American University Press, 1973), p. 90.

4. Manuel Maldonado-Denis, *Puerto Rico: A Socio-Historic Interpretation* (New York: Vintage, 1972), p. 229. See also Pedro Juan Rúa, *Bolívar ante Marx y otros ensayos* (Río Piedras: Ediciones Huracán, 1978), pp. 83–85.

5. A. G. Quintero-Rivera, *Conflictos de clase y política en Puerto Rico* (Río Piedras: Ediciones Huracán, 1976), pp. 71, 137–38. Manuel Maldonado-Denis, in his *Hacia una interpretación marxista de la historia de Puerto Rico y otros ensayos* (Río Piedras: Editorial Antillana, 1977), p. 51, uses the term "intermediary bourgeoisie" to denote this relationship.

6. Quintero-Rivera, *Conflictos;* Rafael Ramírez, *El arrabal y la política* (Río Piedras: Editorial Universitaria, 1977), pp. 28, 153; and Ramos, "The Development of Annexationist Politics," p. 268.

7. Ramos, "The Development of Annexationist Politics;" "La revista 'El Estado' en la historia del anexionismo puertorriqueño, 1945–1960," *Revista de Historia* 1, no. 2 (July–Dec. 1985), pp. 215–21; and his introduction to Aarón G. Ramos, ed., *Las ideas anexionistas en Puerto Rico bajo la dominación norteamericana* (Río Piedras: Ediciones Huracán, 1987), pp. 11–53. A good analysis of the evolution of the annexationist movement is also given by Villar Martínez and Dilla Alfonso, "Las tendencias anexionistas."

8. Ricardo Campos and Frank Bonilla, "Bootstraps and Enterprise Zones: The Underside of Late Capitalism," paper delivered at the XIV Latin American Congress of Sociology, held in San Juan, October 5–12, 1981, p. 5; Frank Bonilla, "Clase y nación: Elementos para una discusión," in Rafael Ramírez and Wenceslao Serra-Deliz, eds. *Crisis y crítica en las Ciencias Sociales en Puerto Rico* (Río Piedras: Centro de Investigaciones Sociales, 1980), p. 165; Centro de Estudios Puertorriqueños, History Task Force, *Labor Migration Under Capitalism: The Puerto Rican Experience* (New York: Monthly Review Press, 1979), pp. 128, 141.

9. Ricardo Campos and Frank Bonilla, "Industrialization and Migration: Some Effects on the Puerto Rican Working Class," *Latin American Perspectives*, 3, no. 3 (Summer 1976), p. 68; Bonilla, "Clase y nación," p. 166–67; Frank Bonilla and Ricardo Campos, "A Wealth of Poor: Puerto Ricans in the New Economic Order," *Daedalus* 110, no. 2 (Spring 1981), p. 167.

10. Bonilla and Campos, "A Wealth of Poor," p. 167.

11. Marcia Quintero, *Elecciones de 1968 en Puerto Rico: Análisis estadístico por grupos socio-económicos* (San Juan: CEREP, 1972), p. 39.

12. Luis E. Agrait, "Las elecciones de 1968 en Puerto Rico," *Revista de Ciencias Sociales* 16, no. 1 (March 1972), p. 41.

13. Arcadio Díaz Quiñones, "Introducción," in A. G. Quintero-Rivera et al., *Puerto Rico: Identidad nacional y clases sociales* (Río Piedras: Editorial Huracán, 1979), p. 10.

14. This includes the works of Quintero-Rivera, Ramos, Campos and Bonilla, Negrón Portillo, Villar Martínez and Dilla Alfonso, and Maldonado-Denis, all previously cited. Also, Wilfredo Mattos Cintrón, *La política y lo político en Puerto Rico* (Mexico City, Mexico: Serie Popular Era, 1980).

15. Maldonado-Denis, *A Socio-Historic Interpretation*, pp. 79, 177; and also, *Hacia una interpretación*, p. 51; Quintero-Rivera, *Conflictos*, pp. 61–62, 138.

16. Gregor McLennan, *Marxism and the Methodologies of History* (London: Verso, 1981), pp. 64, 43–44.

17. Kelvin Santiago, "Algunos aspectos de la integración de Puerto Rico al interior del Estado metropolitano: los orígenes de la nueva estructura estatal colonial: 1898–1929," *Revista de Ciencias Sociales* 23, nos. 3–4 (July–Dec. 1981), pp. 292–346; Miriam Muñiz Varela, "Análisis del capital monopólico azucarero y el papel del Estado en el proceso de transición al capitalismo en Puerto Rico: 1898–1920," Revista de Ciencias Sociales 23, nos. 3–4 (July–Dec. 1981), pp. 443–94.

CHAPTER TWO

Annexationism in Nineteenth-Century Puerto Rico

Annexationist tendencies in nineteenth-century Puerto Rico were a reaction to the existing economic and political structures and the social conflicts prevailing under the Spanish regime. The social basis of nineteenth-century annexationism is found in those (predominantly Creole) sectors that were most affected by the Spanish regime: the sugar planters, some coffee *hacendados,* the professional and commercial petty bourgeoisie. The development of these sectors was limited by the barriers imposed by Spanish colonialism: a monopoly on trade and banking, the retarded social and economic development of the island, and restrictions on the political participation of Creoles.

The central proposition of this chapter is that support for the annexation of Puerto Rico to the United States emerged after the mid–nineteenth century as a nonorganized political tendency within the two political movements that represented the Creoles—liberal autonomism and separatism. The former sought a liberal regime within an autonomist framework under Spain, while the latter demanded total independence. The alliance between the sugar bourgeoisie and the petty bourgeoisie, who dominated the Republican Party during the first three decades of the twentieth century, dates back to the latter part of the nineteenth-century.

Nineteenth-century proannexationist sectors represent more than opposition to the Spanish regime in Puerto Rico. They played a critical role in the implantation of the American regime in the island: they were a vital source of support for the new socioeconomic and political structures of the new American regime.

POLITICS AND SOCIETY IN NINETEENTH-CENTURY PUERTO RICO

The state structure during the nineteenth century was characterized by the control of all colonial affairs by the metropolitan state, the monopoly of government jobs by Spaniards, and the Creole elite's lack of power and participation in the political and economic affairs of the island. The Spanish policy of political and economic exclusivism prevented Creoles' access to the government and politics while it monopolized the mechanism of trade to assure the maximum appropriation of the agricultural surplus.[1] Toward the last third of the century the Creole elite began more actively to demand participation in the economic and political decision making of the colony, while the more radical sector attempted a rebellion against the metropolis (the *Grito de Lares* in 1868). Spanish policies to foment agricultural production in the island made it possible for the hacienda to become the main social and economic unit by the latter part of the century. Through this policy the metropolitan state sought to make the colony profitable by taxing the island's increasing agricultural exports.[2]

For most of the century the colonial government safeguarded the conditions for the reproduction of the hacienda. But after the 1870s the growth of the hacienda and of the hacendado class came into conflict with Spain's colonial regime in Puerto Rico. The metropolitan state maintained a mercantilist policy that limited the growth of the hacienda and trade by the Creoles, while favoring the Spanish commercial interests in Spain and Puerto Rico. The growth of agricultural production during this period brought to the fore the conflicts between the Creole hacendados and merchants and the metropolitan state. During the early 1870s the hacendados' "ties of dependency" to the metropolitan state were broken. After 1873, with the abolition of slavery and the termination of the workbook system, the hacendados were forced to stop relying on the colonial state as their guarantor of labor. The colonial state used to guarantee the hacienda's labor needs through land expropriation from peasants, vagrancy laws, the workbook regime (where labor was regulated through the use of a workbook), and the enforcement of slavery. After 1873 the hacendados had to satisfy their labor needs mostly through their own means, mainly through the *agregado* system (sharecropping), increased indebtedness of laborers to the hacienda, and wage labor.[3] The increased opposition to the colonial structures by the Creoles and the demise of the Spanish empire, under heavy attack in Cuba, led to a series of reforms in the late nineteenth century that ended in the Autonomist government of 1897, formed months before the U.S. invasion of July 1898.

Political conflict during the late nineteenth century was largely determined by the conflicts between the Creole elite (hacendados and merchants) and big merchants (mostly Spaniards). The latter controlled not only the island's trade but credit and finance as well, a privileged status that was protected by the colonial state. A great number of hacendados and medium and small merchants went into heavy debt and bankruptcy due to this situation.[4] Those that depended on the permanence of the metropolitan state to maintain their privileged positions supported the conservative pro-Spanish parties, while those mostly affected by the Spanish regime supported the Liberal/Autonomist parties or separatism. The merchants, the government officials, and all those that benefited from the colonial regime in Puerto Rico supported the Inconditional parties. The Creoles were grouped first around the Liberal Reformist Party, founded in 1870, and later in the Autonomist Party, formed in 1887. These parties responded to the basic demands of the Creole groups: free trade, a liberal regime, self-government, credit, and access to modern technology.[5]

The main Creole political movement during the last three decades of the nineteenth century was liberal, reformist, and autonomist. Liberalism provided the ideological tools against Spanish absolutism in Puerto Rico. Its economic and political objectives were decentralizing reforms of the Spanish regime in Puerto Rico and not total separation from Spain. Autonomism was a political movement led by and representing the interests of the Creole hacendado class. The major demands of this political movement were the economic defense of the Creoles and of the hacendados particularly, free trade, mainly with the United States, political autonomy, and control over the bureaucratic apparatus of the island. The political movement of the Creoles in the late nineteenth century was determined by the configuration of its main social sector, the hacendados. Their rally behind reformism and autonomy, staying away from radical alternatives like independence, has to be explained on the basis of their structural weakness as a class.[6] This is important to understand not only the political movement of this period but also of the socioeconomic and political evolution of the island after the American invasion. This structural weakness underlies the facile and rapid consolidation of a capitalist economy dominated by American capital in alliance with sectors of the Creole proprietary class and the petty bourgeoisie.

THE POLITICAL BASIS OF NINETEENTH-CENTURY ANNEXATIONISM

Any reference to nineteenth-century annexationism in Puerto Rico has to treat the phenomenon as merely a political tendency; there are no clear indications that it existed as an organized political movement during that period. There is evidence of proannexationist inclinations within the political movements opposing the Spanish regime, namely, the liberal/autonomist and separatist movements of the nineteenth century.

Puerto Rican liberalism was a historical source of annexationist tendencies. As a reaction to Spanish absolutism in Puerto Rico, liberalism represented the political aspirations of the Creole elite. The liberal alternative to Spanish absolutism was incarnated in the great "Colossus of the North." Liberal, economically strong, and expansive, the United States became the political model of the Puerto Rican liberals. This attraction to American liberalism by Creole sectors fueled proannexationist sentiments throughout the period.[7]

But the United States was also an example to the Creole elite of a great industrial power, which Spain would never be. Agricultural producers wanted to penetrate its immense market; merchants desired its innumerable manufactured commodities; landowners and business people wanted its aggressive capital. Studies about the local perception of the United States during the period show the great admiration that the Creoles felt toward the economic system of that country.[8]

This admiration of the American economic system was related to the economic relations between the Spanish colony and its powerful northern neighbor. When the United States invaded the island, commercial and financial relations between them had been going for more than a century. Commercial contacts between the United States and Puerto Rico go back to the colonial days and increased through contraband as the American economy grew. Once economic relations between Puerto Rico and other countries were legalized at the beginning of the nineteenth century, the United States achieved a privileged position; by 1830 it was the island's major source of imports (with 27.2 percent) and market for exports (with 49 percent).[9] Spain replaced the United States through the imposition of tariffs, but the latter remained among Puerto Rico's major trade partners. The United States was the major buyer of Puerto Rican sugar by the end of the century. Since the predominance of commercial agriculture prevented the cultivation of staples, and its low industrial capacity did not allow the production of manufactured goods, and since Spain lacked the capacity to satisfy the demands of its market, Puerto Rico needed to trade with other, more advanced industrial economies, including the United States. Toward the end of the nineteenth century Puerto Rico was buying a fourth of its imports from the United States, including machinery, manufactured goods, and foodstuffs like wheat and beef.[10] These commercial relations strengthened the ties between some Creoles and the United States, particularly those with commercial houses or products linked to American trade.

ANNEXATIONIST TENDENCIES

The admiration for the United States' political and economic system was felt in the island's politics. A letter from José P. Morales to José Julián Acosta, then leader of the Liberal Party, outlined the division within the party between the admirers of "the Latin race" and "the followers of the protestant propaganda and admirers of the North American civilization."[11] In 1891 Luis Muñoz Rivera, then Autonomist leader, proposed annexation to the United States as one of the alternatives available to Puerto Rican autonomists.[12] Nevertheless, it is hard to speculate on the nature of the annexationist tendencies within the liberal/autonomist movement since there is hardly any documentation of such phenomena.

There are references to the existence of a so-called annexationist party, but its evolution and destiny are unknown. One such reference is given by Pilar Barbosa in her study of nineteenth-century autonomism. A Juan R. Ramos declared in a letter that his father's "sympathy for the Northern States led him to affiliate to the annexationist party, which was the only one here that was fighting Spanish domination."[13] Ramón Emeterio Betances, the most outstanding figure of the nineteenth-century separatism movement, also referred to this "annexationist party," arguing that "during the first days of the [1868] insurrection, there existed in Cuba and Puerto Rico a party that wanted to annex the islands to the United States of America." The letters of Betances are full of important references to the Cuban and Puerto Rican annexationists and their political role throughout the century.[14]

Another reference to the annexationist party was given by the U.S. consul in Puerto Rico. In 1867 he acknowledged the existence of an independence party and "another party, much more considerable, anxious for a republican government, but with annexation to the United States or under its protection without slavery."[15] Nevertheless, the whereabouts of this annexationist party are not known after 1868. It has been noted that revolutionary clubs of annexationist tendencies participated in the organization of the 1868 Lares rebellion. The Spanish governor at the time complained that in May of 1868 a number of confiscated pamphlets demanded the annexation of Puerto Rico to the United States.[16] According to the U.S. consul, the annexationist clubs participating in the organization of the Lares rebellion decided to retire from the attempt because the conspirators could not agree on the final political form of the would-be republic—independence or annexation to the United States. The consul argued that the withdrawal of the annexationist club was one of the elements that led to the failure of the rebellion.[17] These annexationist clubs at the time of the Lares rebellion are probably the same or related to the annexationist party discussed earlier. The relationship between the supporters of annexation and the evolving separatist movement during the nineteenth century needs to be studied further. The most clear manifestation of this phenomenon is found, nevertheless, in the Section Puerto Rico of the Cuban Revolutionary Party.

THE SECCIÓN PUERTO RICO—PARTIDO REVOLUCIONARIO CUBANO

The Sección Puerto Rico–Partido Revolucionario Cubano (SPR-PRC) was formed in December of 1895 in New York City by a group of Puerto Ricans, most of them exiles. Its aim was realizing one of the objectives of the PRC: that of "auxiliar of the independence of Puerto Rico."[18] The relationship between the Section Puerto Rico and the PRC leadership was very close, even though the Section had wide autonomy over its organizational duties and actions. The leadership of the SPR "was mainly made up of educated persons or of those who had lived for a long time in the United States, and that had internalized the ways of life of this society, particularly the Republican concept of government. Some of them had ties to the American and Puerto Rican commercial community. Ties which would become closer after the change of sovereignty."[19] Among its leadership and members were found key figures of the statehood movement after 1898: its president, Julio H. Henna, Roberto H. Todd, Pedro J. Besosa, Félix Matos Bernier, Eduardo Lugo Viña, Manuel del Valle Atiles, Antonio Mattei Lluveras, Mateo Fajardo, and others.

The SPR was internally divided between supporters of independence and those seeking annexation to the United States. The latter had a great influence in the day-to-day affairs of the organization, sometimes being the dominant voice in the SPR's executive council. Nevertheless, they were restricted by PRC statutes and politics from engaging in proannexationist activities within the organization. Betances wrote: "I know that Henna is an annexationist and he has confessed it to me; but I know also that he does not engage in annexationist politics, for he does not have that right."[20] At the time of the invasion, Henna, a U.S. citizen, believed that its government would recognize Puerto Rico's right to self-determination, including that of annexation. Henna's "profound deception at" the United States' outright annexation of the island without consulting its population and the implantation of a colonial regime was a position not fully shared by the majority of the SPR leadership, as Todd's account shows.[21]

Among the actions taken by the PRC involving the SPR was an attempted military invasion to Puerto Rico during 1895–96. The attempt was never carried out due to military difficulties and lack of political support in Puerto Rico.[22]

Among the most significant actions of the SPR was its participation in the organization and activities of the U.S. invasion of Puerto Rico in 1898. The members of the SPR were conspicuous "for their activities leading to facilitate the invasion of the North American forces and, above all, for their collaboration with the latter in the consolidation of their power over the island."[23] At the beginning of the confrontation between Spain and the United States, the SPR contacted the American government and asked to participate in the organization of the invasion. On July 12 the SPR agreed to participate in the invasion and offered a regiment of volunteers to go along with the American troops. They also wrote a *Manifesto* to the people of Puerto Rico asking their support for the U.S. invasion and their collaboration with the American government.[24]

The bay in the town of Guánica was the chosen site for the U.S. invasion. The town, located in the southwest corner of the island, had a very small Spanish military presence, and its bay was appropriate for the entrance of ships and the landing of troops. But a very important reason was also political: the southwest region of Puerto Rico was known "during the last years [as] a refuge and general headquarters of the majority of Puerto Rican separatists."[25] The area was not only strongly separatist, but annexationist as well; many of the annexationist members of the SPR came from there. In 1897 there was a separatist rebellion in the town of Yauco, next to Guánica, where known annexationists had a leading role in the uprising.[26]

According to historian Rosario Natal, the town of Guánica was chosen not only because of its bay and poor defenses but also because of the knowledge that "a good number of the inhabitants of the near towns were dissatisfied with Spain. They were expected to collaborate with the initial operations." He argues, furthermore, that one of the factors explaining the "enchanting and infantile disposition" of the Puerto Ricans in acclaiming the U.S. invasion forces was "the rising wave of annexationist sentiment" in the island.[27] All the way along the southwestern coast, from Guánica to Ponce, the U.S. troops received the support of the local administrative bodies and the population. In Guánica and Yauco, the first two towns to be taken by U.S. troops, the mayors thanked God for the invasion, offered their loyalty to the United States, and proclaimed "Viva Puerto Rico americano."[28] The war in Puerto Rico took only thirteen days and 3,415 men, with the United States controlling at the time of armistice over twenty-three of the island's seventy towns. U.S. troops found no major resistance from the Puerto Rican population and generally received support in all of the towns taken.[29] The Creole elite was conspicuous in their support of the invasion. On July 29, four days after the invasion, the *Casino de Ponce,* an institution of the local elite, held a sumptuous dance in honor of General Miles, commander in chief of the invasion.[30] Puerto Rican annexationists (many of them from the SPR landing with U.S. troops) worked as guides and translators for the advancing U.S. troops and as administrators of the occupied towns. In most occupied towns the American military left them in charge of organizing new local governments.[31]

LA TORRE DEL VIEJO

The continuity of nineteenth-century annexationism and its materialization after the American regime was established in Puerto Rico is found not in any ideological conception, but in the social basis and the political program of the forces that gave life to it. The early twentieth-century Republican Party was formed around a programmatic alliance between the professional and commercial petty bourgeoisie and the local bourgeoisie (particularly its sugar sector). This alliance came into being a decade before the American regime was established in Puerto Rico, within the most radical faction of nineteenth-century Puerto Rican autonomism.

The most common assertion among students of nineteenth-century Puerto Rican politics is that the basis of the Republican Party (and thus of modern annexationism) is found in the Orthodox Autonomist Party, which is correct to a certain extent (we have to remember the existence of the SPR-PRC). But the basis of the Orthodox Party, and of organized annexationism as such, lies farther back, in the year 1887, in a secret society named La Torre del Viejo (The Old Man's Tower). There, for the first time, the representative leadership of what became the axis sectors of the Republican Party were joined in a common political program.

In 1887 the Autonomist Party was formed in the city of Ponce, stronghold of the Creole elite. The year is also known as "the terrible year of 1887," due to the brutal repression that the colonial government and the Spanish Incondicionales unleashed against the Creole population—particularly against the Autonomist Party. The formation of the party was the general cause of the repression; the immediate cause was the actions of a group of anti-Spanish secret clubs that came to be known as La Torre del Viejo.[32] The best historical account by a member of the society is given by José Celso Barbosa. This is no coincidence, for from the most conspicuous members of that society came the leadership of the Orthodox Autonomist Party and later the Republican Party: Barbosa, Gómez Brioso, Matienzo Cintrón, Todd, Ricardo Natal, José Guzmán de Benítez, Julián Blanco Sosa, Pedro del Valle Atiles, Juan Hernández López, and others. Barbosa described the formation and objectives of the society as follows:

> And in that secret but magnanimous and patriotic assembly, the economic problem of the *boricuas* was extensively discussed; and as the only remedy, born of desperation, a vast secret society for the assistance, protection, defense, and progress of the Puerto Ricans was organized and brought to life. . . . The primordial end, the ideal that that secret society aimed for, was the assistance, protection, and mutual defense between the Puerto Ricans for their material and moral progress, in order to safeguard their precarious economic situation, and so that *they could once again be the owners,* even of a small portion, *of the sources of wealth of their land.*[33]

The recuperation of the "sources of wealth" of the country became the basis of this group's political program. If the Autonomist Party gathered around it the majority of the hacendados and the petty bourgeoisie in 1887, a most radical sector gathered around the secret societies and would later on form the Orthodox Autonomist Party.

The secret societies were linked to and nourished from the formation and growth of the Autonomist Party. Its main action was a boycott by their members of Spanish merchants; they were required to trade with Creole establishments only, or to create them where none existed. Cooperatives and associations of mutual aid were formed and no business was to be conducted with establishments that did not employ Creoles. Their merchant members had to buy their merchandise from Creole farmers, who had to sell their products to Creole merchants. The secret society grew dramatically around the island, but particularly in the southern and western areas.[34] The Autonomist Party leadership's position toward it was a difficult one. They could not be opposed to it both because many of its members were party militants and because its economic objective of breaking the commercial monopoly of Spaniards in the island was part of the Autonomist program. On the other hand, the party leadership was not in total agreement with the actions of the society, primarily its violent acts (for example, the burning of Spanish businesses). The Inconditionals and the government linked the society to the Autonomist Party, even when its leadership disowned the society's actions. Increasing popular support for the Autonomist Party and the success of the boycott against Spanish merchants led to a reign of terror against the Creoles in general and the Autonomist leadership in particular.[35]

The most radical sectors of the hacendados and of the commercial and professional petty bourgeoisie, the basis of the Autonomist Party, supported the secret societies and later were grouped around the Orthodox Autonomists. The goal of recapturing the "main sources of wealth" joined these different social classes and groups in a common political program. Hacendados and centralists, merchants and professionals were united in a political bloc whose program was not reform but the total transformation of the existing society. This bloc was formed in 1887 under La Torre del Viejo and was the central axis of the Orthodox Autonomists; their program will take on greater importance in the Republican Party, under the economic and political regime of the United States.

THE SOCIAL BASIS OF NINETEENTH-CENTURY ANNEXATIONISM

Three social groups were notable in their support for annexation to the United States during the last third of the nineteenth century, at least in terms of leadership: the sugar growers, a group of coffee growers in the southwest, and the professional and commercial petty bourgeoisie. The nineteenth-century proannexationist tendency had its deepest roots in the sugar sector of Puerto Rico. The reason for this position is clear: the sugar industry was the island's most hard-pressed economic sector in the last third of the century, and annexation to the United States was seen as the logical solution to their economic woes. During this period three main problems affected the hacendados: the lack of credit to finance their crops, the lack of labor, and Spain's tariff policies. These problems affected differently the two main sectors of the hacendado class, coffee growers and sugar producers, hurting the latter more. For example, when the *central* (sugar mill) emerged in the 1870s as the alternative institution to the crisis-ridden sugar hacienda, it faced tremendous limitations due to lack of credit and labor. The crisis of sugar production deepened at a time when much of the credit available for the sugar industry moved toward coffee production, whose growth began precisely during this period; this also coincided with a pattern of migration from the coast (sugar cane production) toward the interior (coffee area), aggravating thus the labor situation of the sugar industry.[36]

Perhaps the greatest impediment to the development of Puerto Rico's sugar industry was the Spanish tariff structure. While Puerto Rican coffee found in the 1870s a market in Europe (including Spain) and Cuba, to which it had access through the metropolis, it was very different for sugar. Puerto Rican sugar was heavily taxed by Spain to protect its own industry, and the European market was saturated by beet sugar. The natural market for Puerto Rican sugar was the United States, and it was so for most of the century. It was precisely during the most critical period for the sugar industry in Puerto Rico that Spain began a tariff war with the United States; a central issue was the export of Puerto Rican sugar to its northern neighbor. The end result of Spain's tariff policy was the continued prostration of the Puerto Rican sugar industry.[37]

The sugar producers in Puerto Rico believed that their critical situation was caused by Spain's economic and political regime in the island. It is not surprising then that they were the most avid supporters of annexation to the United States. Statements by Ricardo Natal before the Carroll Commission in 1899 exemplify this; according to him, the sugar interests were "the determining point in favor of annexation to the United States," and the possibility of free entrance to the U.S. market "has done much to arouse interest in Porto Rico [sic] in favor of annexation."[38]

Nineteenth-century Puerto Rican annexationism flourished in the southwestern part of the island, centered around the area of Ponce, where sugar production and trade were the important economic activities. It is important to mention the Creole merchants of this area, who maintained trade relations with the United States and whose economic growth was prevented by Spain's limitations on trade.[39] Another proannexationist group of economic importance were coffee hacendados of Corsican descent centered around the town of Yauco. They were part of the small group of coffee hacendados who were able to move into trade and even provide credit to other hacendados. They are best known for their affluence and their modernization of coffee production.[40] They were characterized politically by their liberal creed (heritage of French Republicanism), their firm opposition to the Spanish regime, and their admiration for American Republicanism. Out of this group came the most outstanding annexationists of the period, many of them members of the SPR-PRC; they were also among the organizers of the Yauco rebellion of 1897.[41]

Professionals (lawyers, doctors, journalists, and others) were an important source of leadership for the SPR-PRC and the Orthodox Autonomists. Why would the professionals support this political path? This social group included intellectuals who had absorbed the liberal creed by having been educated in Europe and in the United States. Many were descendants of the hacendados and empathized with the situation of this class. Furthermore, the limitations imposed by the Spanish regime hindered their own development as a social group: the taxes on professionals imposed by the government; the general poverty of the country, which limited the market for services; the lack of schools and hospitals; restrictions on the press, and so on. Also, as an intermediate social group, they were prevented from moving to higher social positions within either the productive and commercial system or the government.[42]

Another important sector that moved politically to the Orthodox Autonomists, and after 1898 to the Republican Party, was that formed by urban workers and artisans. These groups expanded in the main cities of the island, stimulated in part by development of commerce. Great numbers of them came to the cities after the abolition of slavery and the termination of the workbook system. Others left the sugar areas after the crisis in the industry or with the breakdown of the *agregado* system with the coming of the sugar mills. Many of these became agricultural wage earners in the centrals; others moved to the cities to sell their labor. This group of wage earners (tobacconists, shoemakers, printers, bakers, and so on), together with the artisans, developed an ideological and political posture of opposition to the Spanish regime. Moved both by a series of general afflictions (inflation, lack of currency, taxes) and some particular to them (prohibition of trade unionism), these wage earners supported the most radical sector of autonomism, the Orthodox Autonomist Party.[43]

ANNEXATIONISM AND THE ORTHODOX AUTONOMISTS

The immediate cause for the formation of the Orthodox Autonomist Party was the pact between Muñoz Rivera's faction of the Autonomist Party and a monarchical party in Spain, merging the Autonomist Party with the Spanish party in return for a promise of autonomist reforms for Puerto Rico in 1897. The opposition to the pact by the Barbosa faction was based on refusal to fuse with a Spanish party, particularly a monarchical one. The faction headed by Barbosa was also opposed to the kind of autonomy demanded by the "fusionists." The Orthodox position was one of complete decentralization within the Spanish regime. The Barbosa faction was characterized by its defense of Republicanism, autonomism, and complete administrative and political decentralization.[44]

Two issues concerning the Orthodox Autonomist Party and its eventual political evolution into the Republican Party need to be discussed. They are the differentiation between the Orthodox Autonomists and the Liberal Fusionist Party headed by Muñoz Rivera, and the degrees of affinities toward annexationism in the Orthodox. With regard to the first issue, it has been argued that the main difference between the parties lay in the clashing of personalities between their leading figures, Muñoz Rivera and Barbosa.[45] This notion, which views politics as the interaction of great individuals, has no analytic power to explain a broad range of political phenomena. The other proposition that tries to explain the differences between the Autonomist forces proposes that the distinction is one of degrees between its leadership, with the Orthodox Autonomists representing "those groups most interested in the 'modernization' of the Puerto Rican society."[46] Though within the leadership of both parties there were a great number of professionals, the main differentiating element between the Orthodox and the Liberals seems to be in the support given by the sugar growers and the radical petty bourgeoisie to the Orthodox, while the coffee hacendados supported mostly the Liberals.[47] This is one of the most important elements for their distinct political programs. To the Orthodox, but not to the Liberal Fusionists, their Republican liberalism was nonnegotiable, and even though the Orthodox wavered on the issue of fusion with peninsular parties, they were opposed steadfastly to uniting with a monarchical party.[48] The Orthodox Autonomist position emphasized a wider and more decentralized autonomy than that of the Liberals. Their opposition to the Autonomist government of 1897 was based not only on the attacks and manipulations by the Liberals against them, but in the limitations imposed upon that autonomy by Spain.[49] According to Barbosa, under Spain, autonomy "was the highest aspiration that our country could have."[50]

The other issue with regard to the Orthodox Autonomist Party and its future evolution is the so-called annexationist vocation that it supposedly concealed. According to W. Mattos Cintrón, due to the lack of "a clear annexationist program, the Orthodox Party had to take cover under the flag of republicanism to conceal its inclination toward the United States. Once the invasion altered the political panorama, the Orthodox discovered their natural political position and formed the Republican Party."[51] However, Republicanism was not a concealing veil but rather one of the elements that would "incline" Orthodox Autonomism toward annexationism after the invasion. The Orthodox Autonomist Party could not have a "clear annexationist program" simply because that was not its goal under the Spanish regime. Although within the party there were many members with known annexationist tendencies, many of them from the SPR-PRC, this was never the position either of its main leadership or of the party itself. It is not surprising, then, that there is neither documented evidence nor any mention whatsoever of any declaration in favor of annexation by the main Orthodox leadership before the invasion of 1898. As a matter of fact, the references made to the United States by the leaders of the party before and during the invasion are negative. When the United States declared war against Spain, *El País,* the newspaper of the Orthodox party, declared that the United States was "the modern Carthage," that they would never be "slaves of the yankees" and that they would be "in a definitive, irrevocable, insurmountable manner and forever united to the destiny of Spain."[52] Barbosa himself in 1918, commenting on the Autonomist Party of 1887, declared: "Maybe, if the success of that program and the realization of those ideals would have changed completely the destinies of this nation, the catastrophe of 1898 would have never taken place."[53]

Nevertheless, on August 27, 1898, little more than a month after the invasion, a group of the best-known leaders of the country—among them the bulk of the Orthodox Autonomist leadership—delivered a document to the military government in which they accepted and defended "the sovereignty of the United States" over Puerto Rico and made public their aspiration to become "one more state within the Union to affirm the personality of the people of Puerto Rico."[54] How can these events be reconciled with the formation of the Republican Party, the backbone of the statehood movement in decades to come? Where, then, lies the continuity of annexationism before and after the invasion?

The element that provides continuity to Puerto Rican annexationism lies neither in any ideological construction (concealed annexationism, assimilationism, and so on), nor in the avowed political opportunism of a group, but in the political program of specific sectors of classes and social groups. As has been argued before, the Orthodox had more affinity for the presence of the United States in Puerto Rico than those sectors within the Liberal Party.[55] The affinity of the Orthodox with annexation lies in the identity of interests of the sectors that formed it, not only in terms of the presence of the United States in Puerto Rico but, more importantly, in the implantation in the island of the United States' economic and political system. In contrast to Spanish absolutism was the Republican democratic system; against the limitations in trade and the worn relations of production that Spain represented, the United States symbolized free trade, the desired market, and capitalist relations of production; to a decadent Spain was opposed a vigorous and powerful United States.

Once Spain granted autonomy to Puerto Rico, the Incondicionales weakened as a political force. The internal political and social conflict before the invasion revolved around the two Creole parties, the Liberals (Barbosa called them the "new Inconditionals") and the Orthodox Autonomists. The invasion "altered the political panorama," not by discovering an "annexationist vocation" in the Orthodox, but by presenting the opportunity to change the power relations between the two main Creole parties and corresponding social forces. On May 28, 1899, the leadership of the Orthodox Autonomist Party presented a *Manifiesto* proposing the creation of a new party; the preamble read: "Dissolved the former parties that struggled for the liberties of Puerto Rico under the Spanish sovereignty, there is now the necessity to group around a new political program those inhabitants of the country that would like to work for the development of local interests under the protection of the glorious American flag."[56]

The affinity toward the presence of the United States in Puerto Rico by the social forces grouped within the Orthodox Party was not limited to the ideology and politics, but extended to economics as well. The so-called gateways to capitalism during the nineteenth century become an important factor in understanding this process. It is precisely among the sectors grouped around the Orthodox Autonomists, later Republicans, that a more acute predisposition to capitalism is found. The late nineteenth-century sugar industry shows the most advanced level of capitalist relations in Puerto Rico.[57] This also applies to the coffee growers of the southwest and some Creole merchants, like those from Ponce, who sought wider trade with the United States and had moved to the

financial area (forming the Banco Crédito y Ahorro Ponceño). These social
sectors were limited by the Spanish colonial regime and saw in American capitalism the necessary conditions for their growth.

ANNEXATIONISM AND THE AMERICAN REGIME

One last issue is the characterization of the Orthodox Autonomist/Republican
Party as the backbone of annexationism in the decades to come. In 1899, after
the Treaty of Paris ceded Puerto Rico to the U.S., the Liberal Party was transformed into the Federal Party and the Orthodox Autonomist Party became the
Republican Party. Both included support for the annexation of Puerto Rico to
the United States and stated their goal of making Puerto Rico a state of the
American Union in their program. The differences in their support for annexation were to be seen after the U.S. regime in the island was established. Once
Puerto Rico had submitted to military government by the United States, with
all the changes that were implemented during this period, and once the colonial
government was implanted in Puerto Rico under the 1900 Foraker Law, the
Federal Party became the political opposition to the regime and the issue of
statehood was subordinated, and even rejected, within its program. The Republican Party remained the supporter of statehood and of the U.S. regime in
Puerto Rico.

Even when both the Federal and the Republican parties showed a favorable
disposition toward annexation during the first years after the invasion, those
groups that coalesced around the Republican Party (Orthodox Autonomists and
SPR members) labored concretely and assiduously to secure the presence of the
United States in Puerto Rico and for the formation of a new state apparatus.
Along with the SPR members who participated in the invasion, many others
joined the U.S. troops in their advance (as trackers, guides, spies, and the
like), served the military in many tasks (translators, provisional governments,
and others), and worked to attain the greatest support possible among the population for the U.S. occupation. In many towns the annexationists negotiated
the pacific surrender to the U.S. troops, created or formed part of the new local
governments, and even circulated proannexationist manifestos.[58] In Ponce the
formation of an "Annexationist Party" was proposed and in a couple of months
numerous newspapers with clear annexationist views appeared throughout the
island.[59] Well-known members of the Orthodox leadership were the first to
publicly declare their support for annexation and statehood for Puerto Rico.[60]
More important yet is the participation of this group "in the consolidation of
North American power in the Island. . . . We do not find in the Liberals
a sincere disposition to cooperate with the invader and to facilitate him a
rapid concretion of its power."[61] When the Republican Party was founded on
July 4, 1899, great sectors of it were already part of the recently imposed state

apparatus. The Republican Party thus became part of the mechanism of U.S. domination in Puerto Rico and its main source of support.[62]

NOTES

1. Gordon K. Lewis, *Puerto Rico: Freedom and Power in the Caribbean* (New York: Monthly Review, 1963), ch. 2.

2. A. G. Quintero-Rivera, *Conflictos de clase y política en Puerto Rico* (Río Piedras: Ediciones Huracán, 1976), p. 14.

3. On the labor regime see Labor Gómez Acevedo, *Organización y reglamentación del trabajo en el Puerto Rico del siglo XIX* (San Juan: Instituto de Cultura Puertorriqueña, 1970).

4. Astrid T. Cubano, "Comercio y hegemonía social: los comerciantes de Arecibo, 1857–1887" (Master's thesis, Dept. of History, UPR, 1979); Laird W. Bergad, "Toward Puerto Rico's Grito de Lares: Coffee, Social Stratification, and Class Conflict, 1828–1868," *Hispanic American Historical Review* 60, no. 4 (November 1980), pp. 619–42; Fernando Picó, *Amargo café* (Río Piedras: Ediciones Huracán, 1981), ch. 2.

5. Dulce M. Tirado Merced, "Las raíces sociales del liberalismo criollo: el Partido Liberal Reformista (1870–1875)" (Master's thesis, Dept. of History, UPR, 1981); Félix Mejías, *De la crisis económica del 86 al año terrible del 87* (Río Piedras: Ediciones Puerto, 1972); Pilar Barbosa de Rosario, *De Baldorioty a Barbosa: Historia del autonomismo puertorriqueño, 1887–1896* (San Juan: Editorial "La obra de José Celso Barbosa," 1974).

6. Tirado Merced, "Las raíces sociales," p. 204; Mariano Negrón Portillo, *Reformismo liberal, reformismo conservador: dos etapas del autonomismo puertorriqueño (1895–1914)* (Río Piedras: Centro de Investigaciones Sociales, UPR, 1981), p. 21.

7. Lidio Cruz Monclova, *Historia de Puerto Rico (Siglo XIX)* (Río Piedras: Editorial Universitaria, 1952), vol. 2, pt. 1, p. 130; Germán Delgado Pasapera, *Puerto Rico: sus luchas emancipadoras* (Río Piedras: Editorial Cultural, 1984), pp. 180–83; Carmelo Rosario Natal, "Betances y los anexionistas, 1850–1870: apuntes sobre un problema," *Revista de Historia* 1, no. 2 (julio–dic. 1985), pp. 113–130.

8. Manuel Alvarado Morales, "Idea acerca de Estados Unidos de América en los periódicos 'La Correspondencia de Puerto Rico' y 'La Democracia' (1890–1898)" (Master's thesis, Dept. of History, UPR, 1975); and Paul Nelson Chiles, "The Puerto Rican Press Reaction to the United States, 1888–1898" (Ph.D. diss., Dept. of History, Univ. of Pennsylvania, 1944).

9. Arturo Morales Carrión, *Albores históricos del capitalismo en Puerto Rico* (Río Piedras: Editorial Universitaria, 1976), pp. 75–131; Julian S. Steward, *The People of Puerto Rico* (Chicago: University of Illinois Press, 1956), p. 52.

10. Henry K. Carroll, *Report on the Island of Porto Rico* (Washington, DC: Government Printing Office, 1899; reprinted by Arno Press, New York, 1975), p. 17.

11. Quoted in Tirado Merced, "Las raíces sociales," p. 37.

12. Luis Muñoz Rivera, *Campañas políticas*, vol. 1 (Madrid: Editorial Puerto Rico, 1925), p. 45.

13. P. Barbosa, *De Baldorioty a Barbosa*, p. 12.

14. Luis Bonafoux, *Betances* (San Juan: Instituto de Cultura, 1970), pp. 102, 288–90. See also Rosario Natal, "Betances y los anexionistas."

15. Centro de Investigaciones Históricas (CIH), *Despachos de los consules norte-americanos en Puerto Rico (1818–1898)*, vol. 1, (Río Piedras: Editorial Universitaria, 1982) p. 760.

16. Delgado Pasapera, *Puerto Rico*, p. 181.

17. CIH, *Despachos*, vol. 1, pp. 810–12, and 917; also P. Barbosa, *De Baldorioty a Barbosa*, p. 15–16.

18. On the SPR-PRC see the following: Partido Revolucionario Cubano, *Memoria de los trabajos realizados por la Sección Puerto Rico del Partido Revolucionario Cubano, 1895 a 1898* (New York: A. W. Howes, n.d.); Roberto H. Todd, *José Julio Henna, 1848–1924* (San Juan: Cantero Fernández, 1930), and *La invasión americana: Como surgió la idea de traer la guerra a Puerto Rico* (San Juan: Cantero Fernández, 1938); also, Carmelo Rosario Natal, *Puerto Rico y la crisis de la Guerra Hispanoamericana (1895–1898)* (Hato Rey: Ramallo Bros., 1975), ch. 3; and P. Barbosa, *De Baldorioty a Barbosa*, ch. 15.

19. Mariano Negrón Portillo, "El liderato anexionista antes y después del cambio de soberanía," *Revista del Colegio de Abogados de Puerto Rico* (October 1972), p. 382.

20. Quoted in Rosario Natal, *Puerto Rico y la crisis*, p. 97.

21. Todd, *José Julio Henna*, pp. 21, 37.

22. Described in PRC, *Memoria*, pp. 7–14; P. Barbosa, *De Baldorioty a Barbosa*, pp. 295–305.

23. Negrón Portillo, "El liderato anexionista," p. 380.

24. Todd, *La invasión americana*, pp. 7–8, 13–19; PRC, *Memoria*, pp. 23–24, 29. The Manifesto, written by Eugenio María de Hostos and Henna, is cited in Todd, *José Julio Henna*, p. 28–29.

25. Angel Rivero, *Crónica de la Guerra Hispanoamericana* (New York: Plus Ultra, 1973), p. 473, also pp. 182–84 for the invasion plans; and Rosario Natal, *Puerto Rico y la crisis*, pp. 68, 102, 219; the U.S. consul report of June 6, 1898, in Centro de Investigaciones Históricas, *Despachos de los consules norteamericanos en Puerto Rico (1868–1898)*, vol. 2 (manuscript, CIH, UPR); and Fernando Picó, *La guerra después de la guerra* (Río Piedras: Ediciones Huracán, 1987), p. 55–56.

26. Negrón Portillo, "El liderato anexionista," pp. 370–79, 394; Rosario Natal, *Puerto Rico y la crisis*, pp. 116–18.

27. Rosario Natal, *Puerto Rico y la crisis*, pp. 219, 241.

28. Rivero, *Crónica*, p. 159–60.

29. Rosario Natal, *Puerto Rico y la crisis*, ch. 6; Rivero, *Crónica*; Picó, *La guerra*, pp. 57–64.

30. Antonio Mirabal, "La invasión norteamericana en Ponce," *El Día* (Ponce), Dec. 18, 1949, p. 39.

31. Ibid.; Rivero, *Crónica*, ch. 28; Rosario Natal, *Puerto Rico y la crisis*, ch. 6; and Mariano Negrón Portillo, *Cuadrillas anexionistas y revueltas campesinas en Puerto Rico, 1898–1899* (Río Piedras: Centro de Investigaciones Sociales, UPR, 1987), pp. 15–28.

32. Lidio Cruz Monclova, *Historia del año de 1887* (Río Piedras: Editorial Universitaria, 1970), p. 187ff.; Antonio S. Pedreira, *El año terrible del 87* (San Juan: Editorial Biblioteca de Autores Puertorriqueños, 1945).

33. José Celso Barbosa, *Orientando al pueblo, 1900–1921*, edited by Pilar Barbosa (San Juan: Imprenta Venezuela, 1939), pp. 242–44.

34. Mejías, *De la crisis económica del 86*, p. 67; J. C. Barbosa, *Orientando al*

pueblo, p. 244–46; Cruz Monclova, *Historia del año de 1887*, pp. 188–95; Delgado Pasapera, *Puerto Rico*, pp. 384–99.

35. Cruz Monclova, *Historia del año de 1887*, pp. 194–95, 222–26, and 228–37.

36. See Andrés Ramos Mattei, *La hacienda azucarera: su crecimiento y crisis en Puerto Rico (siglo XIX)* (San Juan: CEREP, 1981); Laird W. Bergad, "Agrarian History of Puerto Rico, 1870–1930," *Latin American Research Review* 13, no. 3 (1978), p. 65–66; and Picó, *Amargo café*, pp. 26, 28, 75, 98.

37. Ramos Mattei, *La hacienda azucarera*, pp. 35–37.

38. In Carroll, *Report*, p. 69.

39. See Rosario Natal, *Puerto Rico y la crisis*, p. 241; Negrón Portillo, "El liderato anexionista," pp. 376–78; and Wilfredo Mattos Cintrón, *La política y lo político en Puerto Rico* (México City: Ediciones Era, 1980), p. 48–49. On the foundation of Banco Crédito y Ahorro Ponceño in 1895 by creoles trying to break the Spanish merchants' monopoly on credit and finance, see "El Banco Crédito y Ahorro Ponceño," *El Día* (Ponce), Dec. 18, 1949, pp. 35 and 40.

40. See Carlos Buitrago, *Los orígenes históricos de la sociedad precapitalista en Puerto Rico* (Río Piedras: Ediciones Huracán, 1976); and Vivian Caro, "La formación de la gran propiedad cafetalera: la hacienda Pietri, 1858–1898," *Anales de Investigación Histórica* 2, no. 1 (1975), pp. 1–111.

41. Negrón Portillo, "El liderato anexionista," p. 370–71.

42. See Barbosa's comments on this regard in J. C. Barbosa, *Orientando al pueblo*, p. 241.

43. Gervasio García and A. G. Quintero-Rivera, *Desafío y solidaridad: Breve historia del movimiento obrero puertorriqueño* (Río Piedras: Ediciones Huracán, 1982), pp. 13–29; and A. G. Quintero-Rivera, "Socialista y tabaquero: La proletarización de los artesanos," *Sin Nombre* 8, no. 4 (Jan.–March 1978), pp. 100–37.

44. Quoted in Pilar Barbosa, *La Comisión Autonomista de 1896* (San Juan: Imprenta Venezuela, 1957), p. 159.

45. Among others, Antonio S. Pedreira, *Un hombre del pueblo: José Celso Barbosa* (San Juan: Instituto de Cultura Puertorriqueña, 1965), p. 169–70; Bolívar Pagán, *Historia de los partidos políticos puertorriqueños* (San Juan: M. Pareja, 1972) vol. 1, p. 15.

46. Negrón Portillo, *Reformismo Liberal*, p. 19.

47. Mattos Cintrón, *La política*, pp. 48, 181–82; Quintero-Rivera, *Conflictos*, pp. 29–31.

48. P. Barbosa, *La Comisión Autonomista*, p. 155.

49. Cruz Monclova, *Historia de Puerto Rico*, vol. 3, pt. 3, p. 201.

50. J. C. Barbosa, *Orientando al pueblo*, p. 136.

51. Mattos Cintrón, *La política*, p. 49.

52. Cruz Monclova, *Historia de Puerto Rico*, vol. 3, pt. 3, pp. 219–21.

53. J. C. Barbosa, *Orientando al pueblo*, p. 241–42. See also Barbosa's rejection of accusations of opportunism held against him in 1899 in *Asamblea Republicana celebrada en San Juan, Puerto Rico, 1 y 2 de julio de 1899* (San Juan: Imprenta de "El País," 1899), p. 33.

54. Luis M. Díaz Soler, *Rosendo Matienzo Cintrón: Orientador y guardián de una cultura* (Río Piedras: Instituto de Literatura Puertorriqueña, 1960) vol. 1, p. 163–64.

55. Mattos Cintrón, *La política*, pp. 49–51; Negrón Portillo, "El liderato anexionista," p. 385.

56. Bolívar Pagán, *Historia,* vol. 1, pp. 34–35. José Tous Soto, then president of the party, made similar comments in 1923; in his "The Republican Party of Porto Rico," in E. Fernández García, *El libro azul de Puerto Rico* (San Juan: El Libro Azul Publishing, 1923), p. 201.

57. A. G. Quintero-Rivera, "Background to the Emergence of Imperialist Capitalism in Puerto Rico," in Adalberto López, ed., *The Puerto Ricans* (Cambridge, MA: Schenkman, 1980), p. 111, and "Socialista y tabaquero."

58. Cruz Monclova, *Historia de Puerto Rico,* vol. 3, part 3, pp. 374–85.

59. Antonio Mirabal, "Ponce y los partidos políticos de Puerto Rico," *El Día* (Ponce), Dec. 18, 1949, pp. 27, 31; Rosario Natal, *Puerto Rico y la crisis,* pp. 242, 249–50, 263.

60. Díaz Soler, *Rosendo Matienzo Cintrón,* p. 167.

61. Negrón Portillo, "El liderato anexionista," pp. 384–85.

62. See Edward S. Wilson, *Political Development of Porto Rico* (Columbus, OH: Fred J. Heer Publishing, 1905), p. 113.

CHAPTER THREE

The Republican Party, 1898–1924: Advent and Rupture of Annexationism

The Republican Party became the main source of support for the American regime on the island during its first decade. Its program and actions within the colonial government were aimed at strengthening the presence of the American state and capital in Puerto Rico. Republican collaboration with the new regime has to be understood as based not on an extreme opportunism or assimilationist mentality, but from the historical project of the party's leading sectors. Republican politics has to be explained on the basis of what I have termed the Republican project: its goal was the total transformation of Puerto Rican society through the absorption of American social, economic, political, and cultural institutions. It defined statehood within the concept of the "regional fatherland" and legitimized the attempt to win control over the local affairs of the island. The legitimacy of the Republican project was questioned as the result of the limitations imposed by the colonial structure and the economic domination of American capital. The Republican Party ruptured in 1924, when the party's leading sectors disagreed about the party's goals and the alliance with other parties.

TRANSFORMATIONS UNDER THE NEW REGIME

The policies of the American government during its first two decades were aimed at securing its presence in the newly acquired territory. The military government of 1898–1900 implemented a series of reforms to eradicate the vestiges of the Spanish state and to facilitate the swift expansion of American capital in the island. These measures included the abolition of the local government formed under the Autonomous Charter and the formation of a centralized government in the hands of the U.S. military. Among the economic policies of the military government were a tax reform, a credit freeze, and the devaluation of the peso; these facilitated the expansion of U.S. corporations and the transfer of land from local landowners to U.S. capital. The military government's policies served as "preparatory instruments" for the colonial system that was created under the Foraker Act in 1900.[1]

The Foraker Act represents the institutionalization of U.S. hegemony in Puerto Rico. It created the new state and economic institutions, building the colonial system that was to exist for the rest of the century.[2] The Foraker Act established an "autocratic" government in order to secure the U.S. administration of the territory and to restrict the political power of the local groups.[3] The centerpiece of the new state structure was the control of the local administration by the American executive, which appointed the colonial governor and the six members of his cabinet. The latter in turn were members of the upper chamber of the local legislature, violating the Constitutional separation of powers existing in the United States, and giving the governor the power to stifle the popularly elected lower chamber, the only state structure open to local groups. The members of the local supreme court were named by the president, while Congress retained the power to annul any law approved on the island. Municipal autonomy, the political bastion of hacendados until then, was heavily curtailed under the new centralized government. At the economic level, the U.S. tariff was imposed on the island, barring trade with any other country; also imposed was the U.S. maritime law, forcing all trade to be carried in U.S. ships. Also included in the 1900 act was the 500 Acres Law, restricting the amount of land held by any agricultural corporation; this law remained a dead letter for four decades because no mechanism to enforce it was provided.[4]

The Jones Act of 1917 conceded U.S. citizenship to Puerto Ricans and reformed the colonial legislature. According to José Cabranes, by bestowing citizenship on Puerto Ricans, the United States prevented any claim for independence and maintained its colonial hold on the territory. The citizenship granted was incomplete, for "it was never intended to confer the Puerto Ricans 'any rights that the American people [did] not want them to have.' "[5] The colonial status of the island was further reinforced by the so-called Insular Cases, the U.S. Supreme Court's decisions on the status of Puerto Rico. The island was declared a "non-incorporated" territory, that is, not part of the United States, with no right to demand statehood or the applicability of the Constitution.[6] This created a contradictory situation for Puerto Ricans: while as citizens they were integrated into the American state, Puerto Rico as a politicojudicial entity was not. The consequences of these policies are crucial for understanding Puerto Rican politics: colonialism and citizenship still remain at the center of the island's political conflict, particularly within the statehood movement.

The other important measure of the Jones Act was the reform of the local legislature: two popularly elected chambers were created. The cabinet was now named by the colonial governor, except the commissioner of education and the attorney general. The reformed structure put the elite closer to the government, but it was still unable to govern. If the new colonial structures limited the access to state power of those creole groups dominant under the Spanish regime, the economic structure that emerged after 1898 destroyed or rearranged their socioeconomic basis.

The economic transformation of Puerto Rico during the first three decades after the invasion was as drastic as its political transformation. The island witnessed the expansion of a capitalist economy under the hegemony of American capital and a process of increasing economic integration to the United States.[7] Supported by the policies of the state, American capital came to control agriculture, finance, and commerce. The center of the new capitalist economy and the major area of investment was the sugar industry, which not only dominated the imports and exports of the island, but transformed radically the pattern of land ownership and cultivation in agriculture in favor of the production of sugar, heavily controlled by four American corporations.[8]

The expansion of a capitalist economy under the hegemony of American capital transformed the class structure and the character of the political conflict during this period in Puerto Rico. The most important changes in the class structure were: the consolidation of a Puerto Rican bourgeoisie linked to the sugar industry, commerce, and finance; the consolidation of a professional and commercial petty bourgeoisie; the weakening of the hacendado class, particularly the coffee growers; and the development of a working class.[9] Of utmost importance here is the development of the Puerto Rican bourgeoisie. During the nineteenth century the small Puerto Rican bourgeoisie—linked primarily to the sugar industry, trade, and the incipient creole banking institutions—suffered from the limitations imposed by the Spanish colonial regime. The arrival of the American state, the expansion of U.S. capital, and the increasing economic integration of Puerto Rico to the United States set the basis for their development as a class.[10] The ranks of the professional and commercial petty bourgeoisie increased, benefiting from the expansion of the capitalist economy.

The emergence of new social actors, coupled with the structures of the new regime, transformed the politics of the island. Important sectors of the emergent sugar, commercial, and financial bourgeoisie and the growing professional and commercial petty bourgeoisie provided the leadership for the Republican Party, the major supporter of the U.S. economic and political presence in Puerto Rico. The landowning class led by the coffee hacendados, whose economic and political position was undermined by the American regime, headed the opposition to that regime through the Union Party, formed in 1904.[11] The working class, led by the sugar proletariat and urban workers, organized in the Socialist Party in 1915, becoming a major actor in Puerto Rican politics during the 1920s.

INSERTION OF THE REPUBLICANS IN THE NEW REGIME STRUCTURES

The Republican Party was founded on July 4, 1899; most of its ranks came from the Orthodox Autonomist Party. Its program proposed the "definitive and sincere annexation" of Puerto Rico to the United States; it demanded recognition of Puerto Rico as an organized territory as a step toward statehood, and stated its goal to "intervene in insular affairs and in national affairs"; it also promised "fidelity to our new nationality." Among its demands were the need for a civilian government for the island, universal suffrage, civil liberties, English instruction, fiscal reform, free trade, change in currency to the U.S. dollar, aid to agriculture, and the transfer of the American judicial system to the island.[12] In general terms, the Republican program was similar to that of the Federal Party. But the Republicans placed a greater emphasis on the Americanization of the island, desiring a more rapid assimilation of the institutions, customs, culture, and political democratic forms of the United States. Both parties conceived statehood as an autonomous status within the American federation. As in the period of the Spanish regime, regional autonomy (this time under statehood within the U.S. federation) represented the aspiration of the Creole dominant sectors to economic and political power on the island.

The Republican and the Federal parties were clearly differentiated in terms of the social composition of their leadership and popular support. The Federal Party presented itself as the party of the "leading classes of the country" representing "the great regional interests" against the "vile populace," against the "scoria of the suburbs."[13] In turn, the Republican Party presented itself as the party of the popular masses. The difference between the parties was also based on race. Already in the municipal elections of 1899 the social differences between the two parties was evident. Edward S. Wilson records that while the white elite voted for the Federals, the "negroes and colored people generally, the poor and unfortunate, the crowded denizens of the cities, and a large contingent of the men who best remembered Spanish cruelty and wanted to stamp out every vestige of it, voted the Republican ticket."[14] Leo S. Rowe in 1904 indicated that the Republican Party "appealed to the more radical element in the native population"; it "was organized with a view to bring to its support the elements hitherto neglected, the poorer whites and the negroes." According to him, the Federal Party grouped "the more conservative elements" of the elite, characterized by their "Bourbon tendencies," and a "horror of negro domination, coupled with the fear of the results of a further extension of the suffrage to the poorer whites."[15] The Republican Party maintained this image as a popular party for most of the period under consideration, while the Union Party presented itself as the party of the big economic interests and of the white elite.[16] This image of the early Republican Party derived from the outstanding position within its leadership of the professionals, the most articulate and progressive sector of the party, together with the support received from the black population and from sectors of the working class.

The political and ideological differences between the two major parties came to the forefront as the new economic and political structures began to be debated in Puerto Rico and in Washington. Initially the two parties' demands were similar: territorial government as a transitory form on the road to statehood, free trade, availability of credit, change in currency, and subsidies to agriculture, among others. However, the Republican representatives were prominent in the Puerto Rican delegations representing trade and finance interests, while the Federals tended to represent the agricultural interests, particularly those of coffee. Furthermore, the Republicans proposed a tutorial regime by the U.S. government over Puerto Rico while the Puerto Ricans were educated in democratic forms, in self-government, and for statehood; the Federals, on the other hand, demanded the immediate concession of self-government and autonomy.[17] Differences between the two parties emerged with the imposition of the Foraker Act in 1900. The Federal Party, whose major supporters were adversely affected by the new economic and political structures, began to oppose the new regime. The Republicans, whose leading sectors saw in the new regime the opportunity to become the local dominant group, supported the colonial regime.[18]

The Republican Party, supported by the U.S. government, gained access to the colonial government during the early years of the century. The Republicans obtained the majority of the Puerto Rican posts in the Executive Council, the upper chamber of the legislature, whose members were named by the U.S. president. From 1900 to 1917 the Republicans held the majority of the Puerto Rican posts in the council, even though after 1904 the Union Party was the dominant electoral party. Furthermore, from 1900 to 1904 the Republicans were the only party to be represented in the legislature. By law, a new electoral distribution for the island was required for the 1900 elections. The Republican members of the Executive Council, supported by its American members and the governor, proposed an electoral redistribution bill, popularly known as the "humpbacked," which openly favored the Republicans. The bill was approved despite opposition by the two Federal members of the council, who quit afterward. The Federal Party abstained from participating in the 1900 elections, giving the Republican Party an absolute victory and control of the colonial legislature. The Republican Party strengthened its control over the colonial government when the Federal vacancies in the Executive Council were filled with Republicans.[19] The importance of having the Republicans in the colonial government was noticed at the time; as an American observer concluded, the lack of opposition "proved a real advantage during the first and second sessions of the Legislative Assembly"; the institutionalization of the new regime was facilitated by "the unqualified support of a party whose faith in American institutions was born of an unquestioned faith in the principles of our government."[20]

The first two civilian governments under the American regime, dominated by the Republicans in the legislature and in the council, promoted the transfer of American institutions to Puerto Rico. Under the first civilian government of

1900–1902, thirty-six laws were approved, including the transfer of the political, penal, and civil rights codes; the reform of the public school system, electoral system, labor regulations, municipal administration, and police. Also approved was a law giving the U.S. government some land, and the right to obtain more land, needed for defense matters.[21] The laws approved in the economic area served to consolidate capitalist social relations and to facilitate the penetration and expansion of American capital on the island. For example, the new tax law favored big capital and the transfer of land from local landholders to U.S. corporations; the new corporate law facilitated the entrance of U.S. absentee corporations.[22] The new laws also helped to undermine the economic and political power of the hacendados, the major force of opposition to the new regime.[23]

THE FIRST REPUBLICAN RUPTURE

The electoral triumph of the Union Party in 1904 grew out of the increased opposition to the policies of the American government and its local allies. One important faction of the new party was formed by Republican dissidents. The Republican Party was able to attract the support of landowners and workers during its early years. The first dissident movement in the party emerged from among some professionals and landowners discontented with the party's policies. The Republican dissidents were headed by Rosendo Matienzo Cintrón and were supported by some municipal committees of the party, particularly those from Ponce and Mayagüez. In 1902, after his proposal was rejected by a Republican Assembly, Matienzo Cintrón publicly proposed the creation of the Puerto Rican American Union. Among its goals were: the regeneration of the political life of Puerto Rico under the unification of all parties, total political autonomy, free elections, the popular election of both legislative chambers, and the rejection of the new fiscal system. His proposal was supported by the Federal Party but again was rejected by the Republicans. After the rejection of Matienzo Cintrón's proposal, the dissident Republicans left the party and were instrumental in the formation of the Puerto Rican Union Party.[24] The Republican dissidents included an important sector of the party's professionals, many of them outstanding ideologues of annexationism like Matienzo Cintrón, José Julio Henna, Federico Degetau (then resident commissioner), Manuel Zeno Gandía, and others.[25]

Another issue that divided the Republican Party was its incorporation into the national Republican Party. Those opposed argued that this incorporation would undermine the "regional" character of the local party. The Republican Assembly of 1902 decided in favor of incorporating to the national party "with the hope of being protected by the Republican Party of the United States."[26] The local Republicans knew their own strength and that of their adversary, and acknowledged that they would not be able to control the legislature for much longer. They were also interested in the local patronage that the Republican administration could provide. The national party, initially opposed to the incorporation, finally agreed to it knowing that they depended on local Republicans for the administration of the island.[27]

The identification of the Puerto Rican Republicans with the national Republicans has been explained in terms of the racial issue: the national Republican Party was the party of Lincoln, of liberty and freedom. Being a black man, and depending upon the support of the island's black population, it was logical for José Celso Barbosa to support the Republicans and to oppose the Democratic party, which supported racism and the Ku Klux Klan in the South.[28] But more important in explaining the identification of the local Republicans with the national Republicans is the fact that the Republican Party was the party in power at the time of the invasion and the "imperialist" party in the United States. It was the national Republicans who probably would support the annexation of Puerto Rico to the United States. The reality, nevertheless, was different, and it furthered the conflicts in the Republican camp.

The local Republican Party became identified with the party that imposed American colonialism in Puerto Rico. While the Democratic Party in its 1900 and 1904 programs attacked the colonial regime imposed on the island and its annexation without incorporation or citizenship, the national Republican Party exalted the civil service it had established in Puerto Rico and the greater share in local government patronage it had given to the natives.[29]

The support by local Republicans of the colonial government and of the party in the United States that had promoted it created dissatisfaction within the ranks of the party. Federico Degetau described the incorporation to the national Republican Party as an "abdication on our part of all those convictions that we upheld as our principles in the constitution of our Puerto Rican Republican Party."[30] For Degetau, who led the opposition to incorporation, the national Republican Party represented the opposite of all their ideals; that party had denied Puerto Ricans self-government, American citizenship, and even the promise of statehood in the national program. Degetau tenaciously opposed incorporation on the basis that "it has been the Democrats who have been more favorable to the recognition of the rights of the island."[31] He argued that incorporation represented a process of "Americanization" of Puerto Rican politics that was contrary to the interests of the population; that incorporation "consisted of the aborted attempt to strip our party of its flag, of its name, and of its regional character."[32] Finally, Degetau echoed the complaints of the Republican landowners by accusing the national Republicans of imposing a tariff that discriminated against the interests of Puerto Rican coffee growers and favored other products.[33]

After the 1904 electoral defeat, the Republicans took a secondary position in Puerto Rican politics as the Unionists won every election and controlled the House of Delegates during the next two decades. But even after this loss, the Republicans continued to function in the government through the Executive Council and other institutions. The Executive Council, whose Puerto Rican

members were mostly Republicans, functioned extensively as a curb on Unionist demands. A study of the legislative process between 1905 and 1914 concluded that the great majority of bills that the council did not approve were
measures to protect the interests of those sectors represented by the Union Party,
particularly the hacendados.[34] Although they were not incorporated into the
national party from 1913 to 1919, the Puerto Rican Republicans celebrated the
national party's victories as their own, because of the expected patronage. But
the repeated electoral defeats, the slow disintegration of the party, and the
change in leadership had their effects on the party, turning it into a "party of
patronage."[35]

THE REPUBLICAN PROJECT

The Republican Party during this period is traditionally viewed as the party
of patronage, of servile collaboration with the American regime, of insatiable
political opportunism, of repression (the "Republican mobs"), of anti-Puerto
Ricanism and obstinate assimilationism. All these characterizations reflect
something of the Republican phenomenon; but as a matter of fact, some of
these characterizations may apply to the Unionists as well. They are inadequate
for understanding the real nature of the Republican Party and of annexationism
during this period. Often subordinate classes are seen as having the capacity to
transform history (through alternative and historical projects), while the same
capacity is denied to the bourgeoisie and allied classes. It is essential to understand that the Puerto Rican bourgeoisie, with considerable economic, political,
and social power, and joined to an intellectually outstanding petty bourgeoisie,
did indeed have a coherent historical project, what I have called the Republican
project. The basis of this project was the total transformation of Puerto Rican
society; a transformation that was to be realized through the absorption of the
economic, social, political, and cultural forms of the United States.

Americanization

The centerpiece of the Republican project was the program of "Americanization." The Republican Party saw itself as the vehicle for the Americanization
of the island. Barbosa, the party's principal leader and ideologue, was known
in American circles as "The Rock of Americanization."[36] Nevertheless, the
annexationist program cannot be reduced to its support for cultural assimilation,
though this figures prominently in the program of Americanization. By Americanization is understood a historical program at all levels: social, political,
economic, and legal, as well as cultural. In 1908 Barbosa defined the politics
of the Republican Party as: "Auxiliary to the American government in Puerto
Rico, protecting U.S. policy furthering the transformation of the sociopolitical
conditions of the country."[37] This is precisely what Americanization meant for
the Republican Party: to transform Puerto Rican society.

The Republican program of Americanization sought the establishment of U.S. economic, social, and political institutions in Puerto Rico. The American economic and political system had been the model for many Puerto Rican liberal autonomists and radicals during the nineteenth century. But Americanization was also rationalized based on the island's annexation to the United States and thus on the need to accommodate Puerto Rican society to the American model. As Barbosa argued, the Republican Party believed "that by being linked to the American people by geographical accidents, by commercial ties, and, finally, by intransigent laws of history, we should make a great effort . . . to breathe in the spirit redemption of that great people."[38] Americanization was necessary to absorb and internalize the political and economic achievements of the United States: "We defend the Americanization of the island because we wish that our future government be grounded in the same democratic institutions in which that great Republic was founded and that our country assimilate all that has made the American people great and powerful."[39] Given the irreversible fact of annexation and the need to absorb American institutions, Americanization was necessary "to coexist at the side of the vigorous race that inhabits the continent."[40]

The Republican support for Americanization was predicated on the belief in the superiority of American society and the Anglo-Saxon race. According to Barbosa, the Anglo-Saxon race created governments of liberty that were rooted in the people: "This is the Anglo-Saxon politics, which produces such wonderful results that there are no better governments than those of the people belonging to that race."[41] Puerto Rico, of a Latin and "tropical" background, should embrace the Anglo-Saxon "spirit." During the Republican Assembly of 1904, the Americanization of Puerto Ricans was proposed so that the American "national spirit influences this insular country producing the beneficial results that it has achieved in the continent."[42]

The Republican Americanization policy, particularly at the cultural level, was highly conflictive. For example, while it controlled the House, the party approved a law making English the official language of Puerto Rico and promoting its use as the language of instruction in the public school system. This policy resulted in a series of conflicts, both political (with the nationalist sector of the Union Party) and pedagogical. Cultural Americanization, including the propagation of English, was crucial for the Republican program and the annexationist process, because there was opposition in the United States to annexing populations foreign to the culture and race of the country. Spanish and English, "Calderón and Shakespeare" can coexist "in the minds of Puerto Ricans" but, argued Barbosa, "it matters to us, and is more convenient to us, to learn about Shakespeare than to neglect him."[43]

But the issue of Americanization surpassed the question of culture, as it was linked to the adaptation to the "economic forces" of the United States. According to an annexationist view of the period, Puerto Rico was thought to be at a lower socioeconomic level than the United States, among other reasons because of its racial-cultural background. There were no industries in Puerto Rico because of the lack of a "capitalist ethic" as in the Anglo-Saxon tradition.[44] There was a need to facilitate the entrance of American economic institutions that would promote the economic development of the island. Already in 1899 Barbosa had stated what eventually became the party's economic policy: "to stimulate the introduction of capital in the form of banks, societies, companies, etc. . . . for the undertaking of new enterprises, bringing the one factor which is necessary for our prosperity, namely, capital."[45]

As discussed earlier, the policies of the Republican-controlled legislature during the period 1900–1904 were aimed at fomenting the conditions needed for the entrance of American capital; for example, the Republican program of 1902 sought to amend the 500 Acres Law "in order to allow [American sugar] corporations to own up to 5,000 acres."[46] As the Union Party increased its political opposition to the colonial government and to the expansion of American capital in Puerto Rico, the Republican Party became the defender of American capital.

> The Republican Party is the only political party in Puerto Rico that is genuinely friendly toward Americans. . . . These men realize that Americans have made large investments in Puerto Rico and they know, too, that there is more capital from similar sources ready to be invested here . . . and believing that the American money that is now invested here is entitled to protection . . . they have not hesitated to stand up and combat the machinations of the enemies of American rule in Puerto Rico.[47]

Economic Americanization and support for the colonial regime went hand in hand in the Republican program.

Independence

The transformation of Puerto Rican society entailed the absorption of all American "forms"; thus the program of Americanization had as its logical outcome the incorporation of Puerto Rico into the American federation. The first issue to be elaborated in the statehood program was the viability of statehood, as against the other status alternative at the time, independence. The rejection of independence was based on the argument that Puerto Rico lacked the elements necessary to be an independent country, for reasons ranging from its territorial size, small and backward population, lack of natural and technological resources to its incapacity for self-government, the tradition of the "Latin blood" toward nondemocratic forms of governments, the need in the modern world to form large societies, and the lack of power to defend itself militarily.[48] Barbosa liked to talk about the conditions of the modern world that demand "the constitution of large social groups that can create an equilibrium to keep order and peace." There is also the need for a country to be big in economic terms and strong in military terms. Barbosa concluded that "it is necessary to agree that the island of Puerto Rico is not in a condition to be an independent republic, strong and vigorous by itself. In this situation, Puerto Rico needs the outside aid that gives it the strength and the consistency that it unfortunately lacks."[49] That this was merely an intellectual smokescreen was to become clear later on, when the Republicans adopted independence as an alternative to colonialism.

Along with the above-mentioned argument for rejecting independence, the early annexationists argued that statehood was inevitable based on the supposed mutuality of interests between Puerto Rico and the United States. Puerto Rico needed the United States for its defense, and the mainland "represents the natural market for the insular products."[50] At the same time, the United States needed Puerto Rico as a strategic bastion in Latin America and as a market for its products. Furthermore, it was argued that the presence of the United States was the only guarantee of the democratic system in Puerto Rico.[51]

Statehood as the "Regional Fatherland"

The Republicans modified the traditional conception of independence and tried to incorporate it to statehood through the conception of statehood as independence, or the *patria regional* ("regional fatherland"). This conception, which goes back to the nineteenth-century Autonomists, sought to establish the economic and political parameters of the creole dominant sectors at the same time that it linked this to the ethnic-cultural configuration of the population. The dominant sectors of the Republican Party sought to delineate their power in Puerto Rico while maintaining the idea of a Puerto Rican personality within the American federation.

The concept of a regional fatherland was elaborated in the Republican Assembly of 1899 by Degetau:

> American patriotism has the twin conception of the profound love for the native region as the basis of the profound love and respect for the general State, its institutions, and its laws . . . ; only by maintaining the personality of our region, freely developed in the midst of that Union of States that constitutes the American Federal Republic, shall we organize our fatherland worthily to live the life of right and Justice.[52]

Also elaborated was the notion that the fatherland is something more than national (that is, the ethnic and cultural personality of a people); it includes the institutions and the way of life of a population. In that same assembly, Manuel F. Rossy stated that "the fatherland is the realization of right: the exercise of liberty; the establishment of justice."[53] Afterward Barbosa declared: "The fatherland is not only the land where you were born. Our liberties and rights are fatherland too."[54] The Puerto Rican personality, whose existence was questioned by some early Republicans (Barbosa once characterized it as "in gestation"), would be protected under the regional fatherland. Puerto Rican patriotism was not thought to be incompatible with American patriotism, for "neither the New Yorker, nor the Marylander, nor the Texan had to sacrifice any of their local patriotism when they became part of the American nation."[55]

The main element within the conception of the regional fatherland was the notion that Puerto Rico would have autonomy, if not independence, in its local affairs within statehood. This conception reflected the prevailing view of the American federal system, which was viewed more as a confederation than as a federation: the United States was a "Republic of Republics, a State of States." This view of federalism was shared by Republicans and Federals/Unionists alike, which may explain their attraction to annexationism. Within this conception, American federalism "has produced the extraordinary progress and stengthening of the Republic." Furthermore, it is because of federalism "that the regional sentiment is never in conflict with the national sentiment." The regional fatherland would guarantee the preservation of the Puerto Rican personality within the American federal structure.[56]

But the regional fatherland meant more: it represented the aspiration of the leading sectors of the Republican Party to become the regionally dominant group under the aegis of the American state. Statehood as independence meant the total control of local affairs within the North American federation:

> As a state, . . . Puerto Ricans will resolve freely and independently all their local problems; with no more ties than those that exist among the several states that form the American Union with the federal government. . . . This is how the [Republican] party organizes the sentiment of independence with the organization of a real independent republic for the locality and a union with the rest of the nation.[57]

> We are regionalists, separatists, independentists but we are regionalists, separatists, independentists in the same way as the nations or states that form the people of the United States of America.[58]

Thus independence, with control over local affairs, was linked to statehood in the Republican program.

THE BREAKING OF THE REPUBLICAN PROJECT

The first great obstacle to the Republican project was placed by the American government itself when it imposed the colonial government on the island, precluding statehood. The Republican policy of supporting the American regime created a contradictory situation for the party: on the one hand, the American government reiterated its opposition to statehood, while on the other hand, the party that supported the American regime on the island had a program whose main demand was precisely statehood. Though this did not immediately affect the relations between the party and the American government, it did limit the possibilities of the Republican project. Not only was the principal Republican aspiration dashed, but the colonial regime limited the economic and political autonomy they wanted.

As a result of this contradictory situation, the Republicans sought reforms to the colonial regime while dropping the demand for statehood and promoting the widest collaboration with the American government. In its 1899 program, before the Foraker Act was approved, the Republicans demanded annexation, with the transitory form of a territorial government. After the Foraker Act, the main demand of the Republican Party was the organization of Puerto Rico as a U.S. territory, and not statehood. The first Republican demand of reforms to the colonial government, in 1902, was the separation between the executive and the legislative branches in the colonial government. In 1906 the Republicans demanded self-government and U.S. citizenship for Puerto Ricans. These were the bulk of the Republican demands before the Jones Act of 1917.

It was primarily the Republican professional sector, which had elaborated the Republican project as a national one and which feared its collapse, that began to criticize the colonial regime during this period. This fear was grounded in the electoral successes of the Union Party and the increasing collaboration between the Unionists and U.S. government, particularly after the Democratic victory in 1912, and the American government's consideration of a number of reforms presented by the Unionists. In 1913 the Puerto Rican Republican Party disincorporated itself from the national party, supposedly because of the latter's opposition to a bill granting Puerto Ricans U.S. citizenship and its opposition to statehood for Puerto Rico. The local Republicans argued that "it has been clearly shown that the national Republican Party, because of its colonial tendencies and purposes, is antagonistic to, and the enemy of, the high ideals that the Puerto Rican Republican Party pursues."[59] The local Republicans began also to redefine their policies toward the colonial regime.

The Reaction Against Colonialism and the "Foreigners"

The most strident attack by the Republican Party against the colonial regime came in response to the Jones Act. The Jones Act reflected the Wilson administration's desire to reform the colonial regime in Puerto Rico and to concede some of the Unionist demands. The Republican Party opposed the bill, which it considered a Unionist project and a reform of the colonial regime. According to Barbosa, it was "a supreme mockery" that after decades of colonial rule "Washington decided to organize Puerto Rico as an American colony, with restrictions greater than those it has today."[60] To this he later added: "We will never accept American tutelage with a permanent character, nor in good will can we accept the idea of . . . becoming 'in eternum' a dependency, a colony, a factory where we should forever suffer the dominion of a foreign people."[61]

The Republicans claimed that to attain self-government "there are only two roads: one, statehood; the other, the independent republic. The Republicans seek and desire the first alternative, preferably over the second one."[62] They characterized the Jones Act as "organizing the possession, the dependency, the dominion as an American colony"; of restricting self-government and of merely reforming the existing colonial government.[63]

Nevertheless, the Republicans supported the act on the basis of one of its measures: the granting of U.S. citizenship to Puerto Ricans. The Jones Act paved the way to statehood, according to the Republicans, by incorporating Puerto Ricans into the American state as citizens. Even though the citizenship granted carried no promise of future statehood, the Republicans took this as a victory for the party.[64] But the Republican opposition to the colonial regime continued. The Republican Assembly of 1917 stated that the party supported the Jones Act as a step toward self-government, and they demanded from Congress "the recognition of the promise to admit Puerto Rico as a state of the Union" and, until statehood was granted, that Puerto Rico be declared an incorporated territory of the United States. The assembly concluded: "We protest any colonial plan, and we declare that if the people of the United States do not want to admit us into the family of States, they do not have any other alternative than granting us independence."[65]

But perhaps the greatest obstacle to the Republican project was economic: the domination of the economy by the *hijos ajenos* ("foreigners"). Barbosa warned of the dangers involved in the control of the economy by the hijos ajenos in a 1910 article dealing with the issue of land tenure: "The real danger is in those industrial corporations if they are not checked, investigated, and repelled in time . . . sugar, tobacco, and later, coffee, could be controlled by those large corporations; small landowners could be turned into servants."[66] But it was not until 1918 that Barbosa launched his harshest critique of the economic domination of foreign capital. In the last of his articles on the hijos ajenos, in which he gives the historical account of La Torre del Viejo, Barbosa concluded:

> It is necessary to unite all sympathies, all efforts of our friends, toward a common goal: . . . to save our children from economic slavery, so that, not being *agregados* ("sharecroppers") anymore, they can become owners and administrators of their own land. . . .
>
> It is necessary to end in Puerto Rico the current situation where only a small number of Puerto Ricans, escapees of the colonial shipwreck, have real influence, wealth, and prestige; and, on the other hand, a foreign colony remains the richest and most influential and occupies the most outstanding position in our country; and the Puerto Rican entity fades away in all that relates to economic life; and the majority of its inhabitants continue in the economic slavery, submitted to the power of money of the foreigners, whose wealth make them the most powerful and influential as in the past. Under the American flag, at the political level, we share the same

liberties, the same rights and powers of any American citizen, but, at the economic level, we have advanced very little, and you cannot be the owner of a country if you do not own its wealth. . . .

If we are to have our own fatherland, if our children are to be free and happy in their land, they must be the owners and masters of the wealth of their land. There is no political independence without economic independence.[67]

What are the reasons, according to Barbosa, for this economic domination of the country by foreigners?

It is due in great part to the fact that we have lived dreaming and constantly pursuing an ideal . . . of making a free fatherland for our children, without realizing that while we were engaged in this duty of high patriotism, the others, the foreigners, those who did not care for our present and future status, took the opportunity of the new dawn to monopolize the industries, the trade, and the land, and they took possession of the country.

The solution Barbosa proposed to this situation is to "stop considering for a while the political problem, as the most important and fundamental, and to devote all our energies to solve the economic problem."[68] The Republican project was thus greatly questioned by the second decade of the century. The hijos ajenos controlled the economic life of the country and the *hijos del país* ("children of the country") had lost all political power. And all this was due to the "pursuing of an ideal." Statehood presented itself now confronting the fundamental element of the Republican project: control of Puerto Rican society.

Social Peace and the Workers Question

The Republican project was haunted by another major problem, one that endangered not only the realization of the project but the social fiber of Puerto Rican society: the struggle between capital and labor. The Republican project required social peace, since it needed a united front of all Puerto Ricans; but this was now menaced by the class divisions on the island. The Republican program of 1920 proposed in typical Barbosian language that the party's main objective was the promotion of "social peace and the equal dignity and just compensation of capital and labor, making Puerto Ricans owners of the land and industries of our Fatherland, and the People itself arbitrator of the production, circulation, and equitable distribution of its wealth, so that it could be also the owner of its own political destiny."[69] The call for social peace between capital and labor is more urgent in the 1923 Republican program, stating that the "current struggle between Capital and Labor demands, more than ever before, that all parties of the country support . . . the measures proposed to regulate the relations between these factors of production." It concluded: "Between Capital and Labor should exist relations of harmony, of peace, and of mutual trust and respect."[70] The maintenance of social peace became the main problem for the Republicans at the beginning of the 1920s. This presented a dilemma: either the Republicans could ally with the Union Party against labor, that is, the Socialist Party; or they could ally with the Socialists. Under the leadership of Barbosa, the Republicans opted for the second alternative.

The search for a "social peace" agreement between capital and labor was a major element in the Republican quest for an electoral agreement with the Socialists between 1920 and 1924. According to Barbosa, both capital and labor had to make concessions: capital had to abandon its goal of totally dominating labor, and labor had to modify its goal of totally transforming society. But capital had to make the first concession, for it had been its economic and political regime that had promoted the economic and political organization of the working class. The labor movement and the Socialists grew because of the "errors committed by the capitalists, their unjust persecution of workers, the lack of equity and justice on the part of the authorities."[71] The maintenance of social peace had to be secured through the unity between capital and labor. It was also necessary to share the government with labor, because "in a not so distant future they could take the reins of government. The better prepared they are to govern the country, the better will be the new political era that will come soon."[72] Collaboration with the Socialists was thus legitimized in political and ideological terms, as part of the Republican project.

Politically, the Republicans needed the support of the working class to stop the electoral advance of the Union Party. Furthermore, the support by sectors of the working class that the Republicans enjoyed during the first decade and a half of the century was decimated by the creation of the Socialist Party. The Republican professional sector, already in conflict with the bourgeois sector over the content of the party's program, elaborated a policy to incorporate the working class and the labor movement into the party: "You are not justified in forming a class party. The American Federation of Labor on the continent provides you with the path to follow."[73] The Republicans expected the working class to restrict its actions to the area of economic reforms and trade-union activity and politically to support the party closest to its program, the Republican Party.

The Politics of Coalitions

By the early 1920s the fissures in the Republican project were evident: statehood, which promised the Republicans the self-government needed to assure their dominion over Puerto Rican society, was discarded by the American government; the desired dominion over Puerto Rican society was at the same time threatened by the control over the "sources of wealth" by the hijos ajenos and by the political subordination coming out of the colonial regime; finally, the struggle between capital and labor threatened to destroy the social structure itself, making any historical project irrelevant. The reaction of the leading sectors in the Republican Party to this situation provoked the first grave fissure within the party. The sector headed by the Republican bourgeoisie made a political alliance with the Union Party based on the quest for self-government and opposition to the Socialist Party. The petty bourgeois sector abandoned the party and concerted an alliance with the Socialists based on the quest for social peace.

Under the leadership of Barbosa, who died in 1921, the Republican Party evaded any political alliance with the Union Party and, after 1919, pursued an agreement with the Socialists. Though no agreement was reached at the national level, there were local pacts between the Republicans and the Socialists, and coalition governments were achieved in the towns of Ponce (under the Popular Party), Arecibo, and Fajardo.[74] In 1924 José Tous Soto, then party president and lawyer for the sugar corporations, renewed talks with the Socialists.[75] These talks exacerbated the conflicts within the party, finally leading to the rupture of 1924.

The immediate cause of the rupture was the introduction in Washington of a bill liberalizing the colonial regime in Puerto Rico and granting the popular election of the governor.[76] Tous Soto and a Republican delegation went to Washington to lobby for the bill. The American representatives conditioned their support for the bill and asked the Republicans to join the Unionists in a broad front for "the defense of the interests of Puerto Rico." Furthermore, John Weeks, then secretary of war, categorically told the Republicans: "If this issue of liberalizing the regime makes you hold onto the alternative of statehood, I will not support this bill. Puerto Rico should not be a state nor can it be a state in the American Union."[77] Finally the American functionaries made it clear to the Republicans that the U.S. government would not support any reform that led to the participation of the Socialists in the colonial government. According to Tous Soto, "after having been oriented in Washington, after weighing the responsibility of a heterogeneous coalition which has brought such bitter results wherever it has been made," the Republicans agreed that the pact with the Socialists was not possible, for "the mere possibility of the pact may determine that Congress could abstain from granting the People of Puerto Rico the right to elect their own Executive; because it would fear the election of a radical element."[78] In their return trip, Antonio R. Barceló, president of the Union Party, and Tous Soto agreed on the basis for the Alliance. Thus the bourgeois sector of the Republican Party, headed by its president, found support in Washington to join the bourgeois sector of the Union Party and to oppose a possible pact with the Socialists. The Republican petty bourgeois sector, opposed to the alliance with its historical enemies, decided to ally with the Socialists. In this way, two essential elements of the Republican project— the search for self-government and the search for social peace between capital and labor—were separated from each other.

The principal reason for the making of the Alliance was the "red menace": the consolidation and growth of the Socialist Party. The party was founded in

1915 and in the 1917 elections it received 14 percent of the votes; this figure increased to 23.7 percent in 1920. The Union Party, confronted with the possibility of an alliance between the Socialists and the Republicans, decided to make the political agreement with its historical enemies. The Alliance Republicans sought a political agreement that could return them to power in local government. But the basis of the Alliance was an accord between the bourgeois sectors of both parties opposing the working class. Once the conservative sector, grouped around the sugar central owners, gained control of the Union Party in the early 1920s, they were in a position to ally with the Republican bourgeoisie. The bourgeoisie of both parties formed what at the time was known as the *fuerzas vivas* (the "live forces").[79] The possible coalition between the Socialist and Republican parties "alarmed greatly the capitalists who dominated the upper councils of both Unionist and Republican Parties"; the Republican bourgeoisie was "a class actively opposed to labor movements in general, and feared the thought of a workingman's party coming to power."[80]

The Alliance was based on a programmatic accord of a very wide and ambiguous nature that incorporated the basic political demands of both parties. The manifesto, signed by party presidents Barceló and Tous Soto, declared that the two parties finally found "a point of convergence, a common idea to join their aspirations, the 'self-government' for Puerto Rico that constitutes our own sovereignty within the sovereignty of the United States." The latter notion was a compromise with respect to the status position of both parties, for both statehood and autonomy were interpreted as falling under the "sovereignty within the sovereignty" umbrella. The issue of political status was put aside to prevent "the separation of the Puerto Rican family into opposing factions," so both parties could "devote our forces, initiatives, and actions to the study and solution of the social and economic problems."[81]

Statehood became an issue of conflict for the Republicans in the making of the Alliance. Although the statehood alternative coexisted within the Alliance program, it was subordinated within the pronouncements of Tous Soto. The demands for the immediate application of the U.S. Constitution to Puerto Rico and for the incorporation of Puerto Rico were left out, based on the argument that Puerto Rico was not economically prepared for statehood. The traditional demand of the Republican Party for the immediate incorporation of Puerto Rico as a transitory step to statehood was thus rejected. Furthermore, Tous Soto argued that Puerto Ricans were in no position to demand statehood given their political division on this issue, and because of opposition to statehood in the United States. For Tous Soto, statehood "is a bitter road if circumstances do not help us. . . . To climb this hill, defeating all obstacles like distance, language, race, customs, and prejudice, we need the union of all wills for the common effort." Tous Soto gave self-government priority over other issues, including statehood. If the United States does not want to grant statehood, as the political form to guarantee Puerto Ricans control over local affairs, then there is no alternative but independence: "If after the people of Puerto Rico are prepared for statehood, they knock at the doors of the National Home and find them systematically closed by prejudice, our only dignified road will be to form our own and free home.''[82]

The Republican fissure came during the "stormy" Republican Assembly of May 4, 1924, in Mayagüez, where the proposal for the Alliance was debated. Tous Soto defended the pact with the Unionists, while the opposition was headed by Rafael Martínez Nadal. The proposal in favor of the Alliance won by a margin of 130 to 55.[83] The petty bourgeois sector (the so-called Barbosista Old Guard), headed by Martínez Nadal, assembled immediately after the meeting and formed the Pure Republican Party.[84] Martínez Nadal characterized the Republican participation in the Alliance as "an imposition of Mister José Tous Soto and of American vested interests." He later characterized Tous Soto as a "man at the service of the corporations in Puerto Rico, who treacherously stabbed to death" statehood and the Republican Party.[85] Manuel F. Rossy, former party president, characterized the alliance with the Unionists, "our natural and continuous adversaries," "a disaster," emphasizing "the great disparity between these collectivities, not only at the political level, but at the economic level as well."[86]

The Pure Republicans made an electoral alliance with the Socialists based on a minimum program that included the goal of permanent union with the United States. The ideal of statehood, supported by the dominant sector within the Socialist Party, was an important factor in the making of the Coalition.[87] The Socialists sought to implement two goals with its participation in the Coalition: to counter the offensive of the fuerzas vivas, the bourgeois coalition in the Alliance, and to enable the party to penetrate the state apparatus through the electoral process, a strategy defined by its dominant reformist leadership and ideology.[88]

The Republican project, the first statehood project in Puerto Rico, was ruptured with the Republican fissure in 1924. The U.S. colonial regime on the island and the hegemony of the hijos ajenos over the local economy were great impediments to the realization of the Republican project. The rupture of 1924 came as a consequence of the contrasting views of the leading sectors of the Republican Party with regard to the alliance with the working class and its party. Although the "Republican family" was reunited once again in 1932 under the Republican Union Party, the differences between the main sectors of the party were not mitigated. The rupture of 1924 began a period of internal conflicts in the Republicans that lasted for over two decades and engulfed annexationism in a political and programmatic crisis.

NOTES

1. The phrase is from Edward J. Berbusse, *The United States in Puerto Rico, 1898–1900* (Chapel Hill: University of North Carolina Press, 1966), p. 109; on the military government see also Consuelo Maldonado, "Developments in the Puerto Rican Politi-

cal-Administrative, Fiscal, and Commercial Structures During 1898–1900'' (Ph.D. diss., Graduate School of Public Administration, Syracuse University, 1974).

2. Lyman J. Gould, *La ley Foraker: Raíces de la política colonial de los Estados Unidos* (Río Piedras: Editorial Universitaria, 1975).

3. On the words of W. F. Willoughby, then Puerto Rico's secretary of state, as quoted in Edgardo L. Martínez Nazario, ''Estudio histórico-teórico sobre el desarrollo administrativo del sector público en Puerto Rico'' (Master's thesis, Sch. Pub. Admin., UPR, 1971), pp. 41–42.

4. Gould, *La ley Foraker;* María D. Luque de Sánchez, *La ocupación norteamericana y la ley Foraker* (Río Piedras: Editorial Universitaria, 1980).

5. José A. Cabranes, *Citizenship and the American Empire: Notes on the Legislative History of the United States Citizenship of Puerto Ricans* (New Haven, Conn.: Yale University Press, 1979), p. 6. The quoted remarks are from Senator Foraker, in 1900, on the issue of Puerto Rico. Truman R. Clark argues that U.S. citizenship was granted to restrain the independence fervor in *Puerto Rico and the United States, 1917–1933* (Pittsburgh, Penn.: University of Pittsburgh Press, 1975), p. 23.

6. The Insular Cases are included in Commonwealth of Puerto Rico, *Documents on the Constitutional History of Puerto Rico* (Washington, D.C.: Office of the Commonwealth, 1964), pp. 117–20, 120–31, and 140–49.

7. Kelvin Santiago, ''Algunos aspectos de la integración de Puerto Rico al interior del Estado metropolitano: los orígenes de la nueva estructura estatal colonial: 1898–1929,'' *Revista de Ciencias Sociales* 23, nos. 3–4 (julio–diciembre 1981), pp. 295–346; and James Dietz, *Economic History of Puerto Rico: Institutional Change and Capitalist Development* (Princeton, N.J.: Princeton University Press, 1986), ch. 2.

8. On the sugar economy see: Arthur Gayer, Paul T. Hormam, and Earle K. James, *The Sugar Economy of Puerto Rico* (New York: Columbia University Press, 1938); Esteban A. Bird, *Report on the Sugar Industry in Relation to the Social and Economic System of Puerto Rico* (San Juan: Bureau of Supplies, Printing, and Transportation, 1941); Bailey W. and Justine W. Diffie, *Porto Rico: A Broken Pledge* (New York: Vanguard Press, 1931).

9. A. G. Quintero-Rivera, *Conflictos de clase y política en Puerto Rico* (Río Piedras: Ediciones Huracán, 1976); Dietz, *Economic History,* ch. 2.

10. Thomas C. Cochran, *The Puerto Rican Businessman: A Study in Cultural Change* (Philadelphia: University of Pennsylvania Press, 1959); Biagio di Venuti, *Money and Banking in Puerto Rico* (Río Piedras: University of Puerto Rico Press, 1950); Quintero-Rivera, *Conflictos.*

11. Mariano Negrón Portillo, *Reformismo liberal, reformismo conservador: Dos etapas del autonomismo puertorriqueño* (Río Piedras: Centro de Investigaciones Sociales, 1981).

12. The Republican program appears in Bolívar Pagán, *Historia de los partidos políticos puertorriqueños* (San Juan: M. Pareja, 1972), pp. 34–37. The formation of the party is discussed in Antonio Mirabal ''Ponce y los partidos políticos de Puerto Rico,'' *El Día* (Ponce), Dec. 18, 1949, pp. 27, 31–32; and Roberto H. Todd, *Patriotas puertorriqueños* (Madrid: Ediciones Iberoamericanas, 1965), pp. 72–73. The assembly is reviewed in Republican party, *Asamblea Republicana celebrada en San Juan, Puerto Rico, 1 y 2 de julio de 1899* (San Juan: Imprenta de ''El País,'' 1899), pp. 10–25.

13. Negrón Portillo, *Reformismo liberal,* p. 36.

14. Edward S. Wilson, *Political Development of Porto Rico* (Columbus, Oh.: Fred

J. Heer Publishing, 1905), pp. 77–78. A similar description is made by Daniel H. O'Leary, "The Development of Political Parties in Puerto Rico Under American Occupation" (Ph.D. diss., Boston College, 1936), p. 12.

15. Leo S. Rowe, *The United States and Puerto Rico* (New York: Longmans, Green and Co., 1904; reprinted by Arno Press, New York, 1975), p. 247–48.

16. A. Hyatt Verrill, *Porto Rico: Past and Present* (New York: Dodd, Mead and Co., 1914), p. 134.

17. Luque de Sánchez, *La ocupación*, pp. 94–108; and Gould, *La ley Foraker*, pp. 75–80.

18. See Matienzo Cintrón's comments in the 1899 Republican Assembly, in *Asamblea Republicana*, pp. 27–28.

19. Pagán, *Historia*, pp. 73–74; Todd, *Patriotas*, p. 81.

20. Rowe, *The United States and Puerto Rico*, p. 254. Similar comments were made by then Governor Hunt in 1902; in United States War Department, *Annual Report of the Governor of Puerto Rico, 1902–1903* (Washington, D.C.: Government Printing Office, 1903), p. 13.

21. Luque de Sánchez, *La ocupación*, pp. 152–59; Pagán, *Historia*, p. 77.

22. Maldonado, "Developments," pp. 18–19. Also Rowe, *The United States and Puerto Rico*, p. 163.

23. Quintero-Rivera, *Conflictos*, pp. 39–49.

24. See Luis M. Díaz Soler, *Rosendo Matienzo Cintrón: Orientador y guardián de una cultura* (Río Piedras: Instituto de Literatura Puertorriqueña, 1960), pp. 218–54. The Republican Assembly of 1904 is reviewed in Julio Medina González, *El escándalo o Revista de la Asamblea celebrada en el teatro de Ponce por el Partido Republicano de Puerto Rico, en los días 25, 26 y 27 de abril del año 1904* (Mayaguez: Tipografía La Voz de la Patria, 1904?).

25. Quintero-Rivera, *Conflictos*, pp. 60–62; Negrón Portillo, *Reformismo liberal*, p. 46.

26. Partido Republicano, *Informe de los delegados del Partido Republicano de Puerto Rico ante la Convención Nacional Republicana celebrada en Chicago el 21 de junio de 1904* (San Juan: Tipografía "El País," 1904), pp. 6–9.

27. Ibid., p. 23.

28. Argued by Pilar Barbosa, *La política en dos tiempos* (np: Editorial José C. Barbosa, 1978?), pp. 31–33.

29. In Reece B. Bothwell, ed., *Puerto Rico: Cien años de lucha política* (Río Piedras: Editorial Universitaria, 1979), vol. 4, pp. 1478–81.

30. Ibid., vol. 2, p. 209.

31. Angel M. Mergad, *Federico Degetau: un orientador de su pueblo* (New York: Hispanic Institute, 1944), pp. 178–79.

32. Bothwell, *Puerto Rico*, vol. 2, p. 212.

33. Ibid., p. 215; and Medina González, *El escándalo*, p. 33.

34. Mariano Negrón Portillo, "Conflictos legislativos en Puerto Rico, 1905–1914," *La Toga* 10, no. 1 (April 1978), pp. 25–27.

35. Clark, *Puerto Rico and the United States*, pp. 78–79. Patronage became so important to the Republican party that in its 1920 bylaws article 39 specifically dealt with the party's patronage policy. See Partido Republicano Puertorriqueño, *Constitución y plataforma del Partido Republicano Puertorriqueño* (San Juan: Tipografía Times Publishing, 1920), p. 10. The article reappeared in the 1923 Republican bylaws.

36. José A. Gautier Dapena, "Nacimiento de los partidos políticos bajo la soberanía de los Estados Unidos: programas y tendencias," *Historia* 3, no. 2 (Oct. 1953), p. 171.

37. José Celso Barbosa, *Orientando al pueblo, 1900–1921*, edited and introduced by Pilar Barbosa (San Juan: Imprenta Venezuela, 1939), p. 59.

38. Ibid., p. 53.

39. Ibid., p. 33 and 163.

40. Ibid., p. 34.

41. Ibid., p. 85. See also Claudio Capó, *¿República independiente o Estado federal?* (San Juan: n.p., 1921), pp. 33 and 77.

42. Medina González, *El escándalo*, p. 5.

43. Barbosa, *Orientando al pueblo*, pp. 33–34.

44. Capó, *¿República independiente . . . ?*, p. 82.

45. In Henry K. Carroll, *Report on the Island of Porto Rico* (Washington, D.C.: Government Printing Office, 1899; reprinted by Arno Press, New York, 1975), p. 115.

46. Bothwell, *Puerto Rico*, vol. 1, pt. 1, p. 277.

47. *El Tiempo*, 1912, as quoted in Luis A. Vélez Aquino, "Puerto Rican Press Reaction to the Shift From Spanish to United States Sovereignty, 1898–1917" (Ph.D. diss., Dept of Education, Columbia University, New York, 1968), p. 112–13.

48. See, e.g., the 1899 Republican program in Pagán, *Historia*, vol. 1, p. 34.

49. Barbosa, *Orientando al pueblo*, pp. 83–84. Also Capó, *¿República independiente . . . ?*, p. 97.

50. Federico Degetau, *Pequeño resumen de sus obras en favor de la ciudadanía y el estado para Puerto Rico*, edited by Ana Degetau (Madrid: n.p., 1916), p. 18.

51. Federico Degetau, *The Political Status of Porto Rico* (Washington, D.C.: Globe Printing Co., 1902), p. 16. Also, Degetau, *Pequeño resumen*, p. 17; Barbosa, *Orientando al pueblo*, pp. 89 and 163; Capó, *¿República independiente . . . ?*, pp. 78, 93–94.

52. *Asamblea Republicana*, p. 29.

53. Ibid., p. 32.

54. Barbosa, *Orientando al pueblo*, p. 37.

55. Ibid., pp. 34–35.

56. Ibid., p. 42.

57. Ibid., pp. 110, 87, respectively.

58. José Celso Barbosa, in *El Tiempo*, 1916, reprinted in *Avance*, July 16–31, 1975, p. 57. The misperception on the nature of American federalism by the Puerto Rican leaders was acutely noted early in the century by Rowe, *The United States and Puerto Rico*, p. 155.

59. Bothwell, *Puerto Rico*, vol. 1, pt. 1, pp. 337–38.

60. Barbosa, *Orientando al pueblo*, p. 117.

61. Barbosa in *Avance*, p. 58.

62. Pagán, *Historia*, p. 155.

63. Barbosa, *Orientando al pueblo*, pp. 118, 128–29, and 134–36.

64. Ibid., p. 139.

65. Pagán, *Historia*, pp. 182–84.

66. Barbosa, *Orientando al pueblo*, p. 253.

67. Ibid., pp. 247–49.

68. Ibid., p. 236–37.

69. In Bothwell, *Puerto Rico*, vol. 1, pt. 1, pp. 373–74.

70. Ibid., p. 415.

71. Interview with Barbosa in *Puerto Rico Ilustrado,* December 25, 1920, p. 6.

72. Ibid. For similar comments by Manuel F. Rossy see Pilar Barbosa, *Manuel F. Rossy y Calderón: Ciudadano cabal* (San Juan: Editorial "La obra de José Celso Barbosa," 1981), pp. 33–36, 111.

73. Bothwell, *Puerto Rico,* vol. 1, pt. 1, p. 372. The Republicans made the same demands to the AFL in *La Respuesta enviada a los Representantes de la Federación Americana del Trabajo* (San Juan: The Times Publishing, 1920), p. 32.

74. Nilsa Rivera Colón, "Los pleitos electorales Socialistas en Fajardo: 1920–1924" (Master's thesis, Dept. of History, UPR, 1981), pp. 55–58.

75. Roberto H. Todd, "Como se formaron la Alianza y la Coalición en el año 1924," part 1, *El Mundo,* May 5, 1940, p. 5.

76. Pagán, *Historia,* p. 226.

77. Roberto H. Todd, "Como se formaron la Alianza y la Coalición en el año 1924," part 2, *El Mundo,* May 12, 1940, p. 4.

78. Bothwell, *Puerto Rico,* vol. 1, pt. 1, p. 436.

79. *Fuerzas vivas* was the name given to a group of bourgeois associations that included the Association of Sugar Producers, the Chamber of Commerce, and the Farmers Association. See Nilsa Rivera Colón, "Los pleitos electorales," ch. 5.

80. O'Leary, "The Development of Political Parties," pp. 86–87. Also, Pilar Barbosa, *La política en dos tiempos,* pp. 92–93. See the comments by Luis Sánchez Morales, representative of the Republican bourgeoisie, in P. Barbosa, *Manuel F. Rossy,* p. 122.

81. Pagán, *Historia,* pp. 230–32.

82. Bothwell, *Puerto Rico,* vol. 1, pt. 1, p. 433–34.

83. Details on the assembly appear in Teófilo Maldonado, *Rafael Martínez Nadal: Su vida* (San Juan: Imprenta Venezuela, 1937), pp. 34–42; and Pagán, *Historia,* p. 237–38.

84. Maldonado, *Rafael Martínez Nadal,* pp. 43–51. Also P. Barbosa, *La política en dos tiempos,* p. 94, and *Manuel F. Rossy,* pp. 79–80.

85. Maldonado, *Rafael Martínez Nadal,* pp. 40–41.

86. P. Barbosa, *Manuel F. Rossy,* pp. 153–54.

87. Rossy argued that statehood was an important element in cementing the Coalition; in P. Barbosa, *Manuel F. Rossy,* p. 255.

88. A. G. Quintero-Rivera, "La clase obrera y el proceso político puertorriqueño," Part 4 *Revista de Ciencias Sociales* 19, no. 3 (1975), pp. 263–98; and the "Introduction" by Blás Oliveras to Epifanio Fiz Jímenez, *El racket del Capitolio* (San Juan: Editorial Esther, 1944), pp. 10–11.

CHAPTER FOUR

Rupture and Crisis of Annexationism, 1924–1952

The fissure of the Republican Party in 1924 began a period of ruptures and crisis of Republicanism that lasted until the 1950s. The causes of the crisis were not entirely internal to the party; after all, the Republican factions were reunited in 1932 and, along with the Socialists, formed a coalition government that lasted until 1940. The crisis of Republicanism must be seen as symptomatic of the transformations in Puerto Rican society during the thirties and after. The collapse of the sugar industry, the rise in political and social turmoil that led to new political alliances by social forces, and the formation of the Popular Democratic Party (PPD) undermined the social and political basis of Republicanism. The crisis of Republicanism during the 1940s transformed the statehood movement from one of total support of the American regime in Puerto Rico to one of opposition to social and political change. The statehood movement lost its popular basis of support and came under the hegemony of the most conservative sector of the Puerto Rican bourgeoisie, its sugar sector. The statehood ideal lost the reformist appeal of its early days and became a symbol of conservative opposition.

The crisis of Republicanism and the rise of conservatism were the main factors promoting a transformation in the statehood program, from the idealistic character of the Republican project to the ultraconservatism of the statehood program of the 1940s. The crisis of Republicanism resulted from the inability of the Republican leading sectors, the petty bourgeoisie and the sugar bourgeoisie, to adapt to the social and economic transformations and political reforms brought by the crisis of the thirties, and to the continuing political and ideological conflicts between these groups within the statehood movement. Despite these changes, new elements were introduced to the statehood discourse that remained as part of the statehood program for decades to come.

THE POLITICAL CRISIS OF REPUBLICANISM

Crisis and Reform in Puerto Rico

The political changes during the thirties have to be understood within the framework of the economic and political crisis of the period.[1] At the economic level the most important precipitant of the crisis was the stagnation of the sugar industry, axis of the economy during the first three decades of the century. Although the sugar industry was not greatly hurt by the depression at the beginning of the thirties, being able to maintain its previous levels in production and profits, two factors affected it in the long run: the inability to maintain an adequate level of investment and the imposition by the United States of a sugar quota with the Costigan-Jones Act in 1934. The lack of an adequate level of investments was the result of the decision by foreign corporations not to reinvest in the island, in spite of the fact that the profit rate remained stable during the depression years; while 75 percent of the profits were paid in dividends, only 25 percent were reinvested.[2]

The U.S. government imposed the sugar quota on Puerto Rico precisely when the sugar industry began to reduce its production costs. The island's sugar industry required the protection of the U.S. tariff, since sugar produced here survived in the American market only because of the tariff protection, which was really a subsidy for American capital on the island.[3] By the end of the thirties the capacity for expansion of the sugar industry was greatly reduced.[4] With the limitations imposed by the quota, the only mechanisms to increase profits were a further decrease in the costs of production and an increase in productivity, both very difficult to achieve under the circumstances. The industry's situation was further complicated by the PPD reformist policy, which in the early years of the 1940s not only promoted an agrarian reform (for example, enforcement of the 500 Acres Law), but also sought an increase in the wage levels of the sugar proletariat. It is precisely during this period that the gradual withdrawal of the U.S. sugar corporations began.[5] The decline of the industry by the end of the forties was reflected in the weakening of its position within the island's economy.[6]

The critical condition of the sugar industry was one major element inducing a structural crisis in Puerto Rico during the 1930s. The inability of the main productive sectors of the economy (sugar, coffee, and tobacco) to expand prior to the depression, along with population growth, promoted what A. G. Quintero-Rivera has called "the structural crisis of unemployment."[7] Unemployment and marginality became the main social problem of the decade; it was estimated that by 1935 only 35 percent of the working population had an in-come-earning employment.[8] The thirties saw a series of long and bitter strikes, involving among others the sugar workers, public drivers, and dock workers. The Free Federation of Workers (FLT), for a long time the guarantor of social peace, lost its influence among Puerto Rican workers, who began to organize themselves in more radical trade unions outside the federation.

The three main political parties of the period (Liberal, Socialist, and Repub-lican) experienced internal schisms that divided all of them, preventing any effective political leadership of the masses and promoting instability within the party system and the colonial state.[9] The colonial legislature, controlled by the Republican-Socialist Coalition, and the government were plagued by corruption and incompetence; this, together with the increasing opposition to the colonial regime, began to take away the legitimacy of the state apparatus on the island. During this period the Nationalist Party under the leadership of Pedro Albizu Campos took a more radical stance against the colonial system, which included violent tactics against the government. The colonial regime on the island was also questioned in the United States, and in 1936 the Tydings Bill to grant independence to Puerto Rico was introduced in Congress. The bill received the support of the Republican and Liberal parties, which together commanded an electoral majority at the time. Although it died of congressional inaction, the Tydings Bill opened a period of political debate that promoted the division among several political parties.

As a reaction to the crisis, a process of political reform was begun during this period. The pressure by local forces to change the status quo led to the redefinition of political alliances that made possible the emergence of the PPD and its reformist-populist program.[10] Furthermore, the U.S. government pro-moted a long process of reform of the colonial government that began with the transfer of the New Deal to the island and culminated with the creation of the Commonwealth.

The main objective of the U.S. reform policy was to guarantee social and political stability in the colony. Two corresponding policies were implemented to attain this objective. The first was the use of repression by the colonial and the federal governments, as exemplified by the administration of Governor Blanton Winship and the campaign against the Nationalist Party, which led to the effec-tive political eclipse of the party. The second policy was the promotion of social and political reform through the direct intervention of the federal govern-ment. This process began with the transfer of the New Deal to the island, which included the creation of two government programs to provide social re-lief and attain social stability: the Puerto Rico Emergency Relief Administration (PRERA) and the Puerto Rico Reconstruction Administration (PRRA). These programs represent the first massive fiscal intervention of the American state on the island (the transfer of federal funds) to promote social stability, a mech-anism to be used effectively in future decades.[11] The local forces interested in reform were joined through the so-called Chardón Plan (the Report of the Puerto

Rico Policy Commission),[12] the participation of the reformist sector of the Liberal Party in the administration of the PRRA, the the initial reform-oriented PPD program (1940).

The reform of the colonial government began in the forties with the administration of Rexford G. Tugwell. The government reforms implemented by Tugwell were important in making possible the social and economic reforms sponsored by the PPD and in creating the political and economic basis for the Commonwealth. Tugwell was clearly aware that his mission in Puerto Rico was to "shape civil affairs" in order to maintain the island within the hegemony of the United States. To attain this objective, and the reforms required to achieve stability, it was necessary first of all to reform the colonial government structures.[13] The Tugwell administration also supported the PPD in bringing about social and economic reforms. By the mid-forties political reforms to the colonial regime were sought in Puerto Rico and the United States. As a result, in 1947 Jesús T. Piñero became the first Puerto Rican to be named governor of the island; in 1948 Puerto Ricans for the first time elected their governor, Luis Muñoz Marín. The U.S. government and the PPD negotiated a number of reforms of the colonial regime that gave Puerto Ricans more participation in the management of local affairs; this process culminated with the approval of the Commonwealth in 1952. The Commonwealth legitimized U.S. hegemony on the island and provided political stability by giving power over local affairs to the dominant sectors grouped in the ruling PPD.[14]

The forties were also a period of economic transition, from a one-crop agroexporting economy to an industrial capitalism. Early in the decade the PPD began a program of industrialization based on an "import substitution" model, in which the process of industrialization would be propelled through the establishment of state-owned industries. The end of the war forced drastic changes in the industrialization program and in 1947 the PPD government began "Operation Bootstrap," in which industrialization would be promoted by private foreign capital (mostly American) attracted to the island by a series of government-provided incentives (tax exemption, cheap labor, and subsidies). The Commonwealth provided the political shell for the new economic model.

This long process of crisis and reform led to a redefinition of the political alliances that were formed before the forties, including the collapse of the existing political parties before the advance of the PPD and its reformist-populist program. The roots of the crisis of Republicanism, nevertheless, are found in the rupture of the party in 1924, which distanced the axis sectors of the Republican Party.

The Republicans and the Politics of Coalitions

The Alliance, the electoral pact between the Republican and Union parties, was an attempt to unite the bourgeoisie and the hacendados in a common political program for the defense of their minimal common interests. But their class and ideological differences made the Alliance a very fragile political pact. Although the Alliance won the elections in 1924 and 1928, it was plagued from the outset by problems like the distribution of public jobs and electoral patronage between Unionists and Republicans, and their incapacity to integrate organizationally and programmatically.[15] In the end, the Alliance was unable to reconcile the differences between the Republican bourgeoisie and the Unionist *hacendados*.

The crisis of the Alliance came as a result both of the political desperation of the Unionist hacendados and of its class antagonisms. In 1928 Antonio R. Barceló and José Tous Soto demanded from President Coolidge a reform in the colonial regime that would grant them more autonomist powers. The Alliance Assembly of that same year demanded from Congress the admission of Puerto Rico to the federation under a "special State" status with a different fiscal and political treatment than that granted to the other states. Confronted by the refusal of the U.S. government to concede reforms and the Republicans' unwillingness to seek any, the Unionists decided to break the Alliance in 1929. Headed by Barceló, the Union Party launched a campaign for independence and against large monopolies and economic absenteeism.[16]

Class differences were also important in the breakdown of the Alliance. By 1925 Barceló was already in conflict with the fuerzas vivas, the representative organizations of the Puerto Rican bourgeoisie. The conflict emerged from the attempts by Barceló to make a pact with the Socialists, and from a number of fiscal reform measures sought by the Unionists that contradicted the interests of the local bourgeoisie, particularly its sugar sector. This alienated Barceló not only from the Republicans but also from the Unionist bourgeois sector, as reflected in his dispute with Eduardo Giorgetti, representative of the sugar interests in the Union Party.[17] This conflict in the Alliance deepened after the 1928 elections, when the Republicans presented a legislative program that represented the interests of the fuerzas vivas. With the departure of Barceló's ranks from the Alliance, only the Republicans and a group of sugar and bourgeois Unionists, the latter known in the party for their annexationist postures, remained in the organization. The sugar sector that remained in the Union Party, which was later transformed into the Liberal Party, became the conservative and proautonomist faction of the party.[18]

Once the Alliance was broken, there was a realignment of political forces that led to an alliance between the party of the working class and the Republican bourgeoisie in the Coalition by the early 1930s. The basis for this alliance lay in the internal transformations within both parties. The important changes from the perspective of the bourgeoisie were related to the formation of the Partido Unión Republicana (PUR—Republican Union Party) in 1932. The withdrawal of the Unionists left the Republicans in control of the Alliance. But both the Alliance Republicans and the Pure Republicans were politically weak. The Pure Republicans knew that they would be subordinated to the Socialists in the Coalition. The Alliance Republicans, after failed attempts to bring the

Unionists back into the Alliance,[19] saw their political survival in the union of the Republican family. Both Republican factions knew that only united could they withstand the Socialists and prevent the electoral triumph of the Liberals (former Unionists). After bitter debates, particularly over the issues of independence, statehood, and collaboration with the Socialists, the factions reconciled in a common political program under the PUR.

The alliance between the Republicans and the Socialists in 1932 was qualitatively different from the earlier one. In 1924 the Socialists entered into a political alliance with the Republican petty bourgeois sector; but in 1932 the alliance included the Republican bourgeoisie that had joined the PUR. Though the PUR was a fragile alliance between the two Republican factions, compromises required for the unification included the defense of the bourgeois/sugar interests. The PUR leadership was shared by both factions (Rafael Martínez Nadal, Pure, was named president, while Alfonso Valdés, of the Alliance, became vice-president); nevertheless, the bourgeois/sugar sector was prominent in PUR's politics.[20]

The Coalition also required that the Republican bourgeoisie accept the political alliance with the working class. One factor that made it easier for them to accept this alliance was the recognition that the Socialist leadership, headed by Santiago Iglesias, was anything but radical.[21] Furthermore, the Republican bourgeoisie came to accept the petty bourgeoisie's belief in the need for harmonious relations between capital and labor as crucial for the maintenance of social peace.[22] But the differences in the social constituencies of the two parties and the conflicts within each party, spurred by their participation in the Coalition, led to continued disputes in the Coalition.

The Coalition was not able to reconcile the divergent interests of two organizations representing different classes. The Coalition's legislative work was plagued with dissent among the parties, particularly in those bills dealing with the betterment of the working class's working conditions.[23] The extension of the New Deal to Puerto Rico created new conflicts in the Coalition. The Socialists tended to support the transfer of federal programs intended to improve the conditions of the working class. The Puerto Rican bourgeoisie was opposed to the extension of these programs because, like their U.S. counterparts, they viewed it as an improper intervention of the state in the affairs of private enterprise.[24] Once the New Deal programs were transferred to the island, the local bourgeoisie struggled to "adapt" them to the "particular conditions" of Puerto Rico, which created further conflicts with the Socialists.[25] Although the Coalition won the 1936 elections, it was already divided by that time. The new administration fell into disrepute, characterized by extensive corruption and political demoralization.[26] By the mid-1930s both parties experienced internal disputes that would lead to ruptures within the decade.

The Opposition to Social Reform

A series of ruptures in the PUR toward the end of the thirties strengthened the Republican bourgeoisie's hold over the statehood movement and program. One of the most significant events in the evolution of the PUR was the departure of the *colonos* (sugar farmers) from the party. Dependent on the growth of the sugar industry in general, the colonos gave their political support to the *central* owners during the first three decades of the century. Because of the community of interests between the colonos and the central owners, the conflicts among them erupted only after the sugar industry experienced critical problems in the 1930s.

Although the colonos controlled 48.7 percent of the land devoted to sugarcane cultivation, their crops produced only 35.5 percent of the sugar cane. The colonos were at the mercy of the centrals to sell their crops; the centrals fixed the price of sugar cane in their own favor.[27] The quota imposed by the Costigan-Jones Law meant a real economic crush for the colonos, who took the full brunt of the new restrictions. They suffered discrimination in the apportionment of the quota, while the centrals received the greatest number of payments for sugar contracts as established by the quota. In 1935 while 98.2 percent of the sugar contracts received only 25.4 percent of the total payments, 0.4 percent of the contracts received 56.2 percent of total payments.[28] This situation, along with the fall in prices, created a precarious economic condition for the colonos, reflected in their chronic indebtedness to the centrals. By the mid-1930s the colonos had become largely dependent on the centrals, as shown by the fact that two-thirds of the colonos were financed by the centrals. The conflicts between the colonos and the centrals extended to the labor contracts with the sugar workers, which tended to favor the centrals. Minimum wages for the industry were determined on the basis of the centrals' wage levels, which could hardly be met by the colonos.[29]

The imposition of the sugar quota and the transfer of the New Deal to Puerto Rico stimulated the conflicts between the colonos and the central owners in the PUR. Although the PUR tried to conciliate all the sugar interests in the party,[30] it did not take long to discover that the central owners were benefiting at the colonos's expense. In 1934 the colonos organized the Asociación de Colonos (Association of Sugar Farmers) to defend their interests against the central owners. The creation of this organization showed the depth of the colonos's alienation from the PUR. It was organized by Jesús T. Piñero, outstanding Republican leader, who became a founding member of the PPD. The Asociación de Colonos supported the PPD program while the Association of Sugar Producers (ASP), historically the representative of all sugar interests but controlled by the sugar central owners, represented the PUR's sugar interests. During the 1940s all ASP presidents were PUR leaders, with Miguel A. García Méndez being the most important example.

The final rupture between the central owners and the colonos in the PUR came with the debate about the Chardón Plan, which promoted New Deal programs in Puerto Rico. Part of this program was an attack on sugar absenteeism, the enforcement of the 500 Acres Law, and a proposal that the centrals acquired by the government should refine sugar cane for the colonos to provide them with greater benefits. Pressured by the central owners, the PUR rejected the Chardón Plan; this finally alienated the colonos, who supported it, from the party.[31] Many colonos left the PUR and joined the Liberal Party, where Muñoz and his group were supporting the Chardón Plan and the New Deal for Puerto Rico; they became an important social force in the PPD.[32]

The politics of the PUR sugar sector also alienated the professional petty bourgeois sector from the party. The professionals had supported the American regime in Puerto Rico, since it was beneficial to their own growth as a class. The expansion of the sugar economy and commerce, the growth of the market for services, and the increase in the state bureaucracy provided the conditions for their reproduction. But the economic stagnation of the thirties limited the employment opportunities for professionals; they suffered increased unemployment and underemployment.[33] Their political loyalties began to change with this situation, mostly because the Republican leadership alienated them with its conservative policies in favor of the status quo. Nothing is more telling than the PUR's opposition to federal programs in Puerto Rico and to the growth of local government, at times the only sources of employment for professionals. By the end of the decade large numbers of professionals were leaving the party and joining the PPD.

The PPD's reforms adversely affected a sector of the Puerto Rican bourgeoisie, the sugar sector.[34] The sugar bourgeoisie launched a campaign of opposition to the PPD reforms, a campaign that united the rest of the bourgeoisie around it. During the 1940s the Puerto Rican bourgeoisie viewed the PPD as a radical movement seeking to change the socioeconomic structures of capitalism on the island and bring independence. This perception of the PPD caused the bourgeoisie to increase its support of statehood as the only alternative to stop social change and independence.[35]

The sugar bourgeoisie took the lead in opposing the PPD reforms. In 1941 they forced the PUR to vote in block against the Land Law, the centerpiece of the PPD agrarian reform program.[36] The sugar bourgeoisie criticized the PPD for what they called the "nationalization" of the sugar industry and the excessive controls imposed by the government.[37] They also attacked the government for intervening in the sugar worker–employer relationship by supporting the syndicalization of sugar workers and for increasing wages.[38]

The bourgeoisie was also united in its attack of the PPD's industrialization program, which it claimed promoted an "increasing trend toward domination of all business by the insular government."[39] The Puerto Rican Manufacturers' Association (PRMA) criticized the government because it "did very little to aid the development of private industry," while it supported the state's intervention in the economy.[40] The bourgeoisie was also opposed to the expansion of government structures; the first plan of the Planning Board was described by the Chamber of Commerce as "a heterodox program whose main objective is the intensification of the Class Struggle." According to them, the newly created public corporations "are gradually taking over every important industrial, commercial, and agricultural private enterprise on the island."[41] In 1948, a year after Operation Bootstrap began, the opposition's pro-statehood candidate for governor accused the PPD government that "with its policy of control over industries it is going straight toward communism."[42] The PPD's political predominance in the 1940s promoted alliances between the opposition parties, based on two elements: opposition to the PPD's reform program, and support for statehood.

But the PPD's electoral growth also stimulated conflicts and fragmentation within the opposition. In 1939 a dissident faction from the PUR's bourgeoisie, headed by García Méndez, broke from the party and formed the Partido Unión Republicana Reformista (PURR—Reformist Republican Union Party). It united with the Pure Labor Party, a Socialist offshoot, and the remains of the moribund Liberal Party in forming the Tripartite Puerto Rican Unification, popularly known as *la Mogolla* (the "Mess").[43] Although the Coalition again won the 1940 elections by a small margin, the PPD nevertheless was able to implement its program with the collaboration of the labor sector of the Unification that supported the Popular Democratic policies.

In 1944 the Reformist Republicans joined the PUR to form the Partido Unión Republicana Progresista (PURP—Progressive Republican Union Party). That year the PURP joined the Socialists and the Liberals in an electoral coalition against the PPD and were defeated overwhelmingly. For the elections of 1948, the PURP, now the Partido Estadista Puertorriqueño (PEP—Puerto Rican Statehood Party), again united with the Socialists and the Liberals against the PPD. The PPD not only increased its electoral margin, but won all the legislative districts and lost only one town; the opposition could only elect one senator and one representative.[44] The electoral and political hegemony of the PPD was such that only one party, the Statehood Party, survived into the 1950s, becoming the main opposition party.

By the beginning of the 1950s the opposition in Puerto Rico was represented by a party promoting statehood under the leadership of the bourgeoisie. One source of its electoral support came from sectors of the commercial petty bourgeoisie, discontented with the PPD's economic policies.[45] It also received the support of World War II veterans and of the increasing number of federal government employees in Puerto Rico.[46] A sector of Socialist workers, allied with the annexationists during the forties, remained within the Statehood Party. This working-class sector and the increasing number of marginals who began to support the party provided the Statehood Party with its small popular base.[47]

THE TRANSFORMATION OF THE STATEHOOD PROGRAM

The Republican Family: A Conflictive Unity

The formation of the PUR in 1932 was an attempt to unite the diverse inter-ests of the Republican family once again. The Republican rupture in 1924 was accompanied by diverse strategies toward self-government, independence, statehood, and the Socialists by both Republican factions. Though these differ-ences did not prevent the reunification of the Republicans, they laid the basis for future conflicts. The final program of the PUR was a compromise, more like an amalgam, of these conflicting views.[48]

While the Alliance Republicans had to accept the political alliance with the Socialists, the Pure Republicans had to accept independence as a Republican alternative. According to Martínez Nadal, the leader of the Pure Republicans, the party "made one of the greatest sacrifices of its political life in order to obtain the union of a great part of the Puerto Rican family . . . [when] the possible demand for independence was included in our platform."[49] In the section dealing with the political status of Puerto Rico, the program demanded statehood for Puerto Rico, and if this alternative was denied "then the Repub-lican Union Party will struggle for full sovereignty, equally compatible with our ideals of liberty and self-government."[50] Other measures were intended to facilitate self-government while the status issue was being resolved; additional demands for social reform were included as a conciliatory gesture to the So-cialists.

The conciliation of the diverse interests in the PUR did not free the party from internal conflicts, since there was opposition to the unification from both Pure and Alliance Republicans.[51] The most fierce resistance came from some Alliance Republicans, headed by none other than José Tous Soto, who as pres-ident of the Republican Party pushed for the alliance with the Unionists. Tous Soto presented, for the first time, a forceful criticism of statehood within Re-publicanism. Already by 1924 Tous Soto had had doubts about the inevitability of statehood (discussed in Chapter 3). But by 1932 his doubts had solidified into opposition. For Tous Soto, statehood offered only "disadvantages." Eco-nomically, Puerto Rico would have to pay federal taxes and would lose its power to regulate foreign trade and to decide issues like Prohibition, which affected the rum industry in the island. Politically, the "advantages" of state-hood were two senators and seven representatives, along with a constitution "made in Borinquen." But these were not real advantages, since Puerto Ricans would not have great power within Congress. Furthermore, the United States was not disposed to grant statehood to Puerto Rico, for political-cultural rea-sons. According to Tous Soto, Puerto Rico "constitutes a danger to national stability . . . Puerto Rico will never be a genuine American community. . . . We will be American at the skin level, but in the depth of our being . . . we will be intransmutable Puerto Ricans [borinqueños]." But more importantly, statehood would not benefit Puerto Rico because it would not provide self-government to the island:

> the invasion of federal powers in the internal life of the states is accentuated every time . . . taking away, in an avalanche, the highly acclaimed state prerogatives. . . . There is no statesman . . . capable of showing the advantages of the status of statehood, not because he is incapable, but due to the impossibility of doing so.[52]

Tous Soto attempted to reorganize the Alliance by allying again with the Unionists, in order to prevent the fusion with the Pure Republicans.[53] The attempt failed, and with it Tous Soto was buried politically.

It was not long before the reunification of the Republican family showed its internal fissures. In 1934 the first dissidence of importance emerged with the creation of the so-called Group of 76. This faction was formed by prominent members of the Alliance, particularly by former Unionists. They attacked the great individual power of Martínez Nadal in the PUR and protested the constant discrimination against former Unionists. The Group also criticized the struggle over government jobs, the unnecessary attacks against the governor, and the undue opposition to the recently transferred programs of the New Deal.[54]

But their most severe critique was against the party's relationship with the Socialists. The Group of 76 attacked the basis of the Coalition itself, arguing that the Socialists wanted to impose their political-ideological creed upon the Republicans, and that the latter had to support measures that were against their program. In a resolution approved by the Group of 76 they argued that "the Coalition pact does not decree to the contracting parties the obligation to tolerate and to make common cause with the other party"; nor was there an "obligation of mutual solidarity in the attainment of . . . political principles" that were in conflict with the party's program.[55] The Group of 76 was expelled from the PUR, ostensibly for their participation in the Civic League, an organization that had been publicly condemned by the party. In 1935 the Group of 76 formed the Regional Party, whose main political issues were administrative reform and self-government.[56] The Regional Party disappeared as quickly as it emerged, and most of its members later joined the PPD.

The Rejection of Independence

The introduction in 1936 of the Tydings Bill for independence brought to the surface the internal conflicts in the PUR. The Tydings Bill presented the PUR with the opportunity to show its support for independence. The bill divided the party once again: the party leadership, headed by Martínez Nadal, supported the bill, while a sector led by García Méndez opposed the bill on the basis that it excluded statehood as an alternative.

The support given by the party's main leadership to the Tydings Bill, and to independence, was circumstantial. It came from the perception that the American government would not grant statehood to Puerto Rico. Nevertheless, independence was one road to the self-government desired by sectors within the PUR. According to Martínez Nadal: "It is evident that the Administration has no disposition to admit us as a state. . . . Given this situation . . . all that we can demand from Washington is that they modify the basis on which we are to be granted the power to constitute the sovereignty of our Republic."[57] But the PUR had no program for independence. The alternative of independence had been elaborated by the Republicans at a philosophical level, as an alternative path to self-government if statehood was rejected. Furthermore, the Pure Republicans had been pushed to support independence by the need to unite the Republicans in one party; this situation gave rise to a very fragmented and idealistic notion of this alternative. According to Martínez Nadal, the PUR "had assigned independence as the refuge of dignity when acts of Congress or of the people of the United States indicate to us the impossibility of becoming a state of the Union; between hunger and dishonor, I point out to my people the road of dignity."[58]

The absence of an independence program in the PUR led Martínez Nadal to argue that once the Republic of Puerto Rico is accepted, the party should retire from the government, because "those men who sincerely defended the Republic should govern."[59] García Méndez, representing those opposed to separation, proposed that along with independence Puerto Ricans should be presented with another alternative for self-government, which he called *Estado-Independiente* (independent-state); this proposal included "a state of the American Union or a Free State following the guidelines of the Autonomous State of Canada." This proposal resembled the Commonwealth formula that would be so bitterly contested by García Méndez and the annexationists in decades to come.[60] With the debate around the issue of independence, García Méndez's group began to distance from the leadership of the party.

The Tydings Bill confronted the Republicans with the possibility of independence, but by the thirties independence confronted the Republicans with another issue: the social character of the republic. Both factions of the party began to question independence because they feared the direction that the republic might take in Puerto Rico. For Martínez Nadal, the Tydings Bill presented the Union Republicans with "the dilemma of independence or colony, this clamor of justice with hunger, misery and desolation; and as the only hope for the future, a Republic made up of oppressing castes and oppressed castes, or a communist or Soviet Republic"; independence carried the spectre of "a revolution of the proletariat, that would put us in the same situation as Spain, Russia and other wretched places of the world."[61] García Méndez was also opposed to independence, arguing that it would give rise to violence, while statehood provided the internal and external security that Puerto Rico required. Independence, he argued, would arouse social conflicts: "the day that the Republic comes the African hatreds will resurrect."[62] Independence, by opening the spectre of social change, had ceased to be a viable alternative for the Republicans.

The Rise of Conservatism

The PUR finally divided in 1940 when its bourgeois/sugar sector, headed by García Méndez, left the party and founded the PURR. The main cause of the schism was not the issue of independence, but the same one that induced the Republican rupture in 1924: the conflicting views of the petty bourgeois and bourgeois sectors with regard to the social question. The Republican petty bourgeoisie was conservative, but its program included some social reforms, for its members saw themselves as mediators in the conflict between capital and labor. This sector largely controlled the PUR organization and its ideology was very influential in the party's program. But the PUR was founded on compromises, including the defense of the interests of the bourgeois sugar sector, particularly the defense of the sugar industry. Throughout the 1930s the PUR was the fiercest opponent of any reform in the sugar industry, constantly proposing measures for its protection. In 1936 the PUR eliminated from its program the clause demanding enforcement of the 500 Acres Law, which was anathema to the sugar sector.

The defense of the sugar industry by the petty bourgeoisie was in its own interest: since the sugar industry was the axis of the Puerto Rican economy, its well-being provided the economic growth required for the development of this class. Hence their interests coincided with those of the sugar bourgeoisie. But the petty bourgeois sector did not want to appear as mere pawns of the sugar interests. In a speech to the PUR membership, Martínez Nadal stated: "The corporations have nothing to do with the Republican Union. . . . If the Republican Union were to be convinced that by substituting other crops for the cultivation of sugar . . . we could better fight the latifundia and absenteeism, we would not hesitate to do so."[63] This sector held onto Barbosa's argument that the best way to maintain social peace was through the conciliation of capital and labor. Martínez Nadal argued that social peace is possible only if inequalities are eliminated, and it is capital that must take the first step. It is necessary, he argued,

> to put an end in Puerto Rico to these [social] inequalities that disturb the
> spiritual peace of our people, and that are born of unconscionable ambition
> bordering on avarice. . . . It is indispensable that a new socioeconomic
> philosophy be the one to regulate the relations between Capital and Labor.
> . . . Capital should initiate a policy of limiting its profits to a moderate
> and reasonable level.[64]

According to Martínez Nadal, the PUR should follow a policy of conciliation of the diverse social classes in order to secure social peace in Puerto Rico:

> The Republican Union . . . should seek a peaceful, free, and happy exis-
> tence for all classes in Puerto Rico . . . this clamor for justice that some-
> times culminates in revolutions and blood shedding, this desire for social
> justice, . . . have surrounded Puerto Rico, and their presence is felt in
> such a way that no one can escape the desire for social justice.[65]

This conception provided the philosophical-political basis for the electoral alliance with the Socialists, an alliance that the bourgeois/sugar sector of the party
adamantly opposed.

The rupture between the PUR's petty bourgeois and the bourgeois/sugar sectors resulted from their differences over the Coalition with the Socialists and
the social philosophy of the party. The bourgeois/sugar sector had accepted the
pact with the Socialists in the belief that this would secure social peace in
Puerto Rico. But by the late 1930s the Socialist Party (PS) had alienated those
sectors of the working class that had given life to it, in part because of its
alliance with the PUR. By the early 1940s the PS could not guarantee social
peace on the side of the working class. Consequently the PUR's bourgeois/
sugar sector opposed the renewal of the Coalition with the PS. They also argued that the Coalition had been a failure in government, and that the Socialists
were the main culprit for its reputation for corruption and immorality.[66]

The bourgeois/sugar sector also began to articulate its differences with the
petty bourgeoisie regarding the social philosophy of the party. For the bour-
geois/sugar sector, the island's social problems were a result, not of social
inequalities, but of the discriminatory economic policies of the federal government (for example, the Costigan-Jones Act) and an inept administration in the
island.[67] For example, countering the attacks on economic absenteeism as one
of the island's economic ills, García Méndez argued that absenteeism did not
exist on the island due to the fact that "in Puerto Rico 91 percent of all farms
are directly managed by their residents"; similarly, latifundium is nonexistent:
"Latifundium could potentially exist, but not latifundium in its proper sense of
'deserted lands', of 'unused land' . . . this could not be even remotely understood to exist here."[68]

The reforms implemented by the PPD and the Tugwell administration during
1940–44 moved the statehood parties to more conservative positions in defense
of the status quo. After the PPD's unexpected electoral success in 1940 both
Republican factions clamored for unity, based primarily on their opposition to
the PPD policies.[69] The unification of the PUR and the PURR came in 1944
with the formation of the Partido Unión Republicana Progresista (PURP—Progressive Republican Union Party). But this time it was the bourgeois/sugar
sector who molded the ideology and program of the party. The PURP's program was one of opposition to the PPD reforms and in favor of statehood.

As Celestino Iriarte stated when calling for the unity of the Republican family, the objective of the new party was to "defeat the Popular Party, which has
taken over Government and which has disturbed our social, political, and eco-

nomic organization as a people.''[70] The PURP's program was an amalgam of incoherent postulates tied together by one common element: the defense of the existing world against the attack by ''revolutionary'' forces. Its socioeconomic platform included a call to regulate capital-labor relations ''through collective bargaining,'' that is, opposition to the government's fixing wages; ''a campaign against subversive, independentist, totalitarian or communist politics; . . . promotion of industrialization; protection of native products [namely, sugar].''[71] The PURP desired social peace, but believed peace should be achieved through the imposition of Christian values rather than by the conciliation of class interests.[72] They believed in ''cooperation'' among classes, promising to ''fight any attempt to divide Puerto Ricans into classes struggling amongst themselves, or to fan social and economic hatred, because such methods are the negation of democracy.'' Their solution to social and economic instability was a strong dose of ''laissez-faire'': everything would go well if the state did not intervene in the economy and allowed the forces of the market free rein. They maintained that ''the efforts of the government . . . [should] never interfere, dominate and compete'' with private capital.[73]

The bourgeoisie's opposition to state intervention was not only ideological but was a reaction to the public policies of the period. For example, the bourgeoisie opposed government regulation of wages and government support for trade unions, which interfered with the free play of the market in determining wages; instead, its members demanded the regulation of worker-employer relations through collective bargaining.[74] The PURP's ''agrarian program'' reflected the preoccupations of its sugar sector with the PPD's agrarian policies. The program was simply a defense of the party's sugar interests; it stated that the PURP would sell the sugar land and centrals under government control to the private sector, and that it ''will maintain the 500 Acres Law, applying it 'in a just and orderly form.' ''[75] Throughout the decade into the fifties, the defense of the sugar industry remained a central element of the program of the statehood parties. Nothing is more telling than the ad by the Association of Sugar Producers of Puerto Rico in the statehood magazine El Estado during this period: ''All is not sugar in Puerto Rico . . . but sugar is everything to Puerto Rico.''

The 1948 program of the Partido Estadista Puertorriqueño reiterated the attacks on the growth of the state, declaring that ''our government is getting closer, in practice, to a totalitarian kind of regime.'' The PEP program decried state ''latifundium and monopoly'' and ''the disloyal competition by the state against the private entrepreneur; the increasing centralization of public power, which leads to political dictatorship.'' Opposing state intervention, the PEP program emphasized ''the encouragement and protection of private initiative to create more abundant means of life, progress, and welfare through the fruitful exercise of private enterprise.'' The program proposed the elimination of the Agricultural Company and the Land Authority, which had been created to implement the PPD's agrarian reform. It also proposed the elimination of the

Transportation Authority and the Communications Authority and the transfer of these services to private enterprise. It reaffirmed the promise to apply the 500 Acres Law in "an orderly, reasonable, and just form" and to reduce taxes "on lands devoted to the cultivation of foodstuffs" (for example, sugar). With regard to worker-employer relations, the program emphasized the need for "maximum cooperation between capital and labor."[76]

Thus by the late 1940s the program of the old Republican Party had changed drastically. That program presented conservatism and statehood as the alternatives to what they perceived as a radical attack against the status quo by the PPD. The crisis of Republicanism and the rise of conservatism within the statehood movement radically transformed the statehood program.

The Transformation of the Statehood Program

This period can be called one of crisis for the statehood movement for several reasons: the striking decrease in electoral support for the statehood parties; change in the basis of support for annexationism, turning the movement into one representative of the interests of the bourgeoisie, with an extremely conservative politics and ideology; and the constant fragmentation of the movement. Together these elements transformed the statehood program.

The first statehood program was elaborated by the Republican Party during the first decades of this century. It was part of what I have called the Republican project (Chapter 3). An essential part of this project was the achievement of statehood, which was defined under the conception of the "regional fatherland" or "statehood as independence"; that is, the view that the local dominant class would have total autonomy over local affairs. This view was transformed with the "new federalism" of the Roosevelt administration, which did not guarantee the total self-government by the states; the increasing intervention of the federal government in the affairs of the states limited the power of the local dominant classes.

As previously discussed, in the debates around the PUR formation Tous Soto opposed statehood precisely because of the limitations on local self-government resulting from the expansion of federal powers. The Republicans had already experienced this federal intrusion into local affairs. The Republican sugar sector had opposed Prohibition in Puerto Rico and pushed the party to fight for its elimination. In 1932 the Resident Commissioner in Washington, a member of the PUR, submitted a bill to grant the island "autonomy in prohibitionist matters"; the bill was seen "as a step to self-government."[77] But the real confrontation came with the extension of Roosevelt's "new federalism" to Puerto Rico. The imposition of the Costigan-Jones Act, the transfer to Puerto Rico of the Agricultural Adjustment Act and the National Industrial Relief Administration (NIRA), and the implementation of the PRERA, PRRA, and other federal programs raised the wrath of the Puerto Rican Republicans. The Republican bourgeois/sugar sector was the most vociferous opponent of this "invasion" of federal power over local affairs. An angry García Méndez stated: "To allow the functions of a supergovernment to be carried out in Puerto Rico, in total disrespect of popular sovereignty—only a degraded people could tolerate this." Responding to charges that the Republicans were opposed to any program of reconstruction promoted by the federal government, García Méndez answered that "we want reconstruction with the intervention of our government agencies, with respect for the little sovereignty that we enjoy."[78]

More threatening yet was the realization by the sugar bourgeoisie that the federal government would act against its economic interests. This was felt during the thirties with programs like the PRRA and the Costigan-Jones Act, but it became an immediate and pressing reality during the 1940s under the Tugwell administration. The social reforms initiated by the PPD and supported by Tugwell harassed the Puerto Rican bourgeoisie. In the Constituent Assembly of the PURP in 1944, a resolution was approved condemning the "National administration" for keeping Tugwell in his post; he was called "undesirable for this country, because of his arbitrary and obstinate conduct against the most sacred interests of our people."[79] The Department of Interior was likewise condemned for its "incorrect" policy toward Puerto Rico and for its complicity with Tugwell.

The realization by Puerto Rican annexationists that American federalism did not guarantee self-government led to a change in their conception of statehood. The belief that statehood represented total self-government was supplanted by the belief that only statehood could guarantee the full participation of Puerto Ricans in Congress, the seat of power in the American federal system. Luis A. Ferré elaborated on this conception of statehood in his speech before the Commonwealth Constituent Assembly in 1951:

> How can a people guarantee its life when its industry is at the mercy of the actions of a foreign body of legislators that . . . could condemn it to death without our people having any resource or right to defend themselves? . . . Only after Puerto Rico has full representation in Congress, with sufficient votes so that its economic interests are taken into account—not as a gift but with all the force of the right to life that 2,200,000 American citizens have—our political status will not be solved. How could it be if it is in Congress, in whose deliberations our representatives cannot participate, wherein lies the supreme authority that guarantees our lives?[80]

The belief that statehood meant self-government was supplanted by a conception of statehood as the only mechanism to guarantee "equality in the sovereignty of federated statehood," as Ferré called it; the only political status that could provide Puerto Rico with "the necessary tools to guarantee our economic progress."[81]

During the 1940s the Republicans realized that independence—previously considered as the second best to statehood—was not an attractive alternative after all. As discussed earlier, Martínez Nadal and García Méndez feared that independence meant a republic riddled with social conflicts, a "Soviet republic." In the 1940s there was an important change in the program of annexationism: the rejection of independence as an alternative to statehood in obtaining self-government, and the development of an anti-independence, anticommunist rhetoric, at the very moment that statehood became the only alternative.

There are several reasons for this change in program. The rise of the PPD, with a proindependence rhetoric in its early years and a program of social reform, promoted a defensive posture among the bourgeoisie. But more important than this was the material weakness of the bourgeoisie, in particular the sugar bourgeoisie. In the 1920s and 1930s the relative economic and political strength of the sugar bourgeoisie allowed its members to toy with independence as a political alternative. But by the early 1940s their economic and political basis was undermined, and the sugar bourgeoisie was in no condition to struggle for the control of an independent state, so it opposed independence. On the other hand, the industrial bourgeoisie was still in its infancy, still politically subordinated to the sugar bourgeoisie and sharing the latter's fear of reform and independence.

Already by 1944, anti-independence, anticommunist rhetoric is evident in the PURP program.[82] There was a prevalent belief that confronted by the "danger" of independence, the only alternative was statehood.[83] Ramiro Colón, an outstanding statehood leader, clearly espoused this belief in his speech to the Commonwealth Constituent Assembly in 1951: "As long as we do not achieve statehood, the phantom of international independence will always be a nightmare in our collective life. As long as we are not a state . . . we will not enjoy social peace."[84] Independence opens the gates to social conflict; only statehood, through the protection afforded by the American state, can secure the reproduction of capitalism for the Puerto Rican bourgeoisie.[85]

The Push for Statehood

As statehood gained a defensive and conservative character, it lost its popular support, as shown by the electoral results since 1940. In 1945 a congressional committee characterized statehood as "a worn-out political issue in Puerto Rico for the time being."[86] The loss of popular support led to a "push for statehood" campaign in the statehood movement, as it stepped up its statehood proselytism and criticism of the PPD.[87]

The push for statehood included the quest for support among diverse civic and social organizations in the United States, and the creation of new organizations for the promotion of statehood. Throughout the decade, the statehooders curried the support of several U.S. organizations, including the American Federation of Labor, the Lions International Association, the American Legion, the Congress of American Teachers, and others. Statehood was supported in the program of the National Republican Party.[88] New statehood organizations were created both to spread the statehood gospel and to reunify all statehooders. These new organizations were created outside the political parties with the sole objective of promoting statehood. In 1940 the Puerto Rican–American Women's League was created to promote the statehood ideal in the United States.[89] The Asociación Puertorriqueña Pro-Estadidad (APPE—Puerto Rican Association for Statehood), the most outstanding statehood organization in the decade, was formed in 1943 and a year later the Asociación Universitaria Pro-Estadidad (AUPE—University Pro-Statehood Association) was created; the purpose of both organizations was to integrate all supporters of statehood. In 1945 Luis López Tizol founded the magazine *El Estado;* its main objective, according to the editor, was to provide statehooders with a forum for debate, in order to resolve their political differences.[90]

The need for the unity of the statehood movement derives from the defensive character and weakness of the movement during this period, and from the conviction that statehood represented the only viable opposition to the PPD program. In 1948 the PURP changed its name to Puerto Rican Statehood Party (PEP), expressing the importance given to statehood above any other consideration. In a speech given weeks after the formation of the PEP, Ramiro Colón, then APPE president and leader of the party, argued that statehood was essential for economic and political reasons: "Without political stability there can be no economic stability and under the American flag there is political stability only in statehood." It was the urgent task of all statehooders to overcome ideological and-political differences and join in a single party to show the PPD and the United States that the Puerto Ricans wanted statehood; he added that "our differences with respect to socioeconomic ideology will vanish when we become a state. . . . It is time to close ranks and to continue with determination the struggle, the difficult struggle for the salvation of the ideal."[91]

The newly defensive and conservative character of the statehood movement yielded some novel conceptions of statehood, such as the aforementioned "statehood as equality." Two other novel conceptions, of great importance for the statehood movement in future decades, were introduced to the annexationist program: "Creole statehood" and "U.S. citizenship as the gateway to statehood."

Creole Statehood

The concept "Creole statehood" became widely known through Ferré's statehood politics in the 1960s. Of particular concern here is the elaboration during this period of one of its constitutive elements: the notion that the Puerto Rican personality would have to be protected even under statehood. This notion had appeared earlier in the concept of the regional fatherland; José Celso Barbosa argued that American federalism provided the necessary conditions for the survival of the "regional characteristics" of the states. But the Republicans also believed that Puerto Rico had to be Americanized in order to become a state. Several factors led the Puerto Rican annexationists to redefine this policy: the persistence of independence sentiments in the population; the emergence of cultural nationalism in the thirties; and the failure of the Americanization policy, particularly of English-language instruction.

Luis Sánchez Morales, one of the "founding fathers" of the Republican Party, was among the first to deal with this issue. According to Sánchez Morales, "Americanization in Puerto Rico has to be Puerto Rican–style." He argued that Puerto Rico would need a particular formula to achieve statehood:

> The classic Territory [status] . . . would turn us into anti-Americans in a country whose Americanization has to be based on respect for the traditions, laws, customs, language, and even the way of walking that form our personality. . . . In one word: on the way to statehood we have to pass through the autonomy of a special government that would not cripple our physiognomy.[92]

Sánchez Morales went even further than most of his fellow statehooders: the defense of the Puerto Rican personality was above any other consideration, including that of statehood: "If we cannot save the soul of our country within the United States, we shall save it outside."[93] Sánchez Morales attacked the nationalist views by arguing that statehood could not transform the Puerto Rican personality because it was already formed and could not be altered.[94] This argument was incorporated into the statehood discourse through leaders like Martínez Nadal, García Méndez, and Ferré.[95]

While all references to self-government and independence were eliminated from the statehood discourse, the belief that the Puerto Ricans' ethnocultural difference should not be an obstacle to statehood persisted. The concept of a regional fatherland reemerged in a somewhat different form, emphasizing the capacity of the multiethnic U.S. federal system to accept ethnocultural diversity. This position was elaborated by Reece Bothwell, one of the foremost statehood ideologues of the period:

> Heterogeneous peoples like Switzerland, . . . Canada, . . . and Soviet Russia, . . . have been forced to use the federal formula of government. Because this formula, of which the best model is perhaps the United States, offers the advantages of a strong central government to take care of the issues of general interest while at the same time allowing political subdivisions . . . complete independence in the internal affairs of local interest. . . . And this is why we believe that Puerto Rico can fit perfectly in the federation of the United States of America, without sacrificing its uniqueness as a people.[96]

Bothwell argued that the ethnocultural difference of the Puerto Ricans was not an obstacle to statehood, but that, on the contrary, it was a powerful tool, an asset to be used. Statehood would not require the assimilation of Puerto Ricans, because the United States is a multiethnic society, a melting pot of diverse cultures, where the knowledge of other languages besides English is an economic and social advantage. He further argued that Puerto Rico benefited from its contact with American culture by its absorption of the elements of progress, democracy, and liberty typical of Anglo-Saxon culture; while on the other hand, the United States benefited from improved relations with Latin America.[97]

The concept of "Creole statehood" was introduced to argue that Puerto Rico required a particular statehood process, including cultural autonomy; the conception that U.S. citizenship was the gateway to statehood was introduced to legitimize Puerto Rican claims to statehood.

U.S. Citizenship: The Gateway to Statehood

An important part of the Republican project was the legitimation of statehood on the basis of the mutual needs of the United States and Puerto Rico. During the period of crisis of annexationism a new conception arose that argued that the United States had an obligation to grant statehood to Puerto Rico. Citizenship became the legitimizing factor for statehood. This is already evident in the 1944 PURP program:

> This citizenship, once granted, cannot be taken away. The Puerto Rican lot is an integral part of the United States, and any person born in Puerto Rico . . . is, by determination of the federal Congress, a native of the United States. This community of juridical-economic relations and spiritual and moral interests bears an indissoluble mutuality of obligations, prerogatives, and rights that bind forever the march of both peoples toward a common destiny.[98]

Statehood was no longer presented as an alternative to be chosen by Puerto Ricans or granted by the United States, but "as the expression of the right of Puerto Ricans to enjoy all the privileges of American citizenship."[99] Statehood and citizenship are interwoven in a single relationship; if statehood is the only way to enjoy the rights of citizenship, then this guarantees the right of Puerto Ricans to statehood: "the time has come when it should be realized that the Puerto Ricans constitute a community of United States citizens and that their *citizenship is,* as has been to others in the past, *the gateway to their admission as a State* of the Union."[100] Citizenship establishes the essential tie between Puerto Ricans and the United States; it grants rights and obligations to both parties. Puerto Ricans have had the duties of citizenship without the rights that go along with it. Puerto Ricans have fulfilled their obligations: they have remained loyal to the United States since the invasion and have met the duties of citizenship with their "blood tax" (that is, by sending its young men to fight in U.S. wars and thus contributing to the federation not with money but with lives).[101]

But the United States has not fulfilled its obligations. Citizenship is seen as a contract binding both parties: while the United States incurred the obligation to accept Puerto Rico as a state, the Puerto Ricans committed themselves to become a state when they accepted citizenship:

> The concession of American citizenship in 1917 and the unanimous acceptance by the people of Puerto Rico was certainly a plebiscite. The accomplishment of that plebiscite in 1917 makes it unusual and absurd and even a scurrilous criticism the idea to consult us in another plebiscite whether we want to maintain ourselves loyal to the pact of that undestructible link.[102]

By granting Puerto Ricans citizenship, the United States incurred a moral obligation to grant them statehood; if it did not, then the United States was falling short of the principles that sustained it as a nation: "The dignity and honor of the American citizenship command no other direction and no other alternative for a community of loyal American citizens [than statehood].[103]

The right of citizenship would become an important element of the statehood discourse and program in decades to come, particularly in Romero's "statehood as equality" program. Although this concept appeared at a time when the statehood movement was primarily defensive, it provided the basis for an offensive program for achieving statehood later on.

NOTES

1. On the crisis see: A. G. Quintero-Rivera, "La base social de la transformación ideológica del Partido Popular en la década del '40," in Gerardo Navas Dávila, ed., *Cambio y desarrollo en Puerto Rico: la transformación ideológica del Partido Popular Democrático* (Hato Rey: Master Typesetting, 1980), pp. 37–119; José J. Baldrich, "Class and the State: The Origins of Populism in Puerto Rico 1934–52" (Ph.D. diss., Dept. of Sociology, Yale University, 1981), ch. 3; and Thomas Mathews, *La política puertorriqueña y el Nuevo Trato* (Río Piedras: Editorial Universitaria, 1975).

2. Esteban A. Bird, *Report on the Sugar Industry in Relation to the Social and Economic System of Puerto Rico* (San Juan: Bureau of Supplies, Printing and Transportation, 1941), pp. 40, 96, 114–15, and 125.

3. Harvey S. Perloff, *Puerto Rico's Economic Future* (Chicago: University of Chicago Press, 1950; reprinted by Arno Press, New York, 1975), p. 144.

4. Arthur Gayer, Paul T. Horman, and Earl K. James, *The Sugar Economy of Puerto Rico* (New York: Columbia University Press, 1938), p. 160; Bird, *Report on the Sugar Industry*, pp. 114–15; José A. Herrero, "En torno a la mitología del azúcar" (mimeo, 1970), p. 67.

5. Perloff, *Puerto Rico's Economic Future*, pp. 164 and 111; Herrero, "La mitología del azúcar," p. 67.

6. While in 1921 sugar represented 64.5 percent of Puerto Rico's exports, by 1948 it was reduced to 48 percent. In 1940 the sugar industry provided 24 percent of all employment; in 1950 it provided only 14.6 percent. Sugar provided 15.7 percent of the

island's net income in 1940, an amount reduced to 10 percent by 1946. Data from Perloff, *Puerto Rico's Economic Future,* pp. 136–37 and 58; and Junta de Planificación, *Informe Económico al Gobernador, 1969* (San Juan: Junta de Planificación, 1970), p. A-22.

7. Quintero-Rivera, "La base social," pp. 53–73.

8. Mathews, *La política puertorriqueña,* p. 133.

9. Baldrich, "Class and the State," ch. 4; A. G. Quintero-Rivera, "La clase obrera y el proceso político en Puerto Rico" (4, part 2), *Revista de Ciencias Sociales* 20, nos. 1–2 (March 1976), pp. 3–48; Blanca Silvestrini, *Los trabajadores puertorriqueños y el Partido Socialista (1932–1940)* (Río Piedras: Editorial Universitaria, 1979).

10. Baldrich, "Class and the State," chs. 5 and 6; Quintero-Rivera, "La base social"; Emilio Pantojas García, "Desarrollismo y lucha de clases: Los límites del proyecto populista durante la década del cuarenta," *Revista de Ciencias Sociales* 24, nos. 3–4 (July–December 1985), pp. 355–90.

11. Mathews, *La política puertorriqueña,* ch. 5; Gordon Lewis, *Puerto Rico: Power and Freedom in the Caribbean* (New York: Monthly Review Press, 1963), pp. 123–42; David F. Ross, *The Long Uphill Path* (San Juan: Editorial Edil, 1976), ch. 2.

12. Puerto Rico Policy Commission, *Report of the Puerto Rico Policy Commission* (San Juan: n.p., 1934), p. 7.

13. Rexford G. Tugwell, *The Stricken Land: The Story of Puerto Rico* (Garden City, NY: Doubleday, 1947), p. 148; and Rexford G. Tugwell, *Puerto Rican Public Papers* (San Juan: Service Office of the Government of Puerto Rico, 1945; reprinted by Arno Press, New York, 1975), pp. 47–48.

14. Carmen Ramos de Santiago, *El gobierno de Puerto Rico* (Río Piedras: Editorial Universitaria, 1970), ch. 4; and Emilio González, "El estado y las clases dominantes en la situación colonial," *Revista Mexicana de Sociología* 40, no. 3 (July–Sept. 1978), pp. 1141–52.

15. Bolívar Pagán, *Historia de los partidos políticos puertorriqueños* (San Juan: M. Pareja, 1972), vol. 1, p. 248.

16. Ibid., vol. 1, pp. 276–310; 317–18 and 336–37.

17. Ibid., p. 250; Truman Clark, *Puerto Rico and the United States, 1917–1933* (Pittsburgh, Penn.: University of Pittsburgh Press, 1975), p. 96; and Nilsa Rivera Colón, "Los pleitos electorales Socialistas en Fajardo: 1920 y 1924" (Master's thesis, Dept. of History, UPR, 1981), pp. 178–82.

18. Pagán, *Historia,* vol. 1, p. 314, and vol. 2, p. 2.

19. *El Mundo,* Jan. 14, 1932, pp. 1, 3.

20. All mill owners elected to the legislature between 1936 and 1944 were Republicans; see Baldrich, "Class and the State," pp. 182–85.

21. See the comments on this issue by a representative of the Republican bourgeoisie, Luis Sánchez Morales, *De antes y de ahora* (Madrid: Centro Editorial Rubén Darío, 1936), pp. 331 and 334.

22. Also the statements by Miguel A. García Méndez in Angel M. Torregrosa, *Miguel Angel García Méndez* (Puerto Rico: n.p., 1939), pp. 37–38; and also, Rafael Rivera Santiago, *Comprensión y análisis* (San Juan: Imprenta Venezuela, 1938), pp. 134–35.

23. Mathews, *La política puertorriqueña,* p. 57 and 78–80; Silvestrini, *Los trabajadores puertorriqueños,* pp. 38–40.

24. Mathews, *La política puertorriqueña,* pp. 123–26.

25. Silvestrini, *Los trabajadores puertorriqueños*, pp. 44–86, passim.

26. Epifanio Fiz Jímenez, *El racket del Capitolio (Gobierno de la Coalición Repúb-lico-Socialista), años 1932 al 1940* (San Juan: Editorial Esther, 1944).

27. Gayer, Horman, and James, *The Sugar Economy*, pp. 78, 136–43.

28. Bird, *Report on the Sugar Industry*, p. 68.

29. Gayer, Horman, and James, *The Sugar Economy*, p. 144 and ch. 5, passim.

30. See García Méndez's speech in his historical debate with Muñoz Marín on the Costigan-Jones Act; reproduced in Torregrosa, *Miguel Angel García Méndez*. See also Mathews, *La política puertorriqueña*, pp. 133–37, 148ff.

31. Mathews, *La política puertorriqueña*, pp. 182–87, 191, 233.

32. In 1936 the Liberal party nominated Piñero on its slate, who remained a state-hooder. See his comments on the transition in Teófilo Maldonado, *Hombres de primera plana* (San Juan, Puerto Rico: Editorial Campos, 1958), p. 180.

33. See Quintero-Rivera, "La base social," pp. 58–65.

34. Pantojas, "Desarrollismo y lucha de clases," pp. 15, 29.

35. Raymond L. Scheele, "The Prominent Families of Puerto Rico," in Julian Stew-ard et al., *The People of Puerto Rico* (Chicago: University of Illinois Press, 1972), p. 446.

36. Baldrich, "Class and the State," p. 184.

37. House Committee on Insular Affairs, *Investigation of Political, Economic, and Social Conditions in Puerto Rico*, 79th Cong., 1st sess., H. Rept. no. 497, May 1, 1945 (Washington, DC: U.S. Government Printing Office, 1945), pp. 26–27.

38. Joselo Sánchez Dergan, "La industria azucarera operada por el gobierno de Puerto Rico: Necesidad de una política pública azucarera" (Master's thesis, Sch. of Pub. Ad-min., UPR, 1975), p. 73.

39. Committee on Insular Affairs, *Investigation*, p. 27.

40. *El Mundo*, Jan 5, 1947, p. 1.

41. Quotes from Charles T. Goodsell, *Administración de una revolución* (Río Pied-ras: Editorial Universitaria, 1978), pp. 179 and 216 respectively.

42. *El Mundo*, Oct. 27, 1948, p. 1.

43. Pagán, *Historia*, vol. 2, pp. 145–50.

44. Ibid., pp. 269–77.

45. Baldrich, "Class and the State," pp. 192, 244.

46. On the support given by the veterans and U.S. federal government employees to the statehood parties, see *El Estado* 1, no. 1 (Sept.–Oct. 1945), pp. 26–27; 1 no. 3 (Jan.–Feb. 1956), pp. 11, 27, 29; 2, no. 7 (Nov.–Dec. 1946), pp. 5, 11, 27; 2, no. 10 (July–Aug. 1947), p. 35; 2, no. 12 (Nov.–Dec. 1947), pp. 23–25; 2, no. 8 (Jan.–Feb. 1948), pp. 5, 24; and 3, no. 15 (July–Aug. 1948), pp. 35, 37.

47. Baldrich, "Class and the State," pp. 228, 230.

48. The debates are in Pagán, *Historia*, vol. 2, pp. 3–12.

49. *El Mundo*, Jan. 2, 1932, p. 10.

50. Reece B. Bothwell, ed., Puerto Rico: *Cien años de lucha politica* (Río Piedras: Editorial Universitaria, 1979), p. 500.

51. Pagán, *Historia*, vol. 2, p. 8; *El Mundo*, Jan. 2, 1939, p. 60, and Jan. 14, 1932, p. 6.

52. *El Mundo*, Jan. 6, 1932, p. 6.

53. Ibid., Jan. 14, 1932, pp. 1, 3.

54. The Group's story is told by member Francisco M. Zeno in *En defensa propia: ante mi partido y ante la opinión pública de mi país* (San Juan: Tip. "La Correspon-

dencia de Puerto Rico,'' 1934). The Group's Manifesto is in Bothwell, *Puerto Rico,* vol. 2, pp. 473–78.

55. Bothwell, *Puerto Rico,* vol. 2, p. 475. For the Group's accusations see Zeno, *En defensa propia,* p. 20.

56. Bothwell, *Puerto Rico,* vol. 2, pp. 449–71; Pagán, *Historia,* vol. 2, pp. 68–70.

57. Bothwell, *Puerto Rico,* vol. 2, p. 562.

58. Quoted from Teófilo Maldonado, *Rafael Martínez Nadal: Su vida* (San Juan: Imprenta Venezuela, 1937), p. 102.

59. Bothwell, *Puerto Rico,* vol. 2, p. 562.

60. Ibid., p. 571.

61. In Bothwell, *Puerto Rico,* vol. 2, pp. 627–28; also vol. 3, p. 159.

62. In Torregrosa, *García Méndez,* p. 165.

63. In Bothwell, *Puerto Rico,* vol. 2, pp. 625–26.

64. In Rivera Santiago, *Comprensión y análisis,* pp. 135–36.

65. Bothwell, *Puerto Rico,* vol. 2, pp. 626–27.

66. In ibid., vol. 3, pp. 250–54.

67. In Torregrosa, *García Méndez,* pp. 218–19.

68. Ibid., p. 133.

69. Bothwell, *Puerto Rico,* vol. 3, pp. 307–9.

70. *El Mundo,* May 1, 1944, p. 6.

71. Ibid., p. 18.

72. In Bothwell, *Puerto Rico,* vol. 2, p. 205.

73. *El Mundo,* Aug. 21, 1944, p. 10. See also Pagán, *Historia,* vol. 2, p. 206.

74. See the article by García Méndez in *El Día* (Ponce), Dec. 18, 1949, p. 23.

75. *El Mundo,* Aug. 18, 1944, p. 5.

76. The PEP program appears in Bothwell, *Puerto Rico,* vol. 1, pt. 1, pp. 674–81; also *El Mundo,* Oct. 31, 1948, p. 12.

77. *El Mundo,* Jan. 5, 1932, p. 1.

78. García Méndez in Torregrosa, *García Méndez,* pp. 137 and 127 respectively.

79. Pagán, *Historia,* vol. 2, pp. 206–7; *El Mundo,* Aug. 21, 1944, pp. 1, 5–6, and 10.

80. Luis A. Ferré, *El propósito humano,* ed. Antonio Quiñones Calderón (San Juan: Ediciones Nuevas de Puerto Rico, 1972), p. 239. Also, ''Ferré afirma Ley 600 deja indefenso a Puerto Rico en el orden económico,'' *El Estado* 4, no. 27 (Nov.–Dec. 1951), pp. 25–27.

81. Ferré, *El propósito humano,* p. 240.

82. See, e.g., *El Mundo,* May 1, 1944, p. 18.

83. Fernando J. Geigel, *El ideal de un pueblo y los partidos políticos* (San Juan: Tipografía Cantero Fernández, 1940), pp. 26–27; Enrique Córdova Dávila ''Por qué votar por el Partido Estadista,'' *El Mundo,* Nov. 3, 1952, p. 25; and Reece B. Bothwell, ''La República–Un espejismo,'' *El Estado* 1, no. 1 (Sept.–Oct. 1945), pp. 17, 19, 21, 23, and 27.

84. ''Puerto Rico tiene necesidad de resolver el problema de soberanía,'' *El Estado* 4, no. 27 (Nov.–Dec. 1951), p. 23.

85. Luis A. Ferré, ''El día de Lincoln,'' in ibid., 3, no. 14 (March–April 1948), pp. 13–21, and 39.

86. Committee on Insular Affairs, *Investigation,* p. 25. In 1944, as an example of statehood's defensive character during this period, García Méndez discussed with Sen-

ator Pepper of Florida the possibility of Puerto Rico being annexed to that state. See *El Mundo,* May 1, 1944, p. 1.

87. Wilfredo Figueroa Díaz, *El movimiento estadista en Puerto Rico* (Hato Rey: Editorial Cultural, 1979), p. 39.

88. Ibid., pp. 38–43; *El Estado* 2, no. 10 (July–Aug. 1947), p. 35, and 3, no. 15 (July–Aug. 1948), p. 1.

89. American Council on Public Affairs and the Puerto Rican Women's League, *Puerto Rican Problems* (Washington, D.C.: American Council on Public Affairs, 1940), p. 15.

90. On APPE see Emilio del Toro Cuebas, *Puerto Rico: Nuevo estado de la Unión* (San Juan: APPE, 1943). On *El Estado*'s goal see "Editorial," *El Estado* 1, no. 1 (Sept.–Oct. 1945), p. 1.

91. Ramiro L. Colón, *Discurso aniversario 25 de julio de 1948* (Ponce: Imprenta Fortuño, 1948), pp. 22–24.

92. Sánchez Morales, *De antes y de ahora,* pp. 278, 280–81.

93. Ibid., p. 348.

94. Ibid., pp. 324–25.

95. Martínez Nadal in Rivera Santiago, *Comprensión y análisis,* p. 40; García Méndez in Torregrosa, *García Méndez,* p. 63, and "El Estado Libre Asociado y la personalidad de Puerto Rico," *El Mundo,* April 21, 1961, p. 24.

96. Reece B. Bothwell, "Puerto Rico en la Federación Americana," *El Estado* 3, no. 18 (April–May 1949), pp. 9 and 11. Bothwell's comparison is incorrect, because in multiethnic federations, as those he cited, the federal structure is designed precisely to fit ethnonational variations within the state. That is, the federal units (cantons, provinces, republics, or territories) are based on ethnic, national, cultural, linguistic, and other differences in the population. This is not the case in the United States and other federations, where the federal units respond to economic and political, and not ethnonational, criteria. On multiethnic federalism, see, Ivo D. Duchacek, *Comparative Federalism: The Territorial Dimension of Politics* (New York: Holt, Rinehart, and Winston, 1970), ch. 9.

97. Reece B. Bothwell, "What are the Social and Political Objections to Statehood?" *El Estado* 2, no. 8 (Jan.–Feb. 1947), pp. 31–45. Also, Ferré in ibid., 3, no. 18 (April–May 1949), p. 19; and J. Colombán Rosario, "Statehood: Fifty Years of Struggle: 1898–1948," ibid., 3, no. 15 (July–Aug. 1948), p. 27.

98. Pagán, *Historia,* vol. 2, p. 215. See also Pedro A. Cebollero, "Statehood for Puerto Rico, Too Late to Go Back on It," *El Estado,* 2, no. 7 (Nov.–Dec. 1946), p. 41; and Ramiro Colón, *Discurso,* pp. 3–4.

99. Pagán, *Historia,* vol. 2, p. 205.

100. Francisco Ponsa Feliú, "United States Citizenship: The Gateway to Statehood," *El Estado* 1, no. 3 (Jan.–Feb. 1946), p. 29.

101. Julio L. Pietrantoni, "Puerto Rico's Plead," ibid., 2, no. 7 (Nov.–Dec. 1946), pp. 15 and 25. Also, "Editorial," ibid., 3, no. 14 (March–April 1948), p. 2.

102. Julio Pietrantoni, "Statehood, Our Supreme Anxiety," ibid., 3, no. 15 (July–August 1948), p. 35.

103. Ibid., p. 37. Also J. Colombán Rosario, "Statehood," p. 33.

CHAPTER FIVE

The Rise of Postwar Annexationism: From the PER to the PNP, 1952–1968

The period between the formation of the Partido Estadista Puertorriqueño and the electoral triumph of the Partido Nuevo Progresista in 1968 was one of great changes for the statehood movement in Puerto Rico. The conservative PER was supplanted by the more progressive and widely supported PNP. The expansion of industrial capitalism in Puerto Rico provided the conditions for the consolidation of a local industrial bourgeoisie and stimulated the growth of the middle classes and of a poor-marginal stratum. These social sectors provided basic support to statehood electoral politics. The victory of the PNP in the 1968 elections gave pro-statehood forces control over the local government for the first time in three decades. The PNP victory not only broke the twenty-eight years' rule of the Popular Democratic Party, but it occurred a year after the Commonwealth status received a majority support in a U.S.-sponsored plebiscite in 1967.

The 1968 PNP electoral victory represented not only the beginning of a new period in Puerto Rican politics, but also a new stage in the development of the statehood movement. Contrary to widely accepted notions, the PNP represents a break in ideology, leadership, and program from its predecessor, the PER. The transformation of the postwar statehood movement leading to the formation of the PNP was the result of political and ideological struggles between social sectors within the Republican Party. Several sectors within the PER challenged the leadership and program of the sugar bourgeoisie, which controlled the organization and program of the statehood party. Middle- and working-class opposition to the reactionary program of the sugar bourgeoisie was important in leading to the rupture of the alliance between the sugar and industrial bourgeoisie in the PER, which provided the basis for the formation of the PNP.

The role of the local industrial bourgeoisie, represented by Luis A. Ferré, is of utmost importance in the formation and program of the PNP. The industrial bourgeoisie's rise to leadership of the statehood movement opened a new stage in the evolution of the movement. The new program of statehood was framed within a wider historical project that sought to stabilize capitalism in Puerto Rico through the amelioration of class tensions by means of social and economic reform. Statehood was seen by the new leading sectors as an instrument to provide political stability through the security guaranteed by the American state. The formation of the PNP represents the rise to a dominant position of the local industrial bourgeoisie over the statehood movement and program; in alliance with sectors of the middle class they were able to gather mass support for statehood while presenting a reformist socioeconomic program.

THE PER AND THE REDEFINITION OF STATEHOOD POLITICS

The Deterioration of Commonwealth

One of the main factors underlying the rise of the statehood movement in the postwar period is the political and economic deterioration of the Commonwealth. The Commonwealth began to be questioned in Puerto Rico and in the United States shortly after its creation in 1952. Furthermore, the federal government began to take charge of more areas of social and economic control due to the incapacity of the local government to fulfill those functions. The weakening of Commonwealth was reflected internally in the PPD, where conflicts regarding the nature and direction of the Commonwealth and the party's program caused its first major rupture.

The Commonwealth's creation served U.S. interests in two distinct ways. Internationally, it sought to free the United States from accusations of colonialism; in 1953 the United States pushed through the United Nations a declaration of "self-determination" for Puerto Rico. On the one hand, the Commonwealth sought to legitimize Puerto Rico's colonial status, since it entailed a degree of consent by the Puerto Ricans to the colonial situation.[1] The "self-government" granted to the island did not change the colonial relationship or reform the U.S. hegemony on the island. Self-government meant that the United States no longer had to carry out the conflictive task of local administration, a task now performed by Puerto Ricans; it also meant limited autonomy in local affairs for those who controlled the local state apparatus.

The PPD's political hegemony in Puerto Rico came to depend on the Commonwealth's well-being. The recently acquired self-government and economic policies of the 1950s legitimized the new political structure and the PPD's authority. By the late 1950s the PPD began to promote two policies they thought were necessary for the strengthening of the Commonwealth. First, the PPD sought to expand the Commonwealth's autonomy by extending its powers over local affairs; second, it actively sought the "culmination" of Commonwealth status, that is, to make it a permanent political structure. Both were deemed necessary to maintain the viability of the local state and the PPD's political hegemony as well. Attempts to realize both objectives failed. In 1959 the U.S. government rejected the PPD-sponsored Fernós-Murray Bill to provide more powers to the Commonwealth. This attempt continued in the 1960s with the PPD trying to negotiate a "culminated" Commonwealth with Washington. The results of a Congress-appointed Status Commission led to the celebration of a plebiscite on the status of Puerto Rico in 1967, which Commonwealth status won by a majority of votes.[2] But it was a Pyrrhic victory for the PPD; not only was Commonwealth narrowly defined in the plebiscite, but the event set the basis for the formation of the PNP, which a year later won the elections and ended the two-decades-long PPD rule.

The creation of the Commonwealth in 1952 laid the political and juridical basis for the PPD's new economic policy initiated in 1947: the industrialization of the economy through the attraction of U.S. capital. The failure of the state industrialization policy of the early 1940s, and the postwar expansion of U.S. capital to foreign markets, created the conditions for the new economic program. According to it, the function of the restructured state apparatus was to provide the necessary incentives to attract U.S. capital and to secure its permanence on the island by guaranteeing high rates of return. The Commonwealth's fiscal autonomy provided the power to exempt U.S. capital from both federal and local taxes. Wages could also be kept lower than in the United States, another crucial incentive to attract U.S. capital. Finally, the Commonwealth's "association" with the United States assured the permanence of Puerto Rico within the American sphere, thereby guaranteeing the political stability needed for sound investment.

By the mid-1960s the majority of industrial plants promoted by the Economic Development Agency (EDA), the agency in charge of the Commonwealth's economic policy, were U.S.-owned; they also provided most of the manufacturing income and employment of the island.[3] The initial industrialization policy was based on the attraction of labor-intensive light industry, mostly textiles. Although these industries were supposed to provide increasing employment, this was not the case, and unemployment was prevented from rising dramatically in the 1950s by the mass migration of Puerto Ricans to the United States. In the early 1960s many of these industries began to leave the island, due mostly to a decline in their rate of profit, expiration of tax exemptions, and U.S. policies (for example, raise in the minimum wage, elimination of import barriers to European textiles). The government began a new industrialization policy based on the attraction of capital-intensive heavy industries, mostly petrochemicals. These were supposed to provide better wages and stimulate the growth of secondary industries.[4] The latter never happened and unemployment began its rising trend, becoming a major problem for the government since.

Commonwealth was hailed as a pact of sovereignty between the United States and Puerto Rico, giving the island more autonomy. But this autonomy has not separated the island from the metropolis; to the contrary, economic and political integration is more evident than during the period of "direct colonialism" (1898–1952). The so-called political integration of the Commonwealth to the metropolitan state has been related to the increased intervention of the federal state in local affairs to guarantee the reproduction of capitalism by providing social and political stability. Nothing reflects this process more than the role of federal funds on the island.

The dramatic increase in the transfer of federal funds to Puerto Rico during the seventies brought attention to the issue of Commonwealth "dependency" on the United States. The first massive transfer of federal funds came during the 1930s with the transfer of the New Deal to provide "social relief" to diffuse social discontent created by the crisis. The transfer of war-related funds during the early 1940s was instrumental in the attainment of economic and social stability during this period,[5] an important contributing element for the creation of the Commonwealth. Furthermore, the continued transfer of federal funds in the postwar period contributed to the Commonwealth's economic success. A study of capital formation in Puerto Rico during 1950–1960 concluded that the $1.3 billion in transfers by the federal government were crucial for the economic expansion and for the success of the industrialization program by providing funds to the local state that made it possible for Puerto Rico to promote its tax-exemption program.[6]

The transfer of federal funds to Puerto Rico has become a crucial tool for providing stability, mostly by subsidizing a large sector of the population, maintaining high demand levels in the economy, and supporting the local state apparatus. The apparent contradiction that the rate of labor-force participation has remained around 40 percent since the seventies and that unemployment has increased steadily as well (reaching 25 percent in 1983), while at the same time the income levels have more than doubled, is solved by the fact that increasing amounts of federal funds kept coming to the island. From around $300 million in 1960, federal funds increased to nearly $700 million in 1970 to $4.4 billion in 1982. Their share of total personal income increased from 5.7 percent in 1960 to 22 percent in 1982. (Federal transfers to individuals represented 76.7 percent of state transfers to individuals in 1982.) Furthermore, the growth of the Commonwealth bureaucracy has been linked to increased federal transfers; these represented 23 percent of Commonwealth income in 1960, reaching 31.7 percent in 1970 and remaining around this figure since then (it reached 36.6 percent in 1980).[7]

The pervasiveness of federal funds in Puerto Rico has affected the workings of the local state apparatus, what is generally characterized as the "loss of autonomy" by the Commonwealth. The local executive has become, in the words of one observer, a "mediator" between the federal government and the population, whose main function has become the procurement and management of federal funds. The management of local affairs, the sacrosanct symbol of Commonwealth autonomy, has been increasingly determined by federal guidelines regulating the use of these funds. The areas of education, social services, health, and even law and order are increasingly scrutinized and regulated by the federal government. In some cases, parallel structures outside the Commonwealth government have been created at the municipal level to manage federal programs.[8]

These limitations on Commonwealth powers were felt inside the PPD during the sixties, creating a rupture in the programmatic unity characterizing the party for over two decades, and providing the conjuncture for its electoral defeat in 1968. A group of young members began to question the nature of the PPD and the Commonwealth since early in the decade. This "new guard," consisting mostly of young professionals and technocrats, criticized the Commonwealth's lack of autonomy and its economic "dependency." They also criticized the control of the party machinery by an "old guard" that curtailed internal participation and democracy, Muñoz Marín's *continuismo* (continuous rule) and *caudillismo* (one-man rule), and the party's abandonment of its early populist program. The rupture between these two sectors materialized in 1968 when the then governor Roberto Sánchez Vilella and his "new guard" followers were forced out of the party; they created the Partido del Pueblo (People's Party) and took sufficient votes from the PPD to allow the PNP to win the elections.[9]

Class Politics and the Formation of the PER

The conflict that divided the Partido Estadista Puertorriqueño (PEP—Puerto Rican Statehood Party) in 1952 took place at the same time that the Commonwealth was being discussed. However, that debate was not the main cause of the schism. It was the result of a struggle between two sectors of the PEP to take command of the party ideologically and programmatically. The conflict came out into the open when the group headed by Miguel A. García Méndez, representative of the party's sugar interests, and industrialist Luis A. Ferré opposed the party's president, Celestino Iriarte, and his group who supported the Commonwealth.

The issue was the nature of Commonwealth: a step toward statehood, or the continuation of subordination to the United States, that is, colonialism. The debate began in 1947 when Puerto Ricans were granted the right to elect their governor. One sector of the party understood that reforms that increased the island's self-government were necessary steps to statehood. They argued that these reforms gave Puerto Rico "the structure of a government more or less similar to that of a state." This sector, headed by President Iriarte, took the same position with regard to the formation of the Commonwealth; the approval of the Commonwealth Constitution in 1950 was seen as a "transitory step toward statehood.''[10] Ferré, a representative of the opposing sector, argued that although the Commonwealth Constitution gave the island powers to deal with its internal affairs, ''the fundamental legislation that controls the island's economic life shall continue being dictated by one Congress where Puerto Rico has no representation to fight for and on behalf of its interests.''[11]

These differences were reflected in the internal organization of the party. Those in opposition to the Commonwealth argued that to vote for it would imply support for the PPD program. The solution to these differences was somewhat contradictory. A resolution was approved stating that the Commonwealth represented more self-government and that it did not preclude statehood. Consequently the PEP voted in favor of the Commonwealth Constitution and condemned any electoral abstention by statehood supporters, but it left its members free to vote as they wished.[12] This did not solve the internal conflict, since García Méndez and Ferré still argued that the Commonwealth ''could have merits as a transitory measure of government, but it still represents the colony by consent.''[13]

The conflict that divided the PEP in 1952 reflected the power struggle between the group led by President Iriarte and that headed by García Méndez and Ferré. Although the bourgeois sector was ideologically and programmatically dominant within the party, it did not have total control over the party machinery. The García Méndez–Ferré group imposed a directive committee on President Iriarte at the August 1951 party assembly in order to coordinate with him the direction of the party's organization and program. Iriarte and his group knew who they were struggling against. In the PEP's 1952 assembly, Iriarte warned the membership that giving the party presidency to García Méndez would mean turning the party over to the sugar interests and corporations.[14]

Iriarte was right, but this had been the case for more than a decade; it was merely exacerbated with García Méndez in the presidency. Trying to resurrect its glorious past, in 1953 the Puerto Rican Statehood Party became the Partido Estadista Republicano (PER—Republican Statehood Party), making its ideology evident in its name: statehood is conservatism, conservatism is statehood. According to García Méndez, the word ''Republican'' was included in the name of the party in accordance ''with the wish of the party.''[15]

The control of the party by García Méndez and Ferré signifies the dominance of the sugar sector but also of the industrial bourgeoisie over the party. The rise to leadership of the industrial bourgeoisie is of crucial importance for the development of Puerto Rican annexationist politics in the following decades. According to Aarón Ramos, the industrial bourgeoisie gave the annexationist movement a ''more aggressive commitment to statehood.'' Furthermore, Ramos argues that the coleadership of the statehood party by these two factions of the Puerto Rican bourgeoisie gave the PER a ''transitional character''; it was ''a transitional organization from the old agrarian world to the new industrial setting. . . . The political life of the PER . . . reflected the tension between these two groups.''[16]

The expansion of industrial capitalism after the 1950s transformed the social structure and the character of political conflict in Puerto Rico. One of the most important social changes to influence the postwar statehood movement was the decline of agriculture and of the sugar bourgeoisie. Agriculture's share of Puerto Rico's gross domestic product declined from 17.5 percent in 1950 to 3.9 percent in 1969; sugar's share of the total value of agricultural production fell from 53 percent to 19.2 percent during the same period. The number of harvested cuerdas, cane production, sugar production, and sugar mills decreased dramatically during the same period.[17] The remnants of the sugar bourgeoisie and other agricultural sectors, particularly the coffee growers, embraced the opposition to the PPD's economic policy. They argued that the industrialization program was detrimental to agriculture, particularly that industrialization and the growing job opportunities in the urban areas were drying up the labor force in rural areas by promoting the migration of skilled and young labor.[18] These sectors supported the PER and statehood.

The expansion of industrial capitalism in Puerto Rico led to the emergence of a new statehood constituency, primarily from the new middle sectors, segments of the working class, and the urban and rural poor. This new constituency was moving the statehood party away from the reactionary program of the PER's sugar bourgeoisie. The middle sectors provided an important source of social support for the postwar statehood movement. The industrialization of the economy led to a rapid growth of intermediate classes, particularly in the large tertiary sector (services, finance, government), who increasingly supported statehood.[19]

Another group of critical importance for statehood politics during this period consists of those linked to the federal government, especially federal employees on the island, whose numbers had grown substantially. Because of their position within the American state, they have traditionally supported statehood and have repeatedly opposed Commonwealth status. This group was among the founders of Estadistas Unidos (United Statehooders), which advocated statehood in the 1967 plebiscite, and of the PNP in 1968.[20] Puerto Ricans in the U.S. military, especially officers, have also been prominent in their support for statehood. Support for statehood among veterans of the U.S. armed forces grew since the end of World War II. The principal veterans' organizations in Puerto Rico at the time (the American Legion, the Veterans' Association of Puerto Rico) were unequivocal supporters of statehood.[21]

The growing electoral support for statehood after the 1950s has come largely from sectors of the working class and the poor. The PPD's industrialization policy (characterized by low wages, structural unemployment, and marginalization) and the identification of the PPD with the capitalists led many sectors of the working class to move away from the PPD and its program. Many workers continued to believe the early-century notion advanced by the Socialists that only statehood could assure the Puerto Rican working class of the rights already obtained by the American working class (minimum wage, labor rights, welfare benefits).[22] Particularly important were the drivers of *carros públicos* (transportation provided by privately owned cars), who had been instrumental both in the radicalization of the labor movement in the forties and in the formation of the PPD. Alienated by the PPD labor policy, these drivers began to support the PER early in the fifties and were also an important group in the formation of the PNP in 1967.[23]

A group that has received great attention by social scientists for its support of statehood has been the "poor," or urban marginals. They populate the poor areas of the cities (public housing, *arrabales*), suffer from chronic unemployment or partial employment, receive subsistence wages, and depend on public welfare and services for their economic survival. Attracted to statehood as a means to raise their standard of living, the urban poor have increasingly supported the statehood parties since the fifties. Less studied, but equally important in their support of statehood, are the rural marginals, those who were displaced from agriculture but remained in the rural areas, outside the labor force. By 1968 both the urban and rural poor supported the PNP, attracted by its program of social reform and greater (federal) welfare benefits.[24]

"Reaction Has Taken Over the PER"

The wider transformations in Puerto Rican society and the appearance of a new basis of social support resulted in drastic changes within the statehood movement. The most important one was the questioning of the sugar bourgeoisie's leadership within the PER.

Aside from the obvious class affinities and support for statehood, the political alliance between the sugar bourgeoisie and the industrial bourgeoisie was founded upon their common opposition to the socioeconomic and political program of the PPD in the forties. But the industrial bourgeoisie was a rising class with a much more liberal philosophy. Ferré's rise in the statehood party reflected the growing influence of this class within the movement. As early as 1948 the PEP program showed Ferré's influence. He rose to leadership in the party by 1952, sharing power with his brother-in-law, García Méndez. Ferré was the outstanding defender of his party's program and of statehood in the Commonwealth Constituent assemblies. Ferré was the PER's candidate for governor in the 1956 election (and again in 1960 and 1964), and the party's electoral program was then known as "Luis Ferré's program." By 1955 a group within the PER pushed Ferré for the presidency of the party and openly criticized García Méndez's leadership. After the 1956 elections the criticism of García Méndez's presidency grew; although Ferré was not involved in this, it signaled the public manifestation of the conflictive differences within the PER.[25]

From 1956 to 1964 two sectors stand out in their opposition to the sugar bourgeoisie's leadership in the PER: the middle sectors and the workers' sector. The first signs of discontent came from the middle sectors after the 1956 elections. Late that year Jorge Luis Córdova Díaz, a statehood leader and former associate judge of the Puerto Rican Supreme Court, launched a virulent attack on the party's leadership and program, specifically against García Méndez. Córdova Díaz argued that the party's strong showing in the 1956 elections was not enough to advance the ideal of statehood. The PER needed a "radical change in its methods and program" and a new image:

> the ideal of statehood will not bring for the Statehood Party the votes of [all statehooders], not even a majority, as long as they carry on their backs the enormous ballast of being identified with the reactionary, with an ultra-conservative economic policy, with the big financial interests. . . . The fact is that the leaders of the Party, with the exception of Luis Ferré, have not made themselves conspicuous for their interest in the welfare of the laborer, of the peasant, of the distressed . . . it is apparent that their economic and social views are that the welfare of the masses is attained through the protection and encouragement of big interests. . . . Such basic worry for capital and the capitalists . . . is and of right ought to be averse to our people. . . . It is imperative, therefore, if we believe in statehood, if we are loyal to that ideal, that it be divorced from the heavy burden of erroneous economic and social theories that now enhance the Statehood Party.[26]

Enrique Córdova Díaz, an outstanding statehood leader and Jorge Luis's brother, launched another attack on the party's leadership and program:

> no minority party can expect to win a general election on the status issue alone. . . . The Statehood Republican Party in Puerto Rico must also shed old guard ideas and programs. In so doing it must sponsor liberal progressive programs . . . [and] it must advocate [these] under a leadership which has no ties with the past and which can win the confidence of the people.[27]

It is no surprise that the liberal middle sectors were closer to Ferré and supported him for the party presidency. But Ferré tried to prevent the rupture with García Méndez, claiming to support his leadership, and limiting himself to relatively mild critiques of the internal organization of the party.[28]

The reaction of the party machinery against this sector, and perhaps Ferré's unwillingness to confront García Méndez for the party leadership, forced the middle sectors to abandon the party. In 1959 they founded Ciudadanos Pro-Estado 51 (CPE-51, Citizens for the 51st State). The organization's goal was the defense of statehood above any other political consideration, outside the ideological and programmatic framework of the PER. Enrique Córdova Díaz described CPE-51 as "non-partisan, and the main reason for its existence is, perhaps, to show that the statehood movement in Puerto Rico is more extensive than the local Republican Statehood Party."[29] Up to the formation of the PNP, the CPE-51 was supported by those opposed to García Méndez's leadership in the PER.[30] CPE-51 was instrumental in getting the supporters of statehood to participate in the 1967 plebiscite, thereby fomenting the rupture in the PER, and in organizing Estadistas Unidos. They were one of the most important sectors in the formation of the PNP and in Ferré's government.[31]

The other social sector to criticize and oppose the PER's conservative leadership and program was the workers' sector, most of whom had come from the Socialist Party through the alliances of the forties and after the disintegration of the party in 1954.[32] Their statehood and conservative ideology and opposition to the PPD moved them to the PER. But this group kept their "socialistic" views, and thus their presence within the PER created tensions within the party. A good account of the existence of this group in the PER is given by José M. García Calderón.[33] A Socialist leader who joined the PER after the PS disbanded, García Calderón was elected to the House of Representatives by the PER in 1956–60. According to him, his problems with the PER leadership during his term in the House were based on one contradiction within the party: "For a long time in the Statehood Party there has been an ideological duel between the people who represent the philosophy and attitudes of the forces of reaction and myself, representing the anti-reactionary social philosophy, ideology, and attitudes." García Calderón argued that the workers' sector had an enormous influence in the organization of the party and in the attraction of the popular vote to the PER, owing the popular measures in the PER platform to them. But the "reactionary" economic interests within the party opposed any measures that would benefit the masses. García Calderón was scorned by the party leadership for his support of measures of aid to the poor introduced by the PPD and opposed by the PER. The final rupture with the PER came after García Calderón submitted a bill to study the antilabor practices of the Roig Central, owned by Antonio Roig, a prominent member of the PER. The *central* owner used his power in the party, including his relative Luis Ferré, to force García Calderón to withdraw the bill. According to García Calderón, "reaction has taken over the PER" and uses statehood to defend its economic interests; only after statehood provides a social program for the masses will it be achieved.

The workers' sector was relatively important in the PER; they handled some of the party's local organizations, particularly in the urban areas, and were responsible for much of the party's popular support. But aside from one or two representatives in the legislature, the workers' sector had no influence in the party leadership. After the 1960 elections the workers' group began to pressure the party leadership for more power in party structures, using the local structures under their control, and trying to obtain more representation in the legislature. In 1963 the group failed in its attempt to oust García Méndez from the presidency of the party, provoking a furious reaction by the party machinery. Prior to the 1964 elections, García Méndez imposed a series of candidates over those of the workers' sector, going against the decisions of the local committees and leaving the local committees out of the party structures. In August 1964 the workers' group left the PER and proposed the creation of a new party: "It will be a Socialist Party, like the one of master Santiago Iglesias Pantín."[34]

The new party never did come to life, and many of its supporters later joined the PNP.

The Rupture in the PER

From the mid-fifties on, García Méndez's conservative leadership of the PER was increasingly criticized within the party. The new social sectors that were joining the statehood movement found themselves in opposition to the sugar bourgeoisie in the PER. The electoral showing of the PER in 1964, the debate around the United States–Puerto Rico Commission on the status of Puerto Rico in 1966, and the issue of statehood's participation in the plebiscite fomented an ideological struggle within the party that led to its rupture in 1967.

After the 1964 election a group from the middle sector began to question openly the ideological basis of the party. Though they were members of the PER, they were close to Ciudadanos Pro-Estado 51. Led by Carlos Romero Barceló, this group played around with the idea of forming another party, to be called the Liberal Reformist Party or Liberal Progressive Party. The idea was discarded and the group decided to stay and try to reform the structures of the PER, while continuing to use CPE-51 as their political and organizational vehicle.[35] In the September 1965 PER Assembly, Romero Barceló argued that the cause of statehood had been harmed by the PER's conservative leadership and the PER's links to the National Republican Party; that there were many supporters of statehood inside and outside the PER who disagreed with its leadership and program, and that statehood needed their support to become a reality:

> In the political arena of Puerto Rico there is no space for any conservative party and any reactionary party. . . . We have to change the name of the party, to eliminate that of Republican Party and change the leadership of this party so that the people can be convinced of the interest and sincere wish of this collectivity of carrying out a total renovation, to which all supporters of statehood in Puerto Rico can belong.[36]

The CPE-51 and Romero's position was clear: statehood needs the masses to succeed and to attract the masses statehood needs a new image. The message was not lost: it was one of the elements that united this group with Ferré's in the formation of the "new vehicle" for statehood, the PNP. But for this to happen, a rupture between Ferré's group and García Méndez's was necessary.

The rupture in the PER came over the issue of the plebiscite, with García Méndez arguing against the participation of the statehood forces in the contest and Ferré arguing in favor of participation. In 1965 a joint United States–Puerto Rico Commission on the Status of Puerto Rico was named by Congress to hold hearings on the political situation of the island. The commission's report concluded that the three political alternatives (commonwealth, statehood, and independence) were equally acceptable solutions to the status of the island if approved by Congress and the Puerto Ricans; it also concluded that the Puerto Ricans should manifest their preference through a plebiscite.[37] The PER leadership had accepted the authority of the Status Commission, but when the possibility arose that a plebiscite on the three status alternatives was to be held, García Méndez abandoned the commission, leaving Ferré as the sole representative of statehood. According to García Méndez, the PPD was using the status commission and the plebiscite to legitimize the Commonwealth; to accept the commission's conclusions and to participate in the plebiscite was to give support to the PPD and to commonwealth status. Furthermore, García Méndez argued that to include statehood in the plebiscite and face defeat would harm their cause.[38] For Ferré, the Status Commission's conclusions had a different meaning: the legitimation of statehood by the U.S. Congress. To participate in the plebiscite was to show Congress that Puerto Ricans desired statehood—one of the prerequisites to statehood that the Status Commission had enumerated. Ferré argued in favor of participation in the plebiscite as the best defense of statehood, since once "this desire to be part of the Union has been expressed, statehood has always been granted."[39] The Status Commission report represented a new opening for statehood that, together with the PER's electoral drive in the 1960s, created the opportunity to push statehood both in Puerto Rico and the United States.

Although the plebiscite was the immediate cause of the rupture in the PER, the underlying cause is found elsewhere, in the social and politicoideological conflicts between different social sectors in the party. This was noticed at the time of the PER Assembly that debated the party's position in the plebiscite: "The outcome of the Assembly will affect the leadership and future orientation of the PER. The confrontation has turned into a struggle between the conservative old guard headed by García Méndez, and the younger Republicans united behind Ferré."[40] The outcome of the assembly did not surprise anyone; García Méndez tightly controlled the party machinery and his victory over the opposition was overwhelming. But it was a Pyrrhic victory, since Ferré began immediately to organize what he had promised in the assembly: an organization to defend statehood in the plebiscite, Estadistas Unidos.[41] In his speech before the PER Assembly, Ferré argued on the need to participate in the plebiscite, but also went further: he put forward what became the political position of Estadistas Unidos and the PNP: the best mechanism to advance statehood is through control of the colonial government, and to achieve this requires mass support.[42]

The conflicts between the different social sectors coexisting in the PER finally erupted in 1967, leading to cleavages in the party and eventually to the formation of Estadistas Unidos, the embryo of the PNP. The new party, dominated programmatically and organizationally by the industrial bourgeoisie and the middle-class sectors of the PER, presented a new program that actively sought mass support. The new party's program evolved around the social philosophy of Ferré. To understand, thus, the PNP's politics and program during its early years, we must depart from an analysis of the politics of the industrial bourgeoisie during the postwar period and of Ferré's social philosophy (as a representative of that class).

THE PNP AND THE POLITICS OF REDEMPTION

The Politics of the Industrial Bourgeoisie

The expansion of industrial capitalism after the war not only eroded the material basis of the sugar bourgeoisie but provided the conditions for the growth of a local industrial bourgeoisie. In the first four decades of the century, the industrial bourgeoisie was extremely small and concentrated in areas of relatively minor economic importance. In the 1930s the only manufacturing activity of importance was in sugar, tobacco, and needlework.[43] The Second World War brought with it important changes for this class: the flow of federal funds and the construction of economic infrastructure related to the war effort, and the general improvement of the economy, created the material basis for the development of a local industrial bourgeoisie.[44] Nevertheless, in its period of growth this bourgeoisie was still weak materially. By 1945 there were only 2,077 manufacturing enterprises in Puerto Rico, most of them small. Over half of these employed fewer than seven workers; only 122 employed over a hundred persons (mostly in sugar and rum, tobacco, and needlework). Over 70 percent were organized as individual enterprises and only 12 percent as corporations.[45]

This local industrial bourgeoisie has its own basis of reproduction; they are not in the strict sense "intermediaries" of American capital, although they coexist with both U.S. capitalists and their local intermediaries. The Puerto Rican industrial bourgeoisie can best be characterized using James O'Connor's conception of "competitive capital." According to O'Connor, in the "competitive sector" of private capital "the physical capital-to-labor ratio and output per worker, or productivity, are low, and growth of production depends less on physical capital investment and technical progress than on growth of employment. Production is typically small scale, and markets are normally local or regional in scope." Labor in this sector is typically low-wage and unorganized; working conditions are poor and unemployment and underemployment are high. Because of this, labor in this sector is increasingly compelled to "look to the state for means of subsistence. Thus they are condemned to be full or partial dependents of the state."[46] The relation between this competitive sector and the other sector of private capital, the monopoly sector, is not a totally contradictory one. On the contrary, though there may be some contradictions between the two sectors, the expansion of monopoly capital benefits the competitive sector:

> The growth of the monopoly sector is based on the expansion of capital and technology. It is the prime accumulating sector of the economy. The

competitive sector grows on the basis of the expansion of labor power which has been "freed" by accumulation and growth in the monopoly sector . . . the competitive sector does not necessarily decline with accumulation but expands because of the growth process in the monopoly sector.[47]

It is argued here that the truly "local" sector of the Puerto Rican bourgeoisie is best characterized as competitive capital, as distinct from an intermediary or dependent bourgeoisie directly linked to U.S. capital. As a whole, the Puerto Rican bourgeoisie as a class was born under the aegis of American capital in Puerto Rico. The economic and political structures promoted under U.S. economic and political hegemony allowed them to reproduce as a class. Its sugar, banking, and commercial sectors benefited from the expansion of U.S. capital in Puerto Rico.[48] This is not to imply that there were no incompatibilities between the local bourgeoisie and U.S. capital and state. But these were subordinated to the fact that the U.S. presence in Puerto Rico secured the expansion and reproduction of capitalism in the island.

The characteristics of competitive capital in the local industrial bourgeoisie are best seen in their concentration in labor-intensive industries like clothing, wood products and furniture; food; stone, ceramic, and glass products; metallurgy; and chemicals. Moreover, their production is for the most part limited to the local market. In 1967, 72 percent of the sales of local firms went to the local market.[49] A 1957 Economic Development Agency (EDA) report argued that "the major deterrents to local manufacturing enterprise seem to be the small size of the local market, lack of competitively-priced raw and semi-finished materials, and scarcity of large pools of locally available capital and know-how for investment in heavy and highly technical industries."[50] Contrary to what EDA argued, the small size of the market was not the problem, for the local market expanded dramatically during the fifties;[51] the problem for local industrialists was competition with American imports and capital in Puerto Rico producing for the local market.

The PPD's industrialization program did not benefit the local industrial bourgeoisie directly, apart from the favorable "industrial environment" that it promoted.[52] During the 1950s and early 1960s, while industrialization advanced and the number of industrial firms increased, there was a decline in the number of local industries. While a group of Puerto Rican capitalists, mostly organized in corporations, did thrive during the period (as evidenced by the fact that the value of local industrial production increased considerably), there was a parallel process of displacement of local capital by foreign capitalists.[53] The number of local manufacturing establishments declined from 95.4 to 65 percent of the total manufacturing firms on the island from 1950 to 1960; their share of the net manufacturing income declined from 97.6 to 46.4 percent from 1948 to 1960.[54]

During the 1940s important sectors of the industrial bourgeoisie opposed the PPD's "populist" program, characterizing it as "socialistic," proindependence, and anti–private enterprise; this class complained that the PPD's state-sponsored industrialization was unfair to local manufacturers because public enterprises were competing with private firms for capital, labor, and markets, while public enterprises were protected by the state and paid no taxes.[55] This rhetoric was abandoned, however, by the early 1950s when the PPD espoused Operation Bootstrap.[56] The bourgeoisie was critical, nevertheless, of the PPD's industrialization program on the basis that it was discriminatory against local capital. The government was criticized for not "protecting" local capital against "unfair competition" from U.S. imports and American manufacturing capital on the island, and for the "exaggerated aid" given to U.S. capital and the government's total disregard of local interests.[57] The Manufacturers' Association on several occasions demanded the extension of Fomento (EDA) subsidies and incentives to *all* industries, local and foreign, and for tax reductions to local industry.[58]

The 1950s was a critical decade for members of the local industrial bourgeoisie. Their main concern during the period was that of competition with American products, imports or locally produced. Competition threatened the local industrial bourgeoisie at the heart of its economic space, the local market. As the local market rapidly expanded during the 1950s, it became highly contested by foreign capital, not only in terms of imports but also by EDA-promoted American firms on the island. According to a 1963 EDA report, the value of shipments to the Puerto Rican market by local manufacturers declined from 85 to 73 percent in the short period of 1954–58; at the same time, the value of shipments to the local market by nonlocally owned manufacturing firms on the island grew by 223 percent.[59] Although the PPD maintained that the main goal of Operation Bootstrap was to attract foreign capital for export-oriented production, the products of a large number of EDA-promoted, tax-exempted industries were in direct competition with local manufacturing.[60]

The PPD, responding to pressures by local capital, began to address the issue of competition in the local market in the early 1960s. In 1960 an EDA-sponsored study on local manufacturing and the local market by Nathan Associates concluded that an expansion of the local market was in itself no assurance that local capital would be the main beneficiary of that growth; and it forecasted a stronger competition on the local market from American capital.[61]

The relations between the local industrial bourgeoisie and the PPD government were very tense during the early 1960s. Competition from U.S. imports and manufacturing capital on the island was hurting local manufacturing and EDA showed no interest in their situation.[62] The number of local firms closing increased, as well as takeovers of local firms by foreign capital and joint ventures between local and foreign capital (a policy promoted by EDA at the time).[63] Local capitalists complained that even for those enterprises that were "Fomento assisted" (Fomento's term for local firms under its program), aid was too little, too late, and always uncertain. In part to respond to the demands of local capitalists, and mostly responding to its own goals, the PPD government created the "Native Industries' Program" within EDA and the "Governor's Investment Committee." The government's goal was to expand local capital's participation in the Puerto Rican economy in order to create an "economically balanced society," able to make its own essential economic decisions.[64] Behind all this apparent effort in favor of local capital was the PPD's new industrialization policy aimed at the attraction of high-tech, capital-intensive industries (particularly petrochemicals) as the centerpiece of the industrialization program.[65] Since these were capital-intensive, not labor-intensive, industries, an employment problem had to be solved; Fomento strategists envisioned local manufacturing as being able to absorb excess labor produced by the new industrialization policy.[66] The new policy's goal was never achieved; not only was unemployment never curtailed, but the decline of local capital accelerated during the period. By 1965, 73 percent of all EDA-promoted firms were owned by foreign capital, mostly American. Between 1961 and 1965 only 205 local firms were EDA-promoted, and the total investment for these, both public and private, reached only $38 million.[67] Local capital's position within the economy deteriorated dramatically; while in 1960 non-EDA-promoted firms accounted for 46 percent of the net manufacturing income, by 1970 that figure was only 18 percent. In 1965, while 36 percent of total employment in manufacturing came from local industry, only 6.8 percent were from local firms promoted by EDA.[68]

The rise of the PPD, which the bourgeoisie saw as radical and proindependence, cemented the alliance between the industrial bourgeoisie and the sugar bourgeoisie against the PPD-promoted reforms and to support statehood as the only political alternative. By the late 1940s the industrial bourgeoisie began to stand out in the statehood movement. For example, the 1948 PEP program emphasized industrial interests (the platform committee was chaired by Ferré). The program promoted industrialization through "inducements to private enterprise, mainly to the small industrialist," and the protection of "native products against the competition of imported goods." The program also proposed a reduction of the tax load of industrial capital, the provision of subsidies for local industrial production, and a revision of the inheritance law to facilitate the reproduction of local capital. The bourgeoisie demanded that the state defend its interests or, if this was not possible, to refrain from interfering in its affairs.[69]

The PER presented as theirs the industrial bourgeoisie's grievances against the PPD industrialization program, particularly on the unfair competition from U.S. competitive capital subsidized by the state. By 1957 the PER argued in a party's newspaper ad: "We believe that Puerto Rican capital, which provides jobs and wages and profits that remain here, deserves at least the same treatment as American capital, which creates jobs and wages but takes its profits back to the United States."[70] Ferré argued that local capital, the only one being taxed in the island, was subsidizing American capital while receiving no benefit at all. He advocated the imposition of a minimum wage on foreign capital; this would increase workers' purchasing power (and sales for local capital), and would also "stimulate high productivity in the worker." This minimum wage would "not apply to local firms, which may continue to pay reasonable wages that allow the consumption of their goods in Puerto Rico."[71] This is one reason the industrial bourgeoisie within the statehood movement supported the federal minimum wage in Puerto Rico; this also furthered the economic integration to the United States.

According to Ferré, furthermore, foreign capital did not provide the conditions for the development of local capital. Aside from advocating the minimum wage for American capital in Puerto Rico, Ferré even demanded the complete elimination of government subsidies to foreign capital.[72] The solution to the local industrial bourgeoisie's concerns arose out of the economic developments within the Commonwealth during the mid-sixties: the supplanting of competitive capital by monopoly capital; and, in the industrialization program, the promotion of heavy industry over light industry. The annexationist industrial bourgeoisie supported these policies, since they would provide the necessary conditions for the development of local capital and eliminate the competition of American capital.[73] The annexationists' strategy was clear: to attract monopoly capital to Puerto Rico and thereby assure the permanence of American capital after statehood.[74] Monopoly capital would not only further the expansion of local capital but, being less dependent on the Commonwealth's subsidies (low wages, tax exemptions, and so on), it would guarantee a stable economic transition to statehood.

Another element of vital importance for the bourgeoisie's statehood program was the dramatic increase of federal funds generated by the "Great Society" program. Created to alleviate social tensions in the big cities in the sixties, the federal funds represented for Puerto Rican annexationists a means to win the support of the masses who would benefit from federal programs. The federal funds issue was not new to the statehood movement; in the 1940s and 1950s the Puerto Rican bourgeoisie had demanded federal funds for "industry, agriculture, and trade," that is, to benefit them. Ferré had supported the extension to Puerto Rico of "the benefits of the federal laws of social security."[75] But these measures affected only certain social sectors, principally the employed working class: the minimum wage, social security, unemployment benefits, and so on. These programs were not as far-reaching as those of the Great Society, which reached the urban poor, whose numerical and political strength was becoming evident by the mid-sixties. The issue was no longer how much money the government would receive for roads, schools, or local welfare programs; now the issue was how large a segment of the population would benefit from social welfare programs. Statehood became synonymous with federal funds and public welfare.[76] The transfer of federal funds to Puerto Rico for public welfare functioned both as a mechanism to obtain popular support and as a very important part of the statehood strategy of the Puerto Rican bourgeoisie—the federal government would provide for the marginal and poor while the American and Puerto Rican bourgeoisie maintained their privileges.[77]

The public debate around the 1967 plebiscite opened the discussion of the relation between the island's political status and the bourgeoisie's position toward it. In the month of April 1967, the PPD organized the so-called Businessmen for Commonwealth to gather support for commonwealth status among the Puerto Rican bourgeoisie. They also obtained support for Commonwealth status from several representatives of American capital on the island, particularly from the growing petrochemical sector.[78] In a speech to the Manufacturers' Association of Puerto Rico, Ferré argued that statehood was the best political alternative for American capital; that Commonwealth was a transitory form on the way to statehood; and he proposed "transition measures" to ease the coming of statehood for American capital. Ferré demanded that the association not get involved in party politics (that is, that they keep their class interests above their political differences) and suggested to the U.S. businessmen that they stay out of Puerto Rican politics.[79] Ferré did not have to go that far. Weeks before the plebiscite, a political survey of the bourgeoisie in Puerto Rico (local and foreign) showed that a majority of the presidents and general managers of industrial enterprises in Puerto Rico supported statehood.[80]

Ferré and the New Statehood Project

The first statehood program, the Republican project, was elaborated at the beginning of the century by the Republican petty bourgeoisie, best represented by José Celso Barbosa. The Republican project was a radical project at the time, seeking to turn Puerto Rico into a capitalist society within the framework of the U.S. federation. The crisis of Republicanism put an end to the first statehood project and turned statehood into a reactionary cause. A new statehood project was introduced by a group of new annexationists headed by Luis Ferré. The new project did not aim at the total transformation of society, like the Republican project, but at the continuation of capitalist society with reforms. The new project expressed the concerns of the local bourgeoisie, particularly of its industrial sector. Ferré, as a social actor, was very important in the emergence of the PNP and its initial program. To better understand its importance and Ferré's centrality to the postwar statehood movement, we have to understand his sociopolitical philosophy.

Ferré's philosophy needs to be understood, first of all, in terms of his class position. He has been conscious of his historical role as an individual and as a member of a social class that is influenced by particular social forces.[81] For Ferré, capitalism is a means and not an end; it is a mechanism at the service of society and not a social system. Capitalism is the means to maintain liberty and increase production in society.[82]

Within his social philosophy, Ferré's principal interest lies in the relation between capital and labor. He has dealt extensively with this issue since his earliest writings. Already in 1929 Ferré had expressed his views on the need for regulation in capital-labor relations. He argues that labor must be seen "as a conscious and integral part" of the capitalist productive process and asserts that labor "as well as capital, has the right to enjoy [its] share of the profits." He argues that capital should provide the workers a system of benefits (job security, health and retirement plans, and so on), because the greater the workers' sense of security, the greater their productivity.[83]

Ferré's interest in labor relations extends to the need for stability of the capitalist system, surpassing the immediate concern of capital-labor relations in the factory. This is the issue that concerns him in one of his most important writings, "Social Justice, Economic Security, and Political Freedom," written in 1941, during the early days of the PPD reforms. The problem that moved Ferré was "the uncertainty, the discontent, the political passions, the hatred, and the *class struggle* that exists at this moment in Puerto Rico."[84] According to Ferré, class struggle within the capitalist system is not produced by the system itself but is the result of human nature; class struggle "is born from an anachronistic atavism that still dominates modern man, inherited from pre-industrial civilization, which has its origins in man's fear of scarcity." But class struggle should no longer exist because the development of the productive forces under capitalism have created the conditions to eliminate scarcity. That this is not so is the result, not of the system itself, but of the men who organize its production, moved by an anachronistic system of values. According to Ferré, man "has created a state of artificial scarcity that has brought as an inevitable result a state of restlessness and social insecurity of such magnitude, that mankind lives forever frightened on the threshold of a revolution." The accumulation of profits is the main stimulus for production in capitalism; but this incentive cannot be unbounded, for it only deepens the social conflicts that cause social revolutions. These "imperfections" in the capitalist system foment a "class hatred" against capital that should not exist, since capital fulfills an important social function: to develop the techniques of production that have benefited the whole of society. The increase in social production is due to one incentive: "the incentive for profit." If the latter is destroyed, the whole of society will suffer.[85]

As a solution to this contradiction between the profit incentive and the danger of revolution, Ferré proposed a series of reforms, including a "subsistence minimum" for all individuals, the regulation of capital to "prevent abuse and exploitation" without "obstructing the natural development of business," and a reasonable minimum wage. Furthermore, Ferré argues that "the wise solution of our socioeconomic problem requires, in the first place, the establishment of a general principle of *social responsibility* in the individual." Capital and the state, in particular, should promote an ethics of social responsibility in order to provide social cohesion by meeting the basic needs of all classes. In this way, capitalism could protect the free initiative of capital, provide "social justice" for the lower classes, and preserve the political freedom needed to maintain stability.[86]

Ferré's conception of capitalist stability and the regulation of the capital-labor relationship includes what he calls *industrial democracy,* a "revolutionary principle" developed in the United States, which "considers as its legitimate goal the exercise of its economic function as an effective means for the fulfillment of a social function." This social function is to provide what Ferré calls "social prosperity" for all classes. To achieve social peace, indispensable for the preservation of "industrial democracy," Ferré enumerated some "indispensable basic principles" to regulate capital-labor relations. First, the workers' right to form trade unions and to enjoy wage increases, not only "as a means to give justice to the worker and to obtain his enthusiastic collaboration," but to increase workers' buying power so as to expand the economy. Second, the workers should limit their demands and recognize the capitalists' right to make profits; the workers' demands should be limited economic demands in order to prevent the intrusion of political and ideological conflicts. Finally, the capitalist and the workers should try to resolve their differences through negotiations and collective bargaining. Capital-labor relations need to be regulated by third parties because "not all the capitalists are ready to accept these principles with a sense of generous social responsibility."[87]

Capital's "social responsibility" is a crucial element in Ferré's view of capitalism. It is the responsibility of capital to limit class conflict by limiting the accumulation of profits. The responsibility for maintaining social peace falls both to capital and to the state, which must provide the necessary conditions for economic growth. An example of this conception is Ferré's views on the struggle against communism in Latin America.[88] He argues that the promotion of social peace and the struggle against communism in Latin America should be the responsibility of capital, particularly of American capital. The prevention of dictatorships in Latin America, a major cause of communist insurrections, is the responsibility of both the American state and capital: the state must promote democratic governments, and capital must not join in the economic exploitation of the masses maintained by local oligarchies.[89] The promotion of economic development for all classes in Latin America benefited American capital both politically, by preventing communist revolutions, and economically, by enlarging the markets for American goods.

Likewise, Ferré demanded that American capital coming to Puerto Rico to take advantage of tax exemption and government subsidies should assume its "social responsibility."[90] This is the basis for Ferré's demand for an increase in wages and for the application of the federal minimum wage to the island. Ferré argued that American multinational capital should be enticed to Puerto Rico because it could pay higher wages; he opposed the penetration of competitive capital (light industry) to Puerto Rico, because it paid low wages, and lacked "social responsibility," and consequently spread "class hatreds" on the island.

Furthermore, Ferré believed that social instability in capitalist society is not only caused by economic contradictions but by the imbalance between the material advances in science and technology and the population's lack of adequate moral values. Inequities in the distribution of wealth under capitalism are accompanied by spiritual backwardness and by the absence of a social ethic that provides cohesiveness to the social fabric. But he believed that spiritual progress, like individual freedom, should be above material progress. The subordination of individual freedom to material progress destroys the "individual moral discipline" needed for democracy. Ferré argues that "mass production within a competitive market," with the increased alienation of the worker from the productive process, "has contributed to this serious conflict [between classes] that confronts us today." For Ferré, the way to assure the "conditions of equilibrium" between capitalist production and human freedom, in other words, to maintain social order, is to guarantee "the right to nonmonopolistic collective bargaining"[91]—that is, the right of workers to organize in trade unions in order to improve their living conditions.

Thus the absence of moral ethics and spiritual values in capitalist society is not merely a humanistic problem but conflicts with the proper functioning of the system. Education provides citizens with the ethics necessary for the reproduction of the system; it serves as a corrective to class hatreds.[92] These are not only the result of imbalances in the capitalist system (capitalist avarice, and so on), but also of ignorance and the lack of proper values. The absence of a "morality of freedom" in contemporary society is the result of the existing educational system, "concerned with the scientific-material aspect of our culture" at the expense of moral values; this has produced "a group of individuals who are unprepared to live within the democratic order that gave them life."[93]

According to Ferré, the lack of a "moral order" to sustain its social fabric is another source of Puerto Rico's instability. The transformation from agrarian to industrial capitalism in the postwar period tore the social fabric without a social ethic to absorb the tensions of this process. In this situation, it becomes necessary to promote "a regime of moral self-discipline to develop in [individuals] a sense of social responsibility."[94] Thus a sense of social responsibility in individuals, the result of a moral self-discipline, is necessary to create a moral order that will in turn provide social order.

Statehood is an essential part of Ferré's social scheme for providing Puerto Rico with social peace and stability. Only statehood could provide social justice in the island. At the Commonwealth Constituent Assembly in 1951 Ferré defended first, not the political and economic advantages of statehood, but "the evolution toward social justice" that statehood represented. He described the evolution of American capitalism from an agrarian to an industrial society, arguing that after the New Deal the American state created a number of measures for the welfare of the worker, with a "new orientation of social responsibility in the functions of government"; and that the American bourgeoisie developed "the principle of a greater social responsibility toward the worker" as part of the spirit of "industrial democracy." Statehood would guarantee that "social justice," which prevails in the United States as the result of the spirit of social responsibility within the American state and bourgeoisie, will be transferred to Puerto Rico—social justice that is needed to ameliorate the social instability caused by imperfections in capitalism.[95]

Statehood is also necessary to create the vital social order that comes from spiritual tranquility. Ferré argued that statehood would provide Puerto Rico with the "calm and peace" needed to "eliminate the uncertainty in which we live, which is in great part responsible for our serious economic problems."[96] Puerto Rico finds itself, according to Ferré, in a state of restlessness, of uncertainty, of spiritual void, with no social ethics to sustain it. This spiritual restlessness would be solved with statehood, which would provide the elements for the establishment of an ethical-moral order.[97] On the one hand, statehood would guarantee the infusion of those values that characterize American civilization: "the sense of social justice that guarantees the principle of equal opportunity for all, and peaceful democratic behavior under a government of law."[98] On the other hand, statehood would provide Puerto Rico the material progress without which the creation of a new social order would be impossible. Statehood solves the economic problems of Puerto Rico through the security provided by the transfer of the American welfare state to the island. Statehood also provides the security of political stability, whereas the Commonwealth gives "no guarantee of permanence and could lead to independence"[99] and possibly to social revolution.

Ferré's statehood program conflicted with the reactionary program of the sugar bourgeoisie in the PER; it was a program that required both political and economic reforms to the existing capitalist system. The formation of the PNP represents the rise of Ferré's program to the fore of the statehood movement.

The Politics of Redemption

Seven days after the plebiscite, Estadistas Unidos met in Ponce and agreed to form a new party that was to fulfill a historical mission that surpassed statehood: it was to be the "instrument of redemption" of Puerto Rico. In his speech to the PNP Constituent Assembly in July 1967, Ferré clearly indicated what was to be the nature and goal of the new party:

> our people want a new instrument of redemption . . . we now have the supreme mandate to defend the statehood ideal for the people of Puerto Rico. . . . This supreme mandate means that we have to create the new instrument. The people create the instruments for their own redemption and salvation at critical moments. . . . We are going to defend the statehood ideal, because the statehood ideal embraces everything. . . . And the second objective will be real social justice for the people.[100]

This was Ferré's central message at the formation of the United Progressive Party (as the PNP was initially known) in August 1967, and in all of the party's subsequent activities.[101]

The PNP became, in Ferré's words, the "instrument of redemption of our people on the economic level, on the political level, and on the moral and spiritual level."[102] For Ferré, the social problems created by capitalism in Puerto Rico led to class conflict, threatening to destroy the social fabric of the island. To prevent this social calamity the "problems" of capitalism need to be "solved": first, by the correct application of social and applied technology; and second, by the creation of a new moral order ("moral and spiritual redemption"). This was the task confronting the PNP in its search for the redemption of Puerto Rican society; the PNP "rejects class hatred and prejudice as instruments of political activity. Our movement believes in human comprehension, in the common effort of all classes and all the professions, to search for the necessary means to solve our problems and to eliminate conflicts destructive of energy, wealth, life, and happiness."[103] Ferré believed that social problems such as class conflict could be solved through the adequate use of state power; this was to be the goal of the new party in government, as he indicated in an interview several years after the end of his term. Asked about his administration's goals, Ferré replied: "To apply the democratic and humanitarian philosophy that I had defended throughout my life. As an industrialist, I sought the understanding between labor and capital. I do not believe, as Marx does, that they have to be in conflict."[104]

The formation of Estadistas Unidos represented the rise to dominance within the statehood movement of the industrial bourgeoisie and the political decline of the sugar bourgeoisie.[105] Ferré's group gained the support of the bulk of the PER as well as the support of those statehooders outside the party. Most of the leaders of Estadistas Unidos came from middle-class organizations like Ciudadanos Pro-Estado 51 and the Statehood Democratic Movement, which gave the new organization a more liberal content than the PER. Estadistas Unidos was also supported by federal employees and by a group of PPD annexationists organized under Movimiento Popular Estadista (Popular Statehood Movement); it also received the support of the statehood youth organized in the Federación de Universitarios Pro-Estadidad (Federation of Pro-Statehood University Students). It also got important support from labor leaders organized under the United Workers Group. Estadistas Unidos was also supported by the Veterans' Association of Puerto Rico and by the statehood sector of the Manufacturers' Association of Puerto Rico.[106]

Estadistas Unidos was the embryo of the PNP. It realized the goal of winning popular support for statehood and introduced a new statehood program representing the leading sectors of the new organization: the industrial bourgeoisie and the middle sectors. The contrast between the 1960 and 1964 PER programs and the Estadistas Unidos and the 1968 PNP programs reflect the differences between the leading sectors of these parties. The PER programs in the sixties, like those of the previous decade, defended statehood in abstract terms ("the guarantee of liberty, justice, and equal opportunity for all"), the "republican form of government," and private enterprise. Most of the measures were of a general character, particularly those favoring the "poor" (transfer of all federal welfare programs) and the labor movement (minimum wage, collective bargaining). The more concrete measures favored the local bourgeoisie: returning the public utilities to private enterprise; tax reform in favor of capital; and, above all, the end of the PPD's agrarian reform program.[107]

The only PER measures adopted by the PNP were those already incorporated in Ferré's program: those dealing with the labor issue and "social justice" and those dealing with the defense of local capital (tax reform, reform of the tax-exemption program, reform of the industrialization program). Unlike the PER, the PNP's program included concrete measures of popular appeal: the federal minimum wage, better public services, labor legislation (for example, Christmas bonus, general health plan, indemnification), housing (more attention to slums, sale of public land), and the creation of a Department of Public Welfare; land reform including agricultural price subsidies, wage subsidies for agricultural labor, and loans for small and medium farmers; reform in public administration including wage increases and job security for public workers, and more participation of private enterprise in public planning (no mention of selling public corporations).[108] The PNP's political campaign in 1967–68 was aimed at winning popular support from the "middle class," the "working class," and the "poor";[109] and in this it succeeded.

The "politics of redemption," the PNP's programmatic axis in 1968, was translated into the language of the electoral campaign as La Nueva Vida (the New Life). Two issues dominated this campaign: social justice and statehood, in that order. Although the PNP was defined as a statehood party, it argued that "status is not at issue," that statehood was not going to be the centerpiece of the campaign as in previous decades. Under the slogan "social justice," the PNP promised a solution to the social problems that the PPD had been unable to solve: drug addiction, unemployment, housing, health, agriculture, poverty; and the PNP attacked the PPD for its violation of democracy (caudillismo, bureaucratization, continuismo). These problems, however, could only be solved with the mechanisms provided by statehood: political dignity, political equality, and federal funds.[110]

The form of the campaign was also new. The PNP introduced to Puerto Rican politics the electoral campaign à la Madison Avenue; they saturated the mass media (particularly TV and radio) to create the image of a party of reform, contrasted to the tired and worn-out PPD.[111]

There was some continuity between the PNP and the previous statehood movement—its anti-independence/anticommunist rhetoric, an issue in both the 1967 plebiscite and 1968 electoral campaigns. For Ferré and other annexationists, the fervor for independence (synonymous with communism) and the radicalization of the movement were the results of "class hatreds." They accused the PPD and Commonwealth of leading to independence. The PNP argued that the PPD administrations were creating the conditions, through political and economic mismanagement, for the rise of independence/communist fervor in Puerto Rico. Statehood was the only safeguard against independence/communism; this was the basis of the PNP slogan "statehood is security"—not only economic security (federal funds, economic growth), but security from independence and communism as well.[112]

The departure of Ferré's group from the PER before the plebiscite shook the party, taking from it the most dynamic leadership. The success of Estadistas Unidos in the plebiscite and the creation of the PNP politically undermined the PER and led to its demise. Already by early 1968 the majority of the PER's members in the House of Representatives had joined the PNP.[113] The PNP attacked the caudillismo of García Méndez and the conservative philosophy of the PER program. The PNP followed a policy of having no political alliance with the PER.[114] Furthermore, the PNP claimed that it was the only party capable of defending statehood, after the PER's retreat in the plebiscite.

The PER and PNP programs differed not only in terms of their social content, but also in terms of their statehood strategy. The PER claimed to be the only statehood party because it demanded that the United States immediately grant statehood to Puerto Rico. By contrast, the PNP maintained that a transition period was necessary in which to move Puerto Rico toward statehood (through the presidential vote, greater economic and political integration, more federal funds), and to create the necessary conditions for statehood, both in Puerto Rico and in the United States (majority electoral support in Puerto Rico, economic and political stability, and approval from Congress). To counter the argument that statehood meant cultural assimilation, the emergent PNP put forward the notion of "Creole statehood." Simply put, this asserted that under statehood there would be no loss of Puerto Rican culture or of the Spanish language.[115]

Another leg of this statehood strategy was the so-called economic transition program. Recognizing that the main attraction for U.S. capital in Puerto Rico were the Commonwealth's economic incentives, the PNP proposed a transition period during which these arrangements would be acknowledged. For example, federal tax exemptions would be phased out in a twenty-year period, while at the same time other kinds of incentives would be offered by the local government.[116]

The "transition to statehood" was the PNP's new statehood strategy. It required the creation of the necessary internal (majority electoral support) and external (support in Congress) conditions to achieve statehood. To accomplish this the PNP needed to win state power, as Ferré stated in a speech at the beginning of the 1968 campaign:

> Our mission consists in convincing our people that statehood is the road to progress and security, and the only status that secures permanent union

> with the United States; the people, by a majority vote, need to show their support for statehood in a plebiscite. . . . Only in this way will Congress be obliged to fulfill its moral duty of accepting Puerto Rico as a state. . . . But to start the plebiscite process we have to defeat the party in power, whose leadership does not believe in statehood. . . . We have to get into power to legislate a new plebiscite.[117]

To win state power, popular support was essential; for this reason, Ferré and his supporters abandoned the reactionary PER and created a new statehood party and program that joined social justice and statehood as the mechanism to win popular support.

Following Ferré's scheme for the attainment of social justice and social peace in Puerto Rico, the PNP was defined as the "instrument of redemption" of Puerto Rican society, a redemption to be achieved under statehood. With the PNP's electoral triumph in 1968, annexationism became a major political current in Puerto Rico. Furthermore, their electoral victory provided the PNP the opportunity to implement its program; thus the PNP administration of Ferré needs to be understood within the framework of the "politics of redemption." This is the subject of the next chapter.

NOTES

1. Carmen Ramos, *El gobierno de Puerto Rico* (Río Piedras: Editorial Universitaria, 1970), ch. 4.

2. Ibid., chs. 5 and 6.

3. Junta de Planificación, *Estadísticas Socioeconómicas, 1980* (San Juan: Junta de Planificación, 1981), p. 3; Eliezer Curet Cuevas, *El desarrollo económico de Puerto Rico: 1940–1972* (Hato Rey: Management Aid Center, 1979), p. 253.

4. James L. Dietz, *Economic History of Puerto Rico* (Princeton, NJ: Princeton University Press, 1986), pp. 247–55.

5. Harvey S. Perloff, *Puerto Rico's Economic Future* (Chicago: University of Chicago Press, 1950; reprinted by Arno Press, New York, 1975), pp. 58, 160, 383, 392, 400–401.

6. Lyman D. Bothwell, "Capital Formation in Puerto Rico, 1950–1960" (Ph.D. diss., George Washington University, 1964).

7. Junta de Planificación, *Informe Económico al Gobernador, 1982* (San Juan: Junta de Planificación, 1983), p. A-26.

8. Juan C. Rosado Cotto, "Fondos federales y la política pública del Estado Libre Asociado de Puerto Rico," *Revista de Administración Pública* 6, no. 2 (March 1974); Richard B. Capalli, *Federal Aid to Puerto Rico* (San Juan: Instituto de Derecho Urbano, 1970); Teresita Picó, "El impacto de los fondos federales en el desarrollo de Puerto Rico" (Master's thesis, Sch. Pub. Admin., UPR, 1976).

9. See Ismaro Velázquez, *Muñoz y Sánchez Vilella* (Río Piedras: Editorial Universitaria, 1974).

10. Quotes from Enrique Lugo Silva, "Roosevelt's Contribution to Puerto Rican

Self-Government," *El Estado* 4, no. 19 (June–July 1949), p. 15, and *El Mundo*, Aug. 28, 1950, p. 1.

11. Luis A. Ferré, "The Puerto Rican Constitution," *El Estado* 4, no. 22 (Sept.–Oct. 1950), p. 25. The PER president agreed on this issue; see Iriarte's statements in *El Estado* 4, no. 27 (Nov.–Dec. 1951), pp. 11 and 15.

12. *El Mundo*, Aug. 22, 28, and 31, 1950, p. 1.

13. Ibid., Aug. 6, 1951, p. 1. See also Robert W. Anderson, *Gobierno y partidos políticos en Puerto Rico* (Madrid: Editorial Tecnos, 1970), p. 106. According to Ferré, the Commonwealth Constitution did not distance the island "juridically or constitutionally from statehood." Luis A. Ferré, *El propósito humano*, ed. Antonio Quiñones Calderón (San Juan: Ediciones Nuevas, 1972), pp. 243–45.

14. *El Mundo*, Aug. 6, 1951, p. 16; R. Anderson, *Gobierno y partidos políticos*, p. 106. After leaving the PER, the Iriarte faction formed the ephemeral Partido Boricua (Puerto Rican Party). See *El Mundo*, Aug. 1, 1952, p. 5.

15. *El Mundo*, July 29, 1953, p. 4, and July 28, 1953, p. 1.

16. Aarón G. Ramos, "The Development of Annexationist Politics in Twentieth Century Puerto Rico," in Adalberto López, ed., *The Puerto Ricans* (Cambridge, MA: Schenkman, 1980), pp. 263–64.

17. Junta de Planificación, *Informe económico al Gobernador, 1969* (San Juan: Junta de Planificación, 1970), pp. 5 and A-26; Junta de Planificación, *Estadísticas socioeconómicas, 1980*, p. 7.

18. *El Mundo*, Nov. 12, 1962, p. 1, and Aug. 28, 1964, p. 29; Ramiro Colón, "Estadidad salvaría industria cafetalera," *El Estado* no. 65 (June–July 1959), pp. 36–38; and José A. Herrero, "En torno a la mitología del azúcar" (mimeo, 1970), pp. 68, 74, and 77.

19. See Juan M. Carrión, "The Petty Bourgeoisie and the Struggle for Independence in Puerto Rico," in A. López, ed., *The Puerto Ricans*, pp. 248–49; A. Ramos, "The Development of Annexationist Politics," pp. 265–66.

20. *El Estado* no. 63 (Jan.–Feb. 1959), p. 14. *El Mundo*, May 31, 1967, p. 1; and June 8, 1967, p. 26.

21. See, e.g., *El Estado* 8, no. 39 (Sept.–Oct. 1954), pp. 14–15, and no. 42 (March–April 1955), pp. 9 and 11; also *El Mundo*, Jan. 26, 1967, p. 46.

22. *El Estado* 6, no. 33 (May–June 1953), pp. 13 and 15; *El Mundo*, Oct. 27, 1964, p. 7; and July 1, 1967, p. 14.

23. *El Mundo*, Nov. 5, 1956, p. 1, and Nov. 10, 1967, p. 2. The only PER mayor to be elected in more than a decade, in San Lorenzo in 1960, was leader of a public drivers' union. Ibid., Nov. 10, 1961, p. 1.

24. Marcia Rivera, *Elecciones de 1968 en Puerto Rico: Análisis estadístico por grupos socio-económicos* (San Juan: CEREP, 1972), p. 39; Rafael L. Ramírez, *El arrabal y la política* (Río Piedras: Editorial Universitaria, 1977); Luis Nieves Falcón, *La opinión pública y las aspiraciones de los puertorriqueños* (Río Piedras: Centro de Investigaciones Sociales, 1970), pp. 237–39. The marginal/poor sectors were supporting statehood parties during the fifties; see Juan J. Baldrich, "Class and the State: The Origins of Populism in Puerto Rico, 1934–1952" (Ph.D. diss., Dept. of Sociology, Yale University, 1981), pp. 227, 229, and 234.

25. *El Mundo*, Nov. 5, 1956, p. 20; ibid., Dec. 20, 1955, pp. 1 and 20. See also the article by Frank Torres in *El Estado* no. 47 (Jan.–Feb. 1956), p. 19.

26. Jorge L. Córdova Díaz, "The 1956 Election and Statehood," *El Estado,* no. 51 (Nov.–Dec. 1956), p. 14.

27. Enrique Córdova Díaz, "Modern Republicanism and the Statehood Party of Puerto Rico," ibid., p. 17.

28. For example, *El Mundo,* Dec. 30, 1955, p. 1, and Jan. 22, 1958, p. 4.

29. Quoted in Wilfredo Figueroa Díaz, *El movimiento estadista en Puerto Rico* (Hato Rey: Editorial Cultural, 1979), pp. 68–69; also *El Mundo,* May 6, 1959, p. 19.

30. Figueroa Díaz, *El movimiento estadista,* p. 68; *El Mundo,* Dec. 16, 1961, p. 32, and Dec. 12, 1960, p. 23.

31. *El Mundo,* Dec. 10, 1962, p. 8; ibid., Jan. 25, 1968, p. 1.

32. A 1954 PS assembly dissolved the party and urged its members to join the PPD. The president's communication informing the PPD of the action described the PS's ideology as one of "social and economic reform and of permanent union between the peoples of Puerto Rico and the United States." The decision was opposed by a sector of the party. See ibid., Aug. 4, 1954, p. 1, and Aug. 10, 1954, p. 10.

33. José M. García Calderón, "La reacción se ha apoderado del Partido Republicano," ibid., Oct. 29, 1960, pp. 18–19.

34. Ibid., Aug. 28, 1964, p. 26; also, July 1, 1963, p. 1; and June 11, 1964, pp. 1 and 12.

35. Antonio Quiñones Calderón, *Del plebiscito a la Fortaleza* (Hato Rey: Ramallo Bros., 1982), pp. 47–49.

36. Ibid., pp. 57, 60, and 62.

37. United States–Puerto Rico Commission on the Status of Puerto Rico, *Commission Report* (Washington, DC: U.S. Government Printing Office, 1966), p. 14.

38. Quiñones Calderón, *Del plebiscito a la Fortaleza,* p. 84.

39. Ferré, *El propósito humano,* pp. 258–59 and 281. The Status Commission report not only for the first time recognized statehood as an acceptable alternative for Congress, but it stated that neither the economic nor the cultural issues were impediments to obtaining statehood; the major problem was political: gaining enough support both in Puerto Rico and the United States. United States–Puerto Rico Commission, *Report,* p. 15.

40. A. W. Maldonado, "Asamblea PER: Confrontación entre García Méndez y Ferré," *El Mundo,* Jan. 21, 1967, p. 1.

41. Ibid., Jan. 23, 1967, pp. 1 and 20; Jan. 24, 1967, p. 1; Jan. 25, 1967, p. 1. The January 22 PER Assembly and the formation of Estadistas Unidos are discussed in Quiñones Calderón, *Del plebiscito a la Fortaleza,* pp. 88–134. Ferré's speech before the assembly is found in *El propósito humano,* pp. 264–75.

42. Ferré, *El propósito humano,* p. 273.

43. Perloff, *Puerto Rico's Economic Future,* p. 97.

44. Thomas C. Cochran, *The Puerto Rican Businessman: A Study in Cultural Change* (Philadelphia: University of Pennsylvania Press, 1959), pp. 64–65.

45. Perloff, *Puerto Rico's Economic Future,* pp. 102–103.

46. James O'Connor, *The Fiscal Crisis of the State* (New York: St. Martin's Press, 1973), pp. 13, 15.

47. David Gold, Clarence Lo, and Erik Olin Wright, "Some Recent Developments in Marxist Theories of the State," *Monthly Review* 27, no. 6 (Nov. 1975), p. 41.

48. See A. G. Quintero-Rivera, *Conflictos de clase y política en Puerto Rico* (Río Piedras: Editorial Huracán, 1976); Esteban A. Bird, *Report on the Sugar Industry in*

Relation to the Social and Economic System of Puerto Rico (San Juan: Bureau of Supplies, Printing, and Transportation, 1941); Cochran, *The Puerto Rican Businessman;* Biagio di Venuti, *Money and Banking in Puerto Rico* (Río Piedras: University of Puerto Rico Press, 1950).

49. Emilio González Díaz, "Political Attitudes and Behavior of Puerto Rican Businessmen: Preliminary Notes of a Research Project" (mimeo, n.d.), pp. 13–14; Cochran, *The Puerto Rican Businessman,* p. 161.

50. Economic Development Administration, *Social Directions in Industrial Development* (San Juan: Office of Economic Research, EDA, 1957), p. 13.

51. See Economic Development Administration, *Locally and Nonlocally Owned Enterprises in Puerto Rican Manufacturing Industries* (San Juan: Office of Economic Research, EDA, 1963), p. 25.

52. Cochran, *The Puerto Rican Businessman,* p. 50.

53. Emilio González, "Political Attitudes," pp. 8–9; and Cochran, *The Puerto Rican Businessman,* p. 64.

54. Gilberto Cabrera, *Historia económica del comercio y la industria en Puerto Rico* (Hato Rey: Fundación Socio-Económica de Puerto Rico, 1980), pp. 56 and 58.

55. "Industriales contra mayor contribución," *El Mundo,* Oct. 29, 1946, p. 1; "Industriales dicen Tugwell no dió ayuda," ibid., Jan. 5, 1947, p. 1; and ibid., Oct. 27, 1948, p. 1.

56. "Industriales dicen"; and ibid., Sept. 10, 1951, p. 1.

57. See the article by Federico Torres Campos in ibid., Oct. 31, 1948, p. 13; and PRMA's criticisms in ibid., Oct. 31, 1948, p. 1.

58. See ibid., April 20, 1953, p. 25; "Industriales contra"; and ibid., Nov. 29, 1955, p. 20.

59. EDA, *Locally and Nonlocally Owned,* p. 25.

60. See the listings of EDA-promoted firms in Economic Development Administration, *Fomento-Promoted Manufacturing Plants, Classified by Industry (as of December 1958)* (San Juan: Puerto Rico: Office of Economic Research, EDA, 1959).

61. Robert R. Nathan Associates, *Local Participation in Manufacturing Industries in Puerto Rico* (Washington, DC: The Associates, 1960), p. 10.

62. See *El Mundo,* June 29, 1962, p. 1; "Ante competencia, otros problemas," ibid., July 2, 1962, p. 1; and ibid., May 27, 1961, p. 29.

63. "Fomento planea mayor atención a industria local," ibid., July 4, 1962, p. 3; "Para encarar competencia Fomento propulsa incentivos más amplios para industria," ibid., Dec. 1, 1962, p. 22.

64. "Asignan $400,000 estimular industria puertorriqueña," ibid., June 29, 1962, p. 24; "Ante competencia"; and ibid., July 5, 1962, p. 1.

65. This change in industrialization policy was already proposed in 1957, in EDA, *Social Directions,* pp. 9–10; also the comments by EDA in *El Mundo,* Oct. 1, 1960, p. 24; and ibid., July 8, 1964, p. 1.

66. "Asignan 400,000"; "Fomento planea mayor atención"; ibid., Nov. 6, 1962, p. 1; and "Para encarar competencia."

67. Antonio J. González, *Economía política de Puerto Rico* (San Juan: Editorial Cordillera, 1971), p. 272; Curet Cuevas, *El desarrollo económico de Puerto Rico,* p. 272.

68. Junta de Planificación, *Informe económico al Gobernador, 1981)* (San Juan: Junta de Planificación, 1982), p. A-8; Salvador Lugo, *Trends and Problems of the Local*

Puerto Rican Owned Manufacturing Industries (San Juan: Interagency Strategy Committee, 1975), p. 8.

69. The 1948 PEP program appears in Reece B. Bothwell, ed., *Puerto Rico: Cien años de lucha política* (Río Piedras: Editorial Universitaria, 1979), vol. 1, pt. 1, pp. 674–81, and in *El Mundo,* Oct. 31, 1948, p. 12. See also Ferré, *El propósito humano,* pp. 21–22.

70. PER newspaper ad in *El Mundo,* Oct. 14, 1957, p. 7.

71. Speech by Ferré in *El Estado,* no. 43 (May–June 1955), p. 16.

72. *El Mundo,* June 1, 1967, p. 3.

73. See the 1964 PER program in *El Mundo,* Aug. 12, 1964, p. 19. This position was reiterated in the 1967 plebiscite campaign by Estadistas Unidos, in Estadistas Unidos, *El ABC de la Estadidad* (pamphlet, published in May 1967), p. 15.

74. This issue emerged during the 1965 United States–Puerto Rico Commission on the Status hearings, in a discussion between Teodoro Moscoso and Congressman O'Brien on the relationship between Puerto Rico's political status and American investments on the island. See United States–Puerto Rico Commission, *Status Hearings,* vol. 3 (Washington, DC: U.S. Government Printing Office, 1966), p. 729.

75. *El Mundo,* July 26, 1956, p. 5.

76. Ferré, *El propósito humano,* pp. 257–58.

77. This issue was debated by Muñoz Marín and Antonio L. Ferré, son of the statehood leader and then president of the Puerto Rican Cement Co., during the 1965 status hearings. See United States–Puerto Rico Commission, *Hearings,* vol. 3, p. 232.

78. *El Mundo,* April 27, 1967; p. 7; July 20, 1967, p. 42; and July 21, 1967, p. 7. See also United States–Puerto Rico Commission, *Hearings,* vol. 3, pp. 41–60, 511–20, and 547–49.

79. *El Mundo,* April 27, 1967, p. 73.

80. Ibid., July 1, 1967, p. 60; July 14, 1967, p. 3; and July 17, 1967, p. 25.

81. For Ferré's own class self-assessment, see *El Estado* no. 49 (June–July 1956), p. 7; and ibid., no. 45 (Sept.–Oct. 1955), p. 5.

On the Ferré family's economic emporium see: Stu Bishop, "The Ferré Family," *NACLA's Latin America and the Empire Report* 6, no. 6 (July–August 1972), pp. 2–19; Luis A. Ferré, "Dinámica de la industria del cemento en Puerto Rico," *El Día* (Ponce), Dec. 18, 1949, pp. 33 and 39; Pepe Ramos, *Ferré: Autobiografía dialogada* (San Juan: Panavox Multimedia, 1976), pp. 54–55.

82. Pepe Ramos, *Ferré,* p. 195.

83. Ferré, *El propósito humano,* p. 12.

84. Ibid., p. 14.

85. Ibid., pp. 15–17.

86. Ibid., pp. 21–23.

87. Ibid., pp. 25–27.

88. Ibid., pp. 30–35.

89. Ibid., pp. 339–44.

90. Luis A. Ferré, *An Engineer Dreams of a Better Puerto Rico* (Address by the Honorable Governor of Puerto Rico before the Puerto Rico Section of the American Society of Mechanical Engineers, Hato Rey, Puerto Rico, Feb. 21, 1969), p. 5.

91. Ferré, *El propósito humano,* pp. 91–92.

92. Ibid., pp. 351–52.

93. Ibid., pp. 92–93.

94. Ibid., p. 95.

95. Ibid., pp. 237–38, and 257–58.

96. Ibid., p. 254.

97. Ibid., p. 321.

98. Pepe Ramos, *Ferré*, p. 194.

99. Ferré, *El propósito humano*, pp. 278–79.

100. Ibid., pp. 285–86.

101. The August 1967 assembly speech appears in ibid., pp. 289–91; the assembly is discussed in Quiñones Calderón, *Del plebiscito a la Fortaleza*, pp. 167–206. The theme is repeated in Ferré's acceptance speech as PNP candidate for governor; also "El Puerto Rico olvidado," (October 1968); "La Nueva Vida," 1968 campaign closing speech; and in his first speech to the legislature, January, 1969, all reproduced in *El propósito humano*.

102. *El Mundo*, Nov. 21, 1967, p. 36. Also ibid., Oct. 8, 1968, p. 34.

103. Ferré, *El propósito humano*, p. 112. This theme is repeated in Ferré's first speech to the legislature, January 1969, in ibid., pp. 147–60.

104. P. Ramos, *Ferré*, p. 216. For Ferré's bourgeois-technocratic view of society see also Ferré, *An Engineer Dreams of a Better Puerto Rico*, pp. 1 and 3; *El propósito humano*, pp. 115–21, and 159.

105. According to Martínez Fernández, most of the funds for the 1967 campaign by Estadistas Unidos were provided by the Ferré family. The author also shows how an important sector of the main leadership of Estadistas Unidos and of the PNP were linked to Ferré by personal, family, and business links. See Luis Martínez Fernández, *El Partido Nuevo Progresista* (Río Piedras: Editorial Edil, 1986), pp. 26, 33, and 110–12.

106. *El Mundo*, Jan. 25, 1967, p. 1; Jan. 26, 1967, pp. 2, 46, and 63; June 6, 1967, p. 1; June 8, 1967, p. 26; July 1, 1967, p. 14; and July 22, 1967, p. 71. Also W. Figueroa Díaz, *El movimiento estadista*, pp. 82–83.

107. *El Mundo*, Sept. 28, 1960, p. 30; and Aug. 12, 1964, p. 19.

108. Bothwell, *Puerto Rico*, vol. 1, pt. 2, pp. 913–23; *El Mundo*, Oct. 8, 1968, p. 34; Oct. 10, 1968, p. 41; Oct. 14, 1968, p. 38; and Oct. 16, 1968, p. 62.

109. *El Mundo*, Sept. 5, 1967, p. 1; Nov. 27, 1967, p. 36; Dec. 19, 1967, p. 20; Feb. 21, 1967, p. 40; April 11, 1968, p. 28; Aug. 6, 1968, p. 23; and Sept. 17, 1968, p. 27.

110. *El Mundo*, Sept. 16, 1968, p. 31; and Nov. 21, 1967, p. 36; Ferré, *El propósito humano*, pp. 296, 308–14.

The 1968 NPP electoral campaign is discussed in Ruth Martínez Saldaña, "Anatomía de un partido político en su lucha por llegar al poder: El caso del Partido Nuevo Progresista" (Master's thesis, Sch. Pub. Admin., UPR, 1972), p. 12; and William Ríos, "La campaña electoral del Partido Nuevo Progresista en 1968," paper delivered at the Puerto Rican Annexationism Conference held in the University of Puerto Rico, April 14 and 21, 1983.

111. W. Ríos, ibid.; and Marina Plaza Arroyo, "Financiamiento de partidos y campañas políticas en Puerto Rico" (Master's thesis, Sch. Pub. Admin., UPR, 1971), pp. 14 and 19.

112. *El Mundo*, July 22, 1967, p. 14; April 6, 1968, p. 4; Oct. 8, 1968, p. 8; Ferré, *El propósito humano*, p. 279; and Estadistas Unidos, *El ABC de la estadidad*, pp. 26–27.

113. *El Mundo*, April 17, 1968, p. 1.

114. Ibid., July 17, 1967, p. 1. Also, Nov. 28, 1967, p. 1; April 10, 1968, p. 26; and Ferré, *El propósito humano,* p. 291.

115. *El Mundo,* Oct. 10, 1968, p. 29; Oct. 12, 1968, p. 14.

116. The program of ''economic transition to statehood'' was introduced by Arthur Burns in his presentation in defense of statehood during the status hearings in 1965. See United States–Puerto Rico Commission, Hearings, vol 3, pp. 623–35.

117. Ferré, *El propósito humano,* pp. 296–97. Also, *El Mundo,* Sept. 1, 1967, p. 12; May 13, 1968, p. 1; and Oct. 8, 1968, p. 34.

CHAPTER SIX

The New Progressive Party and the Politics of Redemption

The electoral victory of the New Progressive Party in 1968 marks the end of the Popular Democratic Party's political dominance since the forties and the advent of the PNP as a major force in Puerto Rican politics. But it was not until very recently that proper attention was given to this political movement so relevant to Puerto Rico. Even an acute observer of Puerto Rican politics raised the question, several years after the first PNP victory, of whether the statehood movement was a "rising force" or whether it was merely a "suggestive slogan" for mass mobilization, deciding in favor of the latter.[1] The attention given to the PNP has been mostly on its relationship to the status (statehood) and cultural (assimilation) issues;[2] more recently, attention has been given to the social basis of the PNP. But even less attention has been given to the PNP administrations, which controlled the Commonwealth government for twelve years during 1968 to 1984. Little interest has been shown in a comparative study of the PNP under the respective leadership of Ferré and Romero. Chapters 6 and 7 attempt to make a contribution in these significant areas of contemporary Puerto Rican politics.

As argued in the previous chapter, the PNP distanced itself from the Republican Statehood Party, in terms of its social base and program, particularly its stand on statehood. At the time of its first electoral victory, PNP's politics and program were heavily influenced by Luis Ferré. Ferré's government attempted to implement a specific socioeconomic and political program, which I have termed the "program of redemption." This program aimed at providing stability for Puerto Rico, a crucial requisite for the attainment of statehood, and, more importantly, for the survival of capitalism on the island. The specific goals of the program were: to attain social stability through the use of state programs; to promote economic stability by strengthening the position of local capital in the island's economy and by redefining the economic role of American capital in Puerto Rico; and to promote political stability by furthering the political integration of Puerto Rico to the United States. The Ferré administration was unable to implement this program because of structural constraints and the internal schisms that plagued the party by the time of its 1972 electoral defeat.

Statehood was an important issue during the first PNP administration, but it was not the immediate concern of Ferré's government. Furthermore, statehood became a divisive factor in the PNP; it was the issue around which the programmatic and ideological differences in the party were fought. Disagreement about what the main goal of the party should be and the party's electoral defeat in 1972 led to a leadership and organizational crisis. The rise of Carlos Romero Barceló to the party helm represented the solution to the party's crisis and the ascendance of a new program in the PNP.

THE WEAKENING OF COMMONWEALTH

By the mid-1960s the PPD's light-industry-based industrialization model, which led to the 1950s "miracle of economic growth," began to deteriorate. The PPD reacted by revising the Commonwealth's economic program to attract capital-intensive industries. The center of the new policy was the attraction of petrochemical firms; they were supposed to stimulate complementary satellite industries and spur economic growth on the island. But the petrochemical industry declined in the mid-1970s due to changes in the world economy (rise in the price of oil) and subsequent changes in U.S. economic policies (tariffs on foreign oil).

The inability to sustain stable economic development lies with the economic model itself. The businesses that settle in Puerto Rico are foreign (mostly American) owned. Production and profits are exported; little money is reinvested in Puerto Rico. Industrialization has rested on attracting American capital seeking fast and large profits. The fragility of this economic model has been noted by economist James Dietz, who argues that the factors accompanying the "economic growth" of the fifties were less a product of the strength of the local economy "than of the transfer of income within the circuit of capital of international firms. The linking of Puerto Rico into this circuit is not intrinsic to the production process, but rather is contingent on the goals of international corporations, the investment climate in Puerto Rico, the tax laws, the wage rates, and so on."[3]

Rising unemployment and social marginality among the masses, and the failure of one type of industry after another questioned Commonwealth's ability to assure social and economic stability in Puerto Rico. Furthermore, the industrialization program required increased state subsidies and incentives and more investments by the local government to keep it working. The Commonwealth's limited capacity to provide social and economic services promoted a more extensive intervention by the federal government in these areas. The Commonwealth's economic policy has been based on the promotion of manufacturing as the main source of employment, but since the early 1970s the predominant areas of manufacturing have been capital-intensive, not labor-intensive. Manufacturing's share of the gross national income rose from 26 percent in 1970 to 47 percent in 1980, but during the same period the share of total employment in manufacture decreased 0.6 percent.[4] During the 1970s manufacturing in Puerto Rico was dominated by the chemical-pharmaceutical and electronics industries. These two sectors provided nearly two-thirds of all the manufacturing income and 30 percent of the total income of Puerto Rico by 1980. As impressive as these figures are, the impact of these industries on the rate of employment was minimal. In 1980 the chemical-pharmaceutical and electronics industries provided only one-third of all employment in manufacturing and only 6 percent of the total employment in Puerto Rico.[5]

This has stimulated what a U.S. Commerce Department study characterized as "structural unemployment," that is, the incapacity of the Commonwealth's economy to provide the proper levels of employment for the population. "Structural unemployment" reflects on the standard of living of the population; the latest census data indicate that 62 percent of the population in Puerto Rico are under the U.S. poverty level.[6] To maintain social and political stability, the state has had to sustain this growing sector of the population, a task that has fallen upon the federal state. The political consequence of this process is crucial: the American state has created its own political constituency in Puerto Rico. If we add those who depend on federal funds for survival, those working for the federal government, and those employed by the Commonwealth government on federal programs or with federal monies, we have a clear notion of the basis of support for the American state in Puerto Rico. The annexationist forces are the main beneficiary of this social support for the American state in the island.

Puerto Rico's economic integration to the United States has increased in the postwar period along with the development of industrial capitalism. Although the economic integration of Puerto Rico to the United States has remained constant throughout the century, its form has changed according to the dominant form of accumulation: production of sugar, light industry, heavy industry, and high technology. The economic consequences have been: American control of the main productive sector, production for the American market, import of capital goods and raw materials for this production and consumer goods for the population, and constant expansion of American finance capital to support all of the above. By the early 1970s there were changes in the dominant kind of production (from light industry to heavy industry) and in the kind of capital controlling the productive process (from competitive capital to monopoly capital). But by the late 1970s two new elements added to the form of economic integration: the preponderant role of the American state as an economic intermediary, and the rise of finance capital as a major sector of the economy—and of U.S. capital in Puerto Rico (to be discussed in the next chapter).

Federal funds fulfill a very important role in Puerto Rico's economy: by 1981 transfer payments represented 25 percent of the disposable personal income and total federal funds were 41 percent of the island's gross product; in 1977 federal funds provided an estimated 11 percent of the island's gross investment.[7] As the U.S. Commerce Department study argues, federal funds "are important in meeting social needs and they spur consumption and demand."[8] The federal government has become an intermediary in the production and circulation of commodities in Puerto Rico. It exempts American capital ventures in Puerto Rico from taxes and subsidizes American capital in the mainland by pumping money into the island's economy that allows consumption of U.S.-made goods. Puerto Rico's economy produces commodities for the American market and consumes American commodities.

The postwar economic and political transformations spurred the growth of the labor and independence movements by the late 1960s. Both movements were critical of the island's economic and political developments, and both experienced a process of growth and radicalization early in the seventies and of stagnation and deradicalization by the end of the decade. The early seventies, with the breakdown of the "labor peace" agreement with the PPD, saw the reemergence of the labor movement in the island. It was characterized by the rise of trade-union activity and the formation of new labor organizations ("independent" unions, confederations) and more overt political participation, particularly in the public sector. These were more militant unions, as shown by the increase in the number of strikes and the struggle for the right to syndicalize (prohibited in Puerto Rico). These efforts were consequences of the attempt to maintain wage levels and employment security in a deteriorating economy.[9] The labor movement became more politicized, with ties to the leftist parties in the island.

After a decade of electoral losses and stagnation, the major independence parties began to revitalize and radicalize in the late sixties. After becoming the second electoral party in 1956, the Puerto Rican Independence Party (PIP), formed in 1947, began to decline electorally and politically. By the early seventies the party began to grow and presented itself as a social-democratic party with strong Marxist rhetoric. The Pro-Independence Movement (MPI), a late fifties' offshoot from the PIP, followed a similar path. After a decade of leading the independence movement in day-to-day struggles, in 1971 the MPI was transformed into the Puerto Rican Socialist Party (PSP), a self-proclaimed Marxist-Leninist party. Both parties had disastrous electoral showings in the decade, the PIP in 1972 and the PSP in 1976, which led to a change in the ideological direction of the parties. The new PIP leadership purged the radical left from the party and accentuated its left-of-center, electoral, and nationalist program. The PSP began a period of internal schisms that moved the party away from its Marxist program to a more nationalist stance.

The evolutions of the labor movement, disciplined by the economic crisis and by successive PNP and PPD governments, and of the independence movement, ideologically and organizationally fragmented, strengthened the statehood alternative to the crisis of Commonwealth in the 1970s. The weakening of the labor movement since the mid-seventies has reduced its political clout and turned it more dependent on political parties.[10] The PPD's antilabor policies during the Hernández Colón administration (1973–77) and Commonwealth's use of low wages as an incentive moved sectors of the working class to support the PNP. On the other hand, facing the crisis of Commonwealth, the ideological and programmatic fragmentation of the independence movement made the statehood alternative an attractive one in Puerto Rico and the United States.

THE FERRÉ ADMINISTRATION

Social Justice

The first PNP government attempted to implement Ferré's program of redemption—the search for stability through the eradication of social conflicts. "Social justice"—increasing personal income, providing services to the masses, and stimulating economic growth through an increase in demand—was the means to achieve "social peace." This was to be implemented through the use of the state apparatus. La Gran Tarea (The Great Task) of the PNP was to lead Puerto Rico to a Nueva Vida (New Life) of social peace and economic prosperity under the American federation.

In his governor's inaugural address in January of 1969, Ferré described the "New Life"'s purpose as "the elimination of explosive tensions—inevitable consequence of injustice—[that] will provide us with a *firm social stability*."[11] The "New Life" would bring progress "without destroying the indispensable incentives to labor and production"; it was to be a "New Life of mutual comprehension and common creative effort" among all social classes.[12] The PNP's Great Task "is to create a better world . . . inspired in a generous and comprehensive sense of justice that allows poverty and necessity to be abolished, the indispensable requisite to achieve a *durable peace*." The Great Task was also to be "oriented toward a future of permanent union with the nation that we are part of," that is, statehood.[13]

The New Life's goal of achieving a "durable peace" ("social peace") was built upon the achievement of social justice. "Social justice" meant the incorporation of those marginal to society into the mainstream to secure stability; it was a bourgeois program to ensure the reproduction of capitalism. This was Ferré's message to the Manufacturers' Association early in his administration; he told them of his social justice program:

with social legislation of this kind are adding to our effort a whole third of
our population that still lives in extreme poverty or that is earning low
wages. It is an investment for future years and that is the way to see it.
. . . I only ask you to trust this administration, headed by someone who
has had experience in the world of industry.[14]

Ferré not only warned the bourgeoisie that this was a bourgeois program but
also demanded their public and material support to achieve social justice as a
matter of class self-interest.[15]

The principal measure of the Ferré administration's social justice program
was wage and income increases. From the beginning of his administration Ferré
gave public employees wage increases, more benefits (increased pensions, retirement plans, health benefits), and better working conditions (for example,
tenure). Ferré also introduced the Christmas bonus: the employer had to give a
fixed percentage of the employee's yearly salary as a bonus in December.[16]
Another measure of social justice was the rise in agricultural wages and the
granting of a wage subsidy to the sugar industry. This was aimed at improving
the standard of living of the agricultural worker and easing the labor shortage
that was hurting agriculture.[17] The Ferré administration also tried to implement
a general health service program, in which all medical institutions and doctors
had to provide services to every person; the government would defray the cost
for those unable to pay.[18] The Ferré administration also passed a law granting
property titles to those living on government lands and giving land to those
with housing needs. This measure was aimed at solving the grave problem of
housing, using government land with no commercial or agricultural value.[19]
Another law granted subsidies of bank loans to university students, designed
not only to increase the loan capacity of the banks but to stimulate higher
education in the lower economic strata.[20] Other measures of the Ferré administration were in the area of drug addiction and crime (to provide social order).[21]

Although these measures gathered support for the PNP, they nevertheless did
not achieve the desired social and economic goals. On the contrary, the Ferré
years saw an increase in social and political conflict, caused in part by these
very measures. The major social problem confronting the Ferré government
was the conflict between labor and capital. Between 1969 and 1972 there were
a total of seventy strikes in Puerto Rico, over half of these in the public sector
(including workers legally unable to strike).[22] One of the causes was precisely
the PNP arrival in government, which undermined the delicate "labor peace"
agreement between the public employees' organizations and the PPD. Also, the
PNP's attempt to penetrate and control the state apparatus alienated large sectors of the public workers.[23] Furthermore, the PNP's rhetoric and measures in
favor of public employees fostered their claim for more rights and benefits
(including the right to organize in trade unions).

Other factors destabilized the social peace sought by Ferré's administration.

The number of land invasions—in both public and private land—increased, stimulated in part by the government's land distribution program. The people involved claimed lack of attention from or discrimination by the government.[24] But perhaps the most crucial political conflict was the confrontation with the independence movement. The growing and radicalized independence movement clashed with the PNP's open annexationism. All the big issues in which the independence movement was involved (the campaign against the U.S. Navy presence in the islands of Culebra and Vieques, the antidraft/anti–Vietnam War campaign, the university strikes and riots, land invasions, labor strikes) ended in direct confrontation with the government. The Ferré administration also coincided with the rise of underground activities by proindependence groups. The response of Ferré's government to this breakdown in "mutual comprehension" between classes and political groups was the use of force against them, particularly by the police.[25]

The failure of the social justice measures to obtain social peace was accompanied by their failure to stimulate economic stability. For the first time in decades there was a big budget deficit, which lowered the borrowing capacity of the government and its power to stimulate investment. The rise of government expenditures did not offset the decline in real investments.[26] Although by 1972 the social justice measures had failed to bring social peace, Ferré tried a last attempt to implement his redemption program: the stillborn "Patrimony for Progress."

The Patrimony for Progress

The Patrimony for Progress, proposed by Ferré in 1972, may be the best example of his attempt to implement his social philosophy through control over local government. The importance of the Patrimony within Ferré's redemption program was stated by Ferré himself years after his electoral defeat of 1972:

Question: What was your most painful legislative defeat?

Ferré: The Patrimony for Progress. Although throughout my life I have defended capitalism, I am a strong supporter of social justice. Capitalism, as it exists today, is an obstacle to justice. . . .

Question: Why was the bill for the Patrimony for Progress defeated?

Ferré: For lack of vision. My goal was to make of every citizen a capitalist, or if you prefer to call it by another name, to socialize capital. My bill . . . pretended to give the citizens of low incomes an additional economic source through their ownership of shares in government-controlled enterprises. . . . We cannot deny history. Humanity is moving toward socialized distributive justice.[27]

The Patrimony aimed not only at materializing Ferré's redemption program, but also "to stop socialism"; it was proposed in Ferré's message to the legislature in 1972 and submitted months later as an executive bill.[28]

The Patrimony was based on Ferré's social philosophy that only social justice through reforms will assure the reproduction of the capitalist system. He defined the philosophical basis of the Patrimony as follows:

> We need a revolutionary change in our socioeconomic structures that maintains the advantages of free enterprise but that provides an opportunity for the worker to participate in the general enrichment of society. Only this way can we *reduce the enormous difference between capital and labor* and achieve a real life of equal opportunity for all Puerto Ricans, and *eliminate the great social tensions* that today make men unhappy. . . . We need to find a solution that modifies democratic capitalism in such a way that its social injustices are corrected, while its advantages are kept.[29]

"Of every citizen a capitalist" was the goal of the Patrimony: to eradicate social conflict by turning society's members into one class, the capitalist.

The mechanism to implement the Patrimony was simple: a corporation would be created with a fund or patrimony whose shares would come from investments by the workers and a proportional share of investment by the government, which would also provide loans for the workers to invest. The fund was to invest in productive activities and its tax-exempt profits would be distributed to the shareholders (the workers) at periodic intervals.[30] The Patrimony was supposed to eradicate class conflict by turning workers with shares in the fund into capitalists; if all workers participated in the Patrimony, the differences between capital and labor were supposed to be eliminated. With no class differences, social peace would be assured.

Aside from the attempt to make every citizen a capitalist, the Patrimony's other main goal was to provide "a strong stimulus to the economy of Puerto Rico through investments in the industrial, commercial, and agricultural sectors."[31] It was an attempt to remedy one of the most serious economic problems at the time: the low rate of investment in the economy, particularly by local capital. If implemented as planned, the Patrimony would have provided capital for "the investment in firms with some interest for Puerto Rico" and whose management would be in the hands of the local capital.

The Patrimony for Progress was stillborn. Outside the inner circle of Ferré's advisers, the majority of the PNP leadership did not understand the nature of the project. But the greatest opposition to the bill came from the PPD-controlled Senate; nothing could be granted to the PNP-controlled Executive in an election year. Furthermore, criticism of the bill by several well-known economists (including Paul Samuelson) raised grave doubts about its viability.[32] The Patrimony for Progress and the rest of Ferré's program of redemption died in November 1972 with the PNP's electoral defeat and the weakening of Ferré's position inside the party.

Management and Control of the State Apparatus

One of the issues that divided the PER in 1967 was Ferré's position on the need to control the state apparatus in order to advance statehood. Likewise, social justice and other measures of the redemption program could only be promoted from the state apparatus. According to Ferré, direct intervention of the state was necessary to abolish the social inequities that endanger the existence of capitalism.[33] The implementation of the redemptionist program and the realization of the New Life made the use of the state apparatus indispensable.

Ferré had a technocratic notion of the government. According to it, one of the functions of the state was to confront social problems, which could be solved with due attention and adequate and available technology. This view was reflected in his statement that, "I think engineers, by temperament, are well suited to be governors."[34] For Ferré, social manipulation is a matter of technology and has nothing to do with social relations. Government should not only be entrusted to solve social problems but to anticipate them as well. To implement his program, Ferré proposed the use of available technology by "a cabinet of technocrats," free of any political influence, that would try to "apply our best scientific and technological skills to the problems of government, with a particular emphasis on keeping a well-balanced social equilibrium."[35]

But Ferré's "technocrats" were not exactly "value free"; his cabinet included several college professors, a banker, a merchant, a hospital-owning doctor, and a sugar-lobbyist "statesman." While during the previous administration of Sánchez Vilella more than two-thirds of the executive administrators were career government bureaucrats and less than 3 percent came from the private sector, under Ferré one-third came from the private sector and less than one-third came from the government bureaucracy.[36] Several reasons account for this. After twenty-eight years of PPD government, the PNP had no trusted high-echelon bureaucrats. Furthermore, Ferré maintained that individuals coming from the private sector were better prepared technically and had a greater ideological affinity with his program. There was also a purely political reason; the PNP realized that it had to achieve the maximum possible control over the state apparatus both to implement its program and to maintain political power.

This process of penetration and control of the state apparatus was carried out at two levels. First was the penetration from below through the increase in government employees identified with the PNP. The second mechanism was the imposition of new decision-making structures over the different government agencies.[37] To this end, the Ferré administration created a number of boards, committees, and research centers under the control of the executive and outside the formal structures of the existing government; it received financial and technical aid from the federal government, M.I.T., and the Ford Foundation. In 1970 Ferré proposed the creation of the Institute for Social Technology, which gathered outstanding figures to "study the important social problems of Puerto Rico with the best and most advanced methods available to modern technology." His government also created the Center for the Study of North and South America, whose function was to "improve the comprehension between the two great cultures of this hemisphere, the North American Saxon culture and the Hispanic culture," with Puerto Rico as the vital link between both.[38] That same year Ferré formed the Governor's Financial Committee as an advisory committee on economic matters.[39] Early in his administration, Ferré created a series of education and health boards to make public policy and check on the affairs of the executive departments. Thus by the end of his administration Ferré had created structures that supplanted or controlled areas of the PPD-created state apparatus, like the Planning Board, the Departments of Health and Education, and the Economic Development Administration.

An important new institution created by Ferré was the Governor's Advisory Committee for the Development of Government Programs, headed by his son, Antonio Luis. The Advisory Committee formed twelve committees to study four areas: economy, public administration, social issues, and environment. Among their main recommendations were two dealing with the reform of the fiscal system: a proposal for a new tax rate for corporations, and a proposal to reform the existing tax-exemption program for EDA-promoted corporations; this included "the design of a more effective system of incentives and the elaboration of programs that stimulate the Puerto Rican local corporations."[40] These proposals reflected the interest of the Ferré administration in reforming the Commonwealth's industrialization program to favor more local capital.

Local Capital and the Program of Redemption

The measures of social justice, the Patrimony for Progress, and others reflected the interest of the Ferré administration in supporting local capital. While the PPD industrialization program favored mostly American capital, the new government attempted to redress this discrimination. From the first days of his administration Ferré's position was clear: "I will not foment nor sign any legislation that I am convinced will place the industry of the island in a disadvantaged position before the industry of the mainland."[41]

This policy was not merely an issue of conflicting economic interests; it was based on Ferré's program of redemption for capitalism in Puerto Rico. The control of the means of production by the local bourgeoisie not only assures the existence of this class but the reproduction of capitalism itself on the island. This is the conception stated in Ferré's first message to the legislature in 1969:

> Since the beginning of the industrialization program, an active policy to attract foreign capital was adopted. The moment has come to adopt a more active policy to attract the participation of the local entrepreneur, particularly in commerce, construction, and finance. The participation of the local

entrepreneur is important not only for economic reasons but also for powerful social reasons. *A people that does not preserve the control of its sources of employment and wealth develops serious political, social, and emotional tensions.* We have to prevent this from happening in Puerto Rico.[42]

This policy was incorporated into the economic program of EDA, the Commonwealth's agency entrusted with the implementation of the industrialization program. A 1971 EDA report argued the necessity to "balance investment, in order that control of an important part of business here should be in the hands of local residents. The purpose is that important decisions which the private sector makes from day to day with respect to the economy respond to the better interest of our society." The same report outlined steps for the defense of local capital; recognizing that local capital concentrates on the domestic market, EDA argued that "the local market and the use of local raw materials constitute the areas in which Puerto Rican industrialists can naturally achieve greater success. Accordingly, Fomento has reserved these areas for the promotion of local businesses and joint ventures in which resident investors have control."[43]

The economic policy of the Ferré administration was elaborated at two levels: first, the defense of local capital in production for the local market; second, the promotion of American capital of "high productivity," whose production was for the American market. This policy was presented in another 1971 EDA report: "Industrial growth will be induced, as in the past two decades, principally by the export of manufactured goods. Nevertheless, an important role is assigned during the coming decade to the import substitution of manufactured goods as a consequence of the expanding local market."[44] This "import substitution" policy represented the defense of local capital before U.S. capital in the local market. Another EDA report, entitled *Action Program to Stimulate Development for the Seventies,* included among its main proposals the promotion of "greater participation of Puerto Rican entrepreneurs in industry"; the promotion of savings—thus establishing an internal basis for investment; and the creation of scientific and technological research institutes (clearly of benefit to local capital, which lacked strong R and D capacity).[45]

Many of the economic measures of the Ferré administration were to favor local capital. The rise in wages and benefits, the Christmas bonus, the increases in public services and government expenditures were all intended to augment the income level of the population and spur consumption, thus stimulating local production of goods and services. Even the policy of getting more federal funds was legitimized in this sense.[46] Under the Ferré administration the number of local firms receiving aid from EDA increased. Since the EDA program was designed to favor American capital, the kind of aid to local capital was different. One of the most important areas of support to local capital was through the loans granted by the Government Development Bank. In 1969 loans to local manufacturing reached $7 million, increasing to $17 million by 1972; similarly, loans to agriculture increased from $6 to $12 million during the same period.[47]

Other issues also reflect Ferré's defense of local capital. Against his beliefs, Ferré opposed a bill in Congress to impose the federal minimum wage in Puerto Rico, solely on the basis that it would hurt local capital the most.[48] EDA opened a branch office in New York to promote the sale of Puerto Rican goods produced by local capital in the U.S. market and to aid local capital in its trade with the United States. The administration also promoted trade between Puerto Rico and other countries, even Puerto Rican investments in the outside.[49]

The other sector of the local economy that received the support of the Ferré administration was agriculture. Agriculture, particularly sugar and coffee, had been alienated under the PPD industrialization program; it was deteriorating rapidly due to higher wages, the lack of a stable and cheap supply of labor, low levels of investments, and inadequate subsidies from government. Although Puerto Rican farmers, particularly in sugar and coffee, were very supportive of the PNP, Ferré's measures in favor of these sectors were also related to the redemption program. The development of agriculture was needed for economic growth, the provision of jobs, and the maintenance of social stability in the decaying rural areas. According to Ferré, solving the "problem" of agriculture was merely an issue of technical planning and the availability of resources.[50]

Ferré's early agricultural measures were aimed at strengthening sugar and coffee production. Along with a new law raising agricultural wages, a new government wage subsidy to agriculture and loans to sugar ($100 million) and coffee ($24 million) were approved; the previous year's aid to agriculture was $2 million. Also, closed sugar centrals were exempted from taxes as an incentive for their reopening. Ferré created the Sugar Industry Rehabilitation Program, whose purpose was to increase sugar production to one million tons and to treble employment in that sector. These measures aimed to alleviate the lack of labor, subsidize centrals and colonos, and solve the low investments in sugar.[51] But none of these measures solved the problems of the sugar industry. It was obsolete, without any capacity for recuperation; its structural problems could not be solved by any monetary infusion. As a result, Ferré almost totally nationalized the sugar industry in the following year: 65 percent of the total sugar-cultivated land and 100 percent of the centrals and sugar refineries were taken by the government.[52]

In 1970, under the Land Administration Authority, Ferré began the process of nationalization with the expropriation of several sugar centrals that had already announced the termination of their operations, including Guánica central (owned by Gulf & Western), and Aguirre and Cortada centrals (owned by the Aguirre Corporation, a Franco-American partnership). It also rented eight other sugar centrals, operated three sugar refineries, and had under its control some forty thousand cuerdas of sugar land.[53] The expropriation of these sugar centrals was financially lucrative for the absentee-owned sugar corporations, who not only recovered their investments but kept the best lands for real estate speculation. However, I do not hold that this was only to save U.S. capital from a huge financial loss.[54] In the first place, the nationalization of the sugar industry secured the continued existence of the rum industry of the island, whose interests were closely linked to the annexationist bourgeoisie and whose excise taxes provided millions to the public purse. Second, it protected the livelihood of thousands of sugar farmers who depended on the sugar centrals and refineries and who gave the PNP massive political support. Third, the nationalization of the sugar industry secured employment and income for thousands of workers in the most economically backward areas of the island, keeping this way "the tranquility and progress of a whole region of Puerto Rico."[55]

None of the attempts to develop local industry and agriculture in Puerto Rico had the long-term effect desired by the Ferré administration. Local capital's share of industrial production in Puerto Rico kept its downward trend during the decade; and the sugar industry has turned into a financial burden for the local government since.

The Ferré Administration and American Capital in Puerto Rico

The Ferré administration pursued an economic policy that sought to promote local capital while attracting foreign industries with high productivity and wages, producing for the foreign market. From the beginning the Ferré administration tried to amend the tax-exemption program to accommodate it to its economic policy.[56] First, the Ferré administration tried to revise the tax-exemption program to force U.S. corporations in Puerto Rico to pay taxes to the local government. Ferré's 1970 message to the legislature proposed that "the tax burden fall more in that sector that is able to pay taxes," with the proviso that there would be "a substantial difference with the federal income tax system, so that investing in Puerto Rico may still be attractive" to American corporations.[57] Although the Ferré administration was not able to reform the tax system to this effect, it did move the exemption program somewhat closer to its economic policy. EDA's policy was aimed at the promotion of heavy industry.[58] A corollary was the reduction in aid and exemptions to foreign light industry; financial aid and subsidies to foreign manufacturing industries by the Government Development Bank and the Puerto Rico Industrial Development Company were reduced after 1969. Between 1969 and 1972 the number of firms and employment created by EDA-promoted nonlocal firms stagnated, while there was an increase in the number of firms and employment created by EDA-promoted local firms.[59]

Under the Ferré administration, the emphasis of EDA's industrialization program was on the attraction of capital-intensive industries: capital with a strong "social responsibility," that can pay high wages and taxes, and promote stability. This particular economic policy was also important for the creation of an economic infrastructure that would provide more areas for the development of local capital, as was indicated in a 1971 EDA report:

> The metal, petroleum, chemical products industries and machinery manu-
> facture are becoming increasingly dependent on other local firms which
> supply components and services. Thus, industrial development is moving
> gradually towards the implementation of interdependent industrial com-
> plexes. . . . These industries represent the core of future large industrial
> complexes. They will produce basic and intermediate materials to be pro-
> cessed into finished goods by other satellite plants.[60]

EDA planned on the creation of an integrated industrial complex whose axis
would be heavy industry and around which locally controlled satellite industries
would develop. The main sectors of heavy industry were to be the petrochemical and the metallic-electronics industries.[61] The promotion of industries by
EDA under Ferré reflected this priority; for example, the number of pharmaceutical firms increased from thirty-four to forty-seven between 1969 and 1972,
while the number of firms manufacturing electronic machinery and precision
instruments increased from thirty-six to sixty-two during the same period.[62]

An important economic issue for the Ferré administration was its support of
the oil industry. During his first year of government Ferré asked President Nixon
to exempt Puerto Rico from the restrictions in imports and production imposed
on the U.S. oil industry and to allow the island to buy oil in new markets.[63]
More impressive yet was Ferré's granting of tax exemption to Union Carbide
for seventeen more years, so that the company would remain in the island, an
action contrary to his policy of not using tax exemption to retain industries in
Puerto Rico. It was during Ferré's administration that the most important oil
and oil-related firms settled in Puerto Rico.[64]

Perhaps the most resounding action in favor of the oil industry was the proposal for the construction of an oil superport on the island of Mona, off the
west coast of Puerto Rico. This proposal was part of a so-called Petroleum
Base Project, whose plans included the construction of a deep-water port and
oil storage and transshipment facilities to stimulate the growth of the oil industry in Puerto Rico. The project was designed to provide cheap electricity to
other industries, stimulate "the expansion and diversification of the petrochemical industry," and "provide new basic materials needed for the development
of Puerto Rican light industry," that is, to promote the expansion of local
capital.[65] Although the Petroleum Base Project was taken up by the Hernández
Colón administration, changes in the world oil market and mass opposition to
the project in Puerto Rico put an end to the proposal.

The other economic area that was strongly supported during Ferré's administration was copper mining. Since the early 1960s the existence of exploitable
mine deposits in the island became an issue of great concern for the government. One of Ferré's first concerns as governor was precisely a search for an
agreement with U.S. mine companies for the exploitation of the mineral. A
1969 EDA report on the chemical and allied products industry mentioned the
future installation of copper smelters in the south coast by American Metal

Climax and Kennecott Copper.[66] Behind these actions lay Ferré's economic policy: to promote foreign industries that could provide the infrastructure for the development of local industry. In this case the exploitation of the copper mines by American copper corporations that would induce the growth of locally controlled satellite refining and processing metal industries that would supply semiprocessed materials to heavy industries, like machinery and electronics.[67] The metals industry in Puerto Rico was one of the economic areas of higher growth in the island, with half of the firms owned by local capital and over 80 percent of its production aimed for the local market.[68] The Ferré administration and the copper companies never reached an agreement on the exploitation of the mineral.

One issue that troubled the Ferré administration's industrialization program was EDA's performance. EDA confronted grave problems in its day-to-day operations during Ferré's government, mostly as the result of the attempt to redefine its goals as a Commonwealth agency. The administration of EDA's first director under Ferré, Juan Rodríguez de Jesús, was extremely chaotic. The agency suffered the loss of key personnel who did not adapt to the new government and its economic policy. The continued disputes between Rodríguez de Jesús and the governor's main adviser, Antonio L. Ferré, separated EDA from the government's economic policy-making process. As a result of this, and coupled with EDA's emphasis on the promotion of heavy industry, employment and the number of EDA-promoted firms declined. Under the direction of Rodríguez de Jesús as well as that of his successor, Manuel Casiano, EDA had to confront the administration's industrial policy; it even had to oppose the PNP's statehood rhetoric that was scaring potential investors away from the island. Rodríguez de Jesús even publicly criticized the governor's economic policies. Casiano's administration represented the return to EDA's traditional objectives of creating employment through the promotion of light industry. Like his predecessor, Casiano emphasized the "benefits" of Commonwealth for the foreign investor and moved away from the PNP statehood rhetoric.[69]

The results of Ferré's economic policy toward American corporations in Puerto Rico were mixed. His administration achieved the transition to an industrialization program based on heavy industry. Nevertheless, the proposals for the development of industrial complexes around oil and copper were never realized. Ironically, spurred by the rising unemployment and the fall in real investment, during his last year as governor Ferré had to desist from imposing taxes on American corporations and reforming the tax-exemption program; during this year the only increases of his administration in the number of firms promoted by EDA and their total employment were achieved.[70]

Although the Ferré administration was primarily concerned with implementing its redemption program, this is not to say that no attention was paid to the issue of statehood. Statehood was important in Ferré's program for it was seen as the ultimate basis for political stability.

The Issue of Statehood

Statehood was one of the most conflictive issues for the PNP during Ferré's administration, as there were internal differences around this issue in the party. The Ferré administration's contradictory management of the statehood issue came from the lack of a clear notion of how to use the state apparatus to promote statehood. Ferré came to power with the notion that statehood is a long-term endeavor that required support both in Puerto Rico and the United States. Several measures, like the promotion of a cultural program ("Creole statehood") and the creation of a political basis of support in the United States (affiliation of PNP members with both the Republican and the Democratic parties) were steps in that direction. The economic measures of the Ferré administration were directed at the strengthening and stability of the Puerto Rican economy as a requisite of statehood.

Ferré's conception of how to achieve statehood was a subjectivist one; the people must be "educated" in order to consciously accept statehood. The PNP's task is to create the "will" of Puerto Ricans for statehood as an indispensable prerequisite for the granting of this status by Congress. Although Ferré acknowledged that his election was not a mandate for statehood, he did argue that his party's task was to promote the advantages of statehood among the people.[71] One of the first issues dealt with in the pro-statehood education campaign was the issue of cultural assimilation. To reply to the charge that statehood meant cultural assimilation, Ferré argued that there was a difference between *patria* (fatherland) and *nación* (nation). Patria is the place of birth, the native country, the people and its customs. Nación is the government to whom the individual must be loyal, the political institutions that unite a people, the authority that rules and guides the lives of the people. For the Puerto Ricans, Puerto Rico, the island and its people, is the patria; but they must be loyal, based on the ties of citizenship, to the nación, to the United States.[72]

The conception of *estadidad jíbara,* which was elaborated during the thirties and forties, became the cultural program of statehood under the PNP. This conception implied that under statehood there would be no cultural assimilation; Puerto Ricans would be able to keep their language and customs.[73] Furthermore, statehood under estadidad jíbara would provide the cultural autonomy required to protect Puerto Rican culture and language. This notion was elaborated by the statehood ideologue Reece B. Bothwell. Bothwell dusted off an article he had written in the 1940s (discussed in Chapter 4) on the relation between statehood and American federalism and presented it as part of the idea of estadidad jíbara. He concluded that statehood "will guarantee our internal autonomy, our personality and identity as a people of Hispanic background."[74] According to Ferré, the goal of the PNP is "to keep preserving the Puerto Rican *patria* within our loyalty to the American nation."[75] Thus, estadidad jíbara is a vital element of the PNP's statehood strategy: it is the essential link between the Puerto Rican patria and the American nación.

Ferré's management of the statehood issue was very cautious. Ferré knew that he did not have a popular mandate for statehood and that the process of "educating" the people for statehood was necessary. This explains why the public promotion of statehood took a subordinate position to the government tasks.[76] This policy follows Ferré's views that priority should be given to the promotion of social and political stability, prerequisite not only for the viability of statehood in the United States, but also, and more important, for the maintenance of capitalism itself in Puerto Rico. This policy was also based on Ferré's "gradualist" approach to statehood—statehood will be achieved through a process of gradual conviction by the population of the advantages of statehood. One of the mechanisms to attain this was through furthering Puerto Rico's political integration to the United States.

Political Integration

The PNP under Ferré elaborated the notion that the road to statehood was through the increased integration of the Commonwealth to the American state. According to the PNP program, the main objective of the Commonwealth is "the strengthening of the ties of union" between the island and the United States; the PNP would oppose any measure "that could weaken or dilute our ties of union."[77] This notion viewed the Commonwealth as a transitional status toward statehood, thus legitimizing any attempt to reform it.[78]

One of the first issues used by the PNP to promote political integration was that of the presidential vote. This was demanded by the PPD in the 1967 plebiscite. Taking advantage of the conflicts in the PPD between annexationists and autonomists, the PNP took the presidential vote as their main pro-statehood reform of the Commonwealth. One of the results of the 1967 plebiscite was the proposal to create some ad hoc committees on the possible areas of growth for the Commonwealth. In May of 1969 Ferré formed these committees, giving priority to those areas favoring statehood. In July of that year Ferré named the members of the committee, including members from Congress, the PNP, and PPD proannexationists. The conclusions of the committee were as expected: a recommendation to seek the presidential vote for Puerto Rico.[79]

Although the debate around the issue of the presidential vote fueled the internal differences in the PNP, there was common agreement that the presidential vote was a step toward statehood. The presidential vote was seen as advancing the political integration of the Commonwealth to the United States. It emphasized the direct ties of Puerto Ricans with the American state. The annexationists presented it as "an inherent right of our citizenship" and as a "legitimate claim" of the U.S. citizens in Puerto Rico.[80] The presidential vote was also seen as the instrument needed to provide Puerto Ricans with the "participation in the federal government to defend there with more force and effectiveness our rights and interests," including a possible petition for "the ulterior development of the Commonwealth or a transition toward statehood or independence''; the presidential vote would also integrate the Puerto Ricans to the American political process and "will make it easier for them to understand statehood."[81] Some sectors within the PNP viewed the presidential vote as an important part of a strategy for statehood. According to Justo Méndez, then PNP vice-president, the electoral victory of 1968 gave the PNP the right to move Puerto Rico toward statehood. Méndez proposed a three-tier plan for statehood: (1) to obtain the presidential vote, (2) to demand two resident commissioners with the power to vote in Congress, and (3) to celebrate a new plebiscite after a 1972 PNP electoral victory.[82] The bill submitted by Ferré asking for the presidential vote died in the PPD-controlled Senate and the PNP lost the election of 1972.

A more successful attempt to increase the Commonwealth's political integration to the United States was the Ferré administration's push for more federal funds for the island. Federal funds were an important part of Ferré's program to provide social stability in Puerto Rico. This notion was central to Ferré's request for more federal funds in his letter to President Nixon in 1969; federal funds were to be the "medicine" to cure the social "diseases" (unemployment, poverty, social marginality) of Puerto Rico.[83] The Ferré administration elaborated for the first time a public policy with regard to federal funds. From early in his administration, Ferré and the PNP Resident Commissioner began a campaign in the United States to include Puerto Rico in new federal programs and increase its share of those in which it already participated. In July 1969 the Division of Federal Aid Programs of the Planning Board was created, charged with the coordination, compilation of data, and assessment of any issue dealing with federal funds.[84]

The push for more federal funds was also part of the strategy to further greater political integration to the United States. The claim for "equal treatment" in the apportionment of federal funds was based on the "right" of U.S. citizens in Puerto Rico to receive the benefits of their citizenship and thus achieve a greater participation in the affairs of the "Nation."[85] Furthermore, federal funds, like the presidential vote, could be used as an instrument to "educate" the people on the advantages of statehood. To obtain a greater share of federal funds was to show Puerto Ricans the benefits of statehood; it was the best mechanism, also, to show the people that only statehood could guarantee the flow of federal funds to Puerto Rico.[86]

The strategy for increasing Puerto Rico's political integration to the United States included the strengthening of the ties of citizenship between Puerto Ricans and the American state through the defense of their rights as citizens. If the PNP's quest for the presidential vote and more federal funds were examples of this, perhaps the best use of this strategy was shown in Ferré's management of the conflict over the U.S. Navy's use of the island of Culebra. By 1970 the quantity and quality of the opposition to the navy presence in the island had increased. The independence movement joined the people of Culebra in demanding the withdrawal of the navy from the island; later on, the PPD-controlled Senate joined the opposition to the navy presence in Culebra. This presented the possibility of a great conflict against the U.S. presence in Puerto Rico. In an astute political maneuver, the Ferré administration intervened and changed the nature of the conflict. According to Ferré, his goal was to "maintain the conflict within its authentic limits, that is to say, a legitimate demand of American citizens that their rights be respected against the arbitrary attitude of a dependency of the federal government."[87] By having the government take charge of the conflict, Ferré took the issue out of the hands of the antiannexationist forces and turned it into a bureaucratic issue. Informed by Ferré of the political consequences that this issue could have in Puerto Rico and Latin America for the United States, President Nixon intervened in the matter and forced the navy to negotiate with the Puerto Rican government; the navy withdrew from Culebra in 1975.[88]

The push to increase the Commonwealth's political integration to the United States was an integral part of the PNP's redemption program. Greater political integration represented a greater flow of federal funds to the island, a crucial element in Ferré's scheme to promote social stability. Political integration meant also the strengthening of the ties of citizenship of Puerto Ricans to the American state, thus furthering the cause of statehood. Greater political integration was a source of political stability, necessary for the reproduction of capitalism in Puerto Rico.

Ferré's redemption program was never realized. The measures for achieving "social justice" and for protecting local capital did not achieve the expected results, the Patrimony for Progress was stillborn, and the role of the American corporations in Puerto Rico was never redefined. These, along with the internal conflicts in the party and the PNP's defeat in the 1972 elections, led to the collapse of the program of redemption and of Ferré's position within the party.

The Downfall of Ferré

The PNP's formation laid the basis for the internal conflicts of 1973–74 and the rise of Romero Barceló to the party leadership. The PNP was formed as a loosely knit coalition of several annexationist sectors coming from distinct organizations (the PER, Citizens for the 51st State, Americans for Democratic Action, *Populares* for Statehood), many of them with clear political and ideological differences. Even among those coming from the PER there were differences between the Liberals (who tended to support the U.S. Democratic party) and the Republicans (more conservative). A former PNP representative, Benjamín Franklin Cerezo, argued that the PNP "was a party that cemented the impossible. The desire to defeat the [PPD] joined many people that otherwise would not have even greeted each other. *They were several parties in one.*"[89] This weak cohesion fomented a lack of programmatic unity among the party leadership. This led an analyst to conclude that "no matter how long you search for it, you cannot find an essence that you can hold and say: This is the New

Progressive Party."[90] This is partly correct; for example, the diversity of legislative bills submitted by the PNP during this period reflected the diversity of interests and ideological positions in the party.[91] But there was a unifying essence in the PNP that was crucial for its formation: the defense of statehood. The PNP emerged as an organization from Estadistas Unidos, founded with the sole purpose of defending statehood in the 1967 plebiscite. Statehood was the only element that provided the party its ideological coherence, and was also a major source of its internal conflicts.

This diversity of interests in the PNP affected the organizational structure of the party. The PNP was a very loose organization, without a clear and precise demarcation of its internal power structure. According to Martínez Saldaña, the PNP was "a weak party in its internal structure"; only Ferré "has indisputable leadership within the party," but all the other leadership positions "are divided on the basis of an intense power struggle, that can lead to the weakening of the party [in 1972]."[92] The conflicts among the PNP legislators were among the main problems of the party during this period. The differences between the conservatives and the liberals prevented approval of legislation and even impeded the approval of bills coming from the governor's office. For example, the liberal Cerezo was ousted from his top position in the House by his conservative PNP colleagues.[93] This disorganization and lack of a central power structure showed itself also in the formation of local power machines with great autonomy from the central party machinery. The most outstanding one was that formed by the mayor of San Juan, Romero Barceló.

The basis of this lack of organizational unity in the party was fomented by the absence of programmatic unity. This is not to imply that the PNP had no program. As we have demonstrated in this and the previous chapter, the PNP under Ferré tried to implement the program of redemption. But this program was not supported or understood by all sectors within the party. In this regard, the statements made by Antonio Quiñones Calderón on the party unity are very important. He is one of the outstanding founders of the party and was press secretary to both Ferré and Romero Barceló; he also remains the most important chronicler-propagandist of the PNP. Describing the attempt by Ferré to implement his redemptionist program, Quiñones Calderón concluded:

> To face this challenge, without any doubt, was the task that don Luis Ferré understood as his first priority. . . .
> Did the party leadership understand this in the same way? Was it understood by the majority or a great sector of the statehooders. . . ? The response to both questions is *no*. I perceived it then and confirmed it later through the period of that anguished administration.
> As a matter of fact, throughout the three decades of struggle against the [PPD] and Muñoz, all the statehooders—the old ones that were members of the group of extremist Republicans and the young ones that came later on—had turned into "die-hard" statehooders, who demanded "Statehood Now" above everything else.[94]

The unifying link of the party was statehood. That explains why most of the conflicts among the PNP legislators came from their differences regarding social issues and why Ferré had so many problems pushing his programs through the legislature, even among his own party members.

This lack of support reflected a reality already evident by the end of the first PNP administration: the existence of two distinct programs in the party, each one grouping around it the leading sectors of the party. As had happened in the PER years before, the clash between these sectors and their programs was fought at the ideological level, primarily around the issue of statehood. The bourgeois sector headed by Ferré argued in favor of a "gradualist" approach to statehood and saw statehood as part of a broader historical project that did not require immediate statehood to be successful. But another statehood program was slowly rising around the intermediate social sectors headed by Romero Barceló. They represented an "immediatist" approach: "Statehood Now." [95] Their differences came out in the debate around the presidential vote. For Ferré, the Puerto Ricans were not yet ready for statehood, so the presidential vote would strengthen the "permanent union" within the commonwealth status, as a measure of education toward statehood. For Romero, the attainment of statehood was the most important task of the PNP, so that the presidential vote was a step toward statehood in the immediate future. Romero supported a status plebiscite after the 1972 elections if the PNP won, an idea that Ferré did not wholeheartedly support. By this time other differences had already come out in the open. Late in his administration Ferré argued for the continuation of tax exemption as part of the industrialization program, particularly as a weapon against unemployment. Romero, on the other hand, argued for the immediate termination of tax exemption as a transitory measure toward statehood. Furthermore, Romero was already arguing that statehood should become the "ideological basis," the only program of the PNP, a position strongly opposed by Ferré. [96]

Up to the 1972 elections Ferré kept organizational and programmatic control of the party. In the 1972 PNP Assembly Ferré was once again named candidate for governor, without any form of opposition. But Romero's power in the party was already evident by this date. After a fierce struggle, Romero was named first vice-president and several of his protégés were named to the top leadership of the organization. [97] The 1972 electoral program still showed Ferré's influence, with emphasis on the "achievements" of the administration in the socioeconomic area and other measures related to the redemption program—The Great Task, the Patrimony for Progress, social justice, and so on. Both the electoral program and the campaign downplayed the issue of statehood, emphasizing the party's goal of achieving statehood "in the shortest possible term," which would "depend fundamentally on the expression of the will of the people of Puerto Rico." [98]

The defeat in the 1972 elections increased the disunity in the party and led to a crisis at all levels of the PNP. Greatly resentful of the defeat, Ferré accused the people of not having voted wisely; people close to him stated that the cause for the defeat lay in the emphasis some party sectors placed on the issue of statehood (a clear reference to Romero). Ferré presented his resignation from the party presidency and promised to move away from public and party politics forever.[99] Romero responded to this claim by stating that the cause of the defeat was the party's "excess of confidence" (clearly referring to Ferré's campaign on the "achievements" of his administration) and argued that the issue of statehood had nothing to do with the electoral results. He also reaffirmed statehood as the "ideological basis" of the party. Party members close to Romero accused Ferré's government of being the direct cause of the defeat and supported his resignation from the party presidency.[100] The PNP disorganization after the 1972 elections reached such a level that members of the party leadership publicly clamored for the party's unity, organization, and revitalization.[101] The party division widened. For example, the conflicts between the PNP liberals and the conservatives in the legislature increased and even some PNP legislators announced their legislative independence from the party.[102] Ferré's self-imposed alienation immediately after the defeat and the exacerbation of differences in the party leadership created an organizational and power void in the PNP that Romero filled.

The Rise of Romero Barceló

Under the banner of the party reorganization, Romero Barceló took control of the party and imposed a new statehood program. He came out of the 1972 elections unhurt, consolidated San Juan as a PNP stronghold, and became the most outstanding party member occupying a public post in that period. Romero had been a founding member of Estadistas Unidos and of the PNP; his organizational capacity was his main political asset. A rude and straightforward politician, he had rivaled Ferré in prowess by defeating the PPD's strongest local political machinery, in San Juan. Immediately after the 1972 elections, Romero's name was mentioned inside and outside the party as the person to replace the "old man" in the top leadership of the party.[103] In his role as PNP first vice-president, the second highest post in the party, Romero was named by the Presidential Council, the PNP's top decision-making body, to direct the party reorganization in November 1972. From the beginning of the process Romero showed a total control of the reorganization campaign, repeatedly clashing with other party leaders. Romero's PNP reorganization was structured at two levels. First, he created party unity at the organizational level, creating a centralized power structure and taking disciplinary actions against those opposed. Second, Romero placed statehood as the party's sole "ideological basis."[104]

Romero's PNP reorganization throughout 1973 was not without opposition. Throughout the process, which culminated in November of that year with the approval of new party bylaws, the internal conflict became known as the "Ferré-Romero conflict." Ferré and his group accused Romero of total control and reorganizing the party in his favor and that in doing so he had alienated several sectors in the party—particularly the liberals. There was also debate between immediate statehood or gradual statehood, and between statehood and social reform.[105] Romero's control became evident with the approval of the new party bylaws at the end of 1973, which reflected the structural reorganization of the party.

First, the position of president-founder was created to prevent a fratricide struggle for the presidency between Ferré and Romero. Second, a party legislative caucus was formed, requiring the strict participation and loyalty of all its members; this was an internal organism to keep in check the work and positions of all PNP legislators. Third, party primaries were required for all positions of the legislature, mayoralties, and municipal assemblies. Fourth, an amendment was introduced to require that no party member could hold any elective position for more than eight consecutive years.[106] Taken as a whole, the reorganization of the party directly benefited Romero and his group. Romero was in control of the party machinery, and the new legislative caucus subordinated the PNP legislators to the party authority. The changes in the bylaws requiring primaries and an eight-year limit for all elective positions guaranteed Romero and his group the majority of the party's elective positions in the 1976 elections and thus the party control, since they had the greatest political and organizational strength in the party. For example, the 1972 elections showed a continuity in the PNP legislative representation, with seventeen out of twenty-three PNP legislators reelected; on the other hand, the results of the 1976 elections show a rupture in the party's legislative representation, with only twelve incumbents of the forty-seven PNP legislators elected.[107]

The PNP 1974 Convention ratified Romero's power in the party, although it was not totally free of conflict. A considerable group supported Ferré for the party presidency and opposed Romero's policy of "Statehood Now," emphasizing the need for a program of social reform. As expected, Ferré was named president-founder and Romero president of the party, with almost absolute powers over the organization; the party's new top leadership was completely loyal to Romero.[108] Both Ferré and Romero demanded the party unity to confront the PPD in the coming elections. Ferré, acknowledging his decreased strength within the party, was resigned, at least publicly, to remain as "founding father and counsellor" of the PNP, and admitted that "Romero has become the propelling force, injecting new blood into the party."[109]

The rise of Romero Barceló to the command of the PNP represented the end of the attempt to implement Ferré's program of redemption. The PNP under Romero, more than any other party ever, turned statehood into a massive political force. The control of the Commonwealth state apparatus from 1977 to 1985 by Romero's group turned *Estadidad ahora* from a partisan statehood program into public policy.

NOTES

1. Robert Anderson, *Gobierno y partidos políticos en Puerto Rico* (Madrid: Editorial Tecnos, 1970), p. 283.

2. E.g., Andrés Sánchez Tarniella, *Los costos de la estadidad para Puerto Rico* (Río Piedras: Ediciones Bayoan, 1980).

3. James Dietz, *Economic History of Puerto Rico* (Princeton: Princeton University Press, 1986), p. 269.

4. Junta de Planificación, *Informe Económico al Gobernador, 1981* (San Juan: Junta de Planificación, 1982), pp. A7, A27.

5. Ibid., pp. A7–8, A27, A57.

6. U.S. Department of Commerce, *Economic Study of Puerto Rico* (Washington, D.C.: U.S. Government Printing Office, 1979), vol. 1, p. 4.

7. Junta de Planificación, *Informe Económico al Gobernador, 1982* (San Juan: Junta de Planificación, 1983), p. 408; Department of Commerce, *Economic Study,* p. 16.

8. Department of Commerce, *Economic Study,* pp. 14–15.

9. Gervasio L. García and A. G. Quintero-Rivera, *Desafío y solidaridad: Breve historia del movimiento obrero puertorriqueño* (Río Piedras: Ediciones Huracán, 1982), ch. 7; Jesse Pou Rivera, "Public Employee Organizations in Puerto Rico" (Master's Thesis, Sch. Pub. Admin., UPR, 1975).

10. Robert Anderson, "The Party System: Change or Stagnation?" in Jorge Heine, ed., *Time for Decision: The United States and Puerto Rico* (Lanham, MD: North-South Publ., 1983), pp. 19–20.

11. Luis A. Ferré, *El propósito humano,* ed. Antonio Quiñones Calderón (San Juan: Ediciones Nuevas, 1972), p. 6.

12. Ibid., pp. 148, 160.

13. Ibid., pp. 176, 195. See also *El Mundo,* June 1, 1970, p. 1A; Aug. 6, 1969, p. 11E.

14. Ibid., p. 54.

15. *El Mundo,* April 25, 1969, p. 8A.

16. Ibid., June 30, 1969, p. 1A; June 16, 1969, p. 3A; July 2, 1969, p. 12A; June 22, 1970, p. 1A; and April 27, 1972, p. 3A.

17. Antonio Quiñones Calderón, *La obra de Luis A. Ferré en La Fortaleza* (Santurce: Servicios Editoriales, 1975), pp. 64 and 66–67. See also *El Mundo,* Nov. 8, 1969, p. 5A.

18. Quiñones Calderón, *La obra,* pp. 82–86; also *El Mundo,* June 21, 1969, p. 1A.

19. *El Mundo,* June 16, 1969, p. 3A; and Oct. 5, 1972, p. 14D.

20. Quiñones Calderón, *La obra,* pp. 76–77; also *El Mundo,* June 25, 1969, p. 1A; and Sept. 2, 1970, p. 14A.

21. Quiñones Calderón, *La obra,* pp. 79–82, 86–88, 120–21, and 139–42. Also *El Mundo,* March 27, 1969, p. 5A; and March 26, 1971, p. 1A.

22. Luis R. Torres Rodríguez, "La intervención policíaca en los conflictos obrero-patronales entre los años 1971 al 1973" (Master's Thesis, Sch. Pub. Admin., UPR, 1975), pp. xvi–xx.

23. Pou Rivera, "Public Employee Organizations," pp. 250–55. Also *El Mundo,* Sept. 20, 1972; p. 17A.

24. *El Mundo,* Feb. 22, 1972, p. 1A.

25. Manuel Maldonado-Denis, *Puerto Rico: una interpretación histórico-social* (México City: Siglo XXI, 1974), pp. 251–95; Torres Rodríguez, "La intervención policíaca," pp. 88–108; and *El Mundo*, Dec. 15, 1969, p. 3A; March 12, 1971, p. 1A; March 11, 1972, p. 1A.

26. Comité para el Estudio de las Finanzas de Puerto Rico, *Informe al Gobernador* (Río Piedras: Editorial Universitaria, 1976), pp. 46–54 and 27–33.

27. Pepe Ramos, *Ferré: Autobiografía dialogada* (San Juan: Panavox Multimedia, 1976), p. 220.

28. Ferré, *El propósito humano*, pp. 210–32; *El Mundo*, March 10, 1972, p. 3A; and Oct. 18, 1972, p. 10E.

29. Ferré, *El propósito humano*, pp. 229 and 77. The image is inevitable: the Patrimony is, of course, Marx upside down.

30. Ibid., p. 230; also Quiñones Calderón, *La obra*, pp. 239–41.

31. Ferré, p. 78. For the support given to the Patrimony by bankers, see *El Mundo*, Feb. 9, 1972.

32. *El Mundo*, April 21, 1972, p. 3A; April 27, 1972, p. 1A.

33. Ferré, *El propósito humano*, pp. 43, 58, and 73.

34. Luis A. Ferré, *An Engineer Dreams of a Better Puerto Rico* (address by the Honorable Governor of Puerto Rico before the Puerto Rico Section of the American Society of Mechanical Engineers, Hato Rey, Puerto Rico, February 21, 1969), p. 1.

35. Ferré, *El propósito humano*, pp. 48 and 60; also *An Engineer Dreams*, p. 3; and P. Ramos, *Ferré*, p. 217.

36. Juan A. Ríos Vélez, "Análisis del diseño de la rama ejecutiva para determinar el tipo de gobierno que se quiere implantar" (Master's Thesis, Sch. Pub. Admin., UPR, 1981), pp. 19, 28.

37. *El Mundo*, April 22, 1972, p. 1A; and Edgardo L. Martínez Nazario, "Estudio histórico-teórico sobre el desarrollo administrativo del sector público en Puerto Rico" (Master's thesis, Sch. Pub. Admin., UPR, 1971), p. 94.

38. Quiñones Calderón, *La obra*, p. 95; Ferré, *El propósito humano*, p. 180.

39. *El Mundo*, Aug. 9, 1970, p. 19A.

40. Quiñones Calderón, *La obra*, pp. 96–100.

41. Ferré, *El propósito humano*, p. 54.

42. Ibid., p. 154.

43. Economic Development Administration, *Economic Development in Puerto Rico During the Last Twenty Years* (San Juan: Office of Economic Research, 1971), pp. 13 and 15–16. See the statements by Ferré's EDA directors in *El Mundo*, Dec. 27, 1968, p. 1; Jan. 24, 1969, p. 30; and Jan. 6, 1971, p. 1A.

44. Economic Development Administration, *Puerto Rico's Industrial Development: Past Performance and Glance at the Future* (San Juan: Office of Economic Research, 1971), pp. 14–15.

45. EDA, *Economic Development in Puerto Rico*, pp. 22–23.

46. Ferré, *El propósito humano*, pp. 5, 212–13.

47. Salvador Lugo, *Trends and Problems of the Local Puerto Rican Owned Manufacturing Industries* (San Juan: Interagency Strategy Committee, 1975), pp. 8, 21, 50; and Juan A. Alcázar, *Aspectos sobresalientes de la industria local* (San Juan: EDA, 1979), p. 18.

48. *El Mundo*, May 5, 1971, p. 6A; April 24, 1971, p. 1A.

49. Quiñones Calderón, *La obra*, pp. 105–6; and *El Mundo*, Aug. 28, 1969, p. 1A; June 23, 1970, p. 1A.

50. Ferré, *An Engineer Dreams*, p. 7; also Ferré, *El propósito humano*, p. 156.

51. *El Mundo*, June 25, 1969, p. 1A; and Feb. 25, 1972, p. 5A. Also Quiñones Calderón, *La obra*, pp. 64, 67, 69; and Joselo Sánchez Dergan, "La industria azucarera operada por el gobierno de Puerto Rico: Necesidad de una política pública azucarera" (Master's Thesis, Sch. Pub. Admin., UPR, 1975), pp. 82, 102–9.

52. Sánchez Dergan, "La industria azucarera," p. 82. Production of sugar cane decreased from 465 tons in 1969 to 287 tons in 1972; Junta de Planificación, *Socio Economic Statistics 1980* (San Juan: Economic Research Division, 1981) p. 7.

53. Sánchez Dergan, "La industria azucarera," pp. 136–40; Quiñones Calderón, *La obra*, pp. 123–25; *El Mundo*, Aug. 21, 1970, p. 19B.

54. View held by Ruth Martínez Saldaña, "Anatomía de un partido político en su lucha por llegar al poder: El caso del Partido Nuevo Progresista" (Master's Thesis, Sch. Pub. Admin., UPR, 1972), pp. 43–44.

55. Ferré, *El propósito humano*, pp. 198, 216.

56. Economic Development Administration, *Planning for a Changing Industrial Structure in Puerto Rico* (San Juan: EDA, 1969), p. 110. Also Ferré, *An Engineer Dreams*, p. 4.

57. Ferré, *El propósito humano*, p. 184; also p. 211. See Quiñones Calderón, *La obra*, p. 98.

58. S. Lugo, *Trends and Problems*, p. 21.

59. Ibid., pp. 49–50. EDA-promoted firms provided only 4,000 jobs between 1969 and 1973, while the number of plants decreased from 930 to 907 during the same period.

60. EDA, *Puerto Rico's Industrial Development*, pp. 13, 15. See also EDA, *Economic Development in Puerto Rico*, p. 12.

61. EDA, *Puerto Rico's Industrial Development*, p. 15; EDA, *Economic Development in Puerto Rico*, pp. 20–21; and EDA, *Toward an Industrial Development Policy for the 1970s: The Key Role of the Petroleum Base Project* (San Juan: EDA, 1973)

62. Economic Development Administration, *The Drug and Pharmaceutical Industry in Puerto Rico* (San Juan: EDA, 1973), p. 5; and Economic Development Administration, *The Measuring, Analysing and Controlling Instruments* (San Juan: EDA, 1975), p. 4.

63. *El Mundo*, April 19, 1969, p. 6A; Nov. 21, 1969, p. 11B.

64. Ibid., Feb. 6, 1971, p. 3A; and Luz E. Echevarría Seguí, "El desarrollo de la industria pesada en Puerto Rico" (Master's Thesis, Sch. Pub. Admin., UPR, 1979), pp. 38–39.

65. EDA, *Toward an Industrial Development Policy*, p. 16. See also *El Mundo*, Dec. 13, 1972, p. 1A.

66. *El Mundo*, Jan. 15, 1969, p. 1A; and EDA, *The Chemical and Allied Products Industry in Puerto Rico* (San Juan: Office of Economic Research, 1969), p. 9.

67. EDA, *Economic Development in Puerto Rico*, p. 21.

68. Economic Development Administration, *The Metal Industry in Puerto Rico* (San Juan: Office of Industrial Economics and Promotional Services, 1975), pp. 3, 6–7.

69. On EDA's problems during Ferré's government see the articles by A. W. Maldonado in *El Mundo*, March 28, 29, and 30, 1970, p. 7A, and Jan. 5, 1971, p. 7A. Also in ibid., May 27, 1970, p. 6C; March 4, 1972, p. 3B; and Nov. 9, 1972, p. 18B.

70. Ferré, *El propósito humano,* pp. 214–15; *Socio Economic Statistics 1980,* pp. 5–6.

71. PNP 1967 Program in Reece B. Bothwell, ed., *Puerto Rico: Cien años de lucha política* (Río Piedras: Editorial Universitaria, 1979), vol. 1, pt. 2, p. 914; *El Mundo,* Jan. 21, 1969, p. 28; Sept. 2, 1970, p. 18A.

72. *El Mundo,* Oct. 13, 1969, p. 1A.

73. Ferré, *El propósito humano,* pp. 61–62 and 50.

74. Reece B. Bothwell, "La estadidad jíbara," in Bothwell, ed., *Puerto Rico,* vol. 4, pp. 478–79.

75. Ferré, *El propósito humano,* p. 178.

76. *El Mundo,* Aug. 9, 1969, 1A; Sept. 25, 1972, p. 14A.

77. PNP 1972 program, in *Guía para las elecciones: programas oficiales* (San Juan: Banco Popular, 1972), pp. 8–9; also *El Mundo,* Nov. 27, 1970, p. 7A.

78. *El Mundo,* July 22, 1969, p. 4A.

79. Ibid., May 13, 1969, p. 1A; Quiñones Calderón, *La obra,* pp., 159–69.

80. Ferré, *El propósito humano,* pp. 325–35 and 202; *El Mundo,* July 26, 1970, p. 1A.

81. Ibid., pp. 201 and 333.

82. A. W. Maldonado, "El plan del PNP sobre el status," *El Mundo,* Feb. 12, 1970, p. 7A; also, PNP 1972 program, in *Guía para las elecciones,* p. 9.

83. In Quiñones Calderón, *La obra,* pp. 221, 223.

84. Ibid., pp. 222–28; *El Mundo,* Feb. 25, 1970, p. 3A; Juan C. Rosado Cotto, "Fondos federales y la política pública del Estado Libre Asociado de Puerto Rico," *Revista de Administración Pública 6, no. 2* (March 1974), p. 119.

85. Quiñones Calderón, *La obra,* pp. 222–23; *El Mundo,* June 3, 1971, p. 1A.

86. Dimas Planas, "The Statehood Dream—Now or Later?" *San Juan Star,* Oct. 11, 1971, p. 3; Ferré, *El propósito humano,* p. 61.

87. Ferré, *El propósito humano,* p. 203.

88. Quiñones Calderón, *La obra,* pp. 188–216; *El Mundo,* Aug. 14, 1970, pp. 1A, 6A, and 19A.

89. Bennie Frankie Cerezo, "PNP—Energías de ilusión," *Avance,* Sept. 17, 1973, p. 9.

90. A. W. Maldonado, "El Partido Nuevo Progresista," *El Mundo,* April 8, 1970, p. 7A.

91. See Jorge Javariz, "Cosas del Capitolio," ibid., June 5, 1969, p. 10A.

92. Martínez Saldaña, "Anatomía de un partido político," p. 50.

93. *El Mundo,* June 5, 1969, p. 10A, May 21, 1970, p. 1A; and Salvador Guzmán, "Trasfondo," ibid., Feb. 13, 1971, p. 7A.

94. Antonio Quiñones Calderón, *Del plebiscito a La Fortaleza* (Hato Rey: Ramallo Bros., 1982), pp. 16–17.

95. *El Mundo,* Aug. 23, 1970, p. 1A.

96. D. Planas, "The Statehood Dream," p. 3; "La estadidad no será relegada— Carlos Romero Barceló," *Avance,* Nov. 25, 1972, p. 9. Also Jaime Collazo, "La estadidad como ideología política," *El Mundo,* Oct. 5, 1972, p. 8A.

97. *Avance,* July 27–Aug. 3, 1972, p. 5.

98. On the PNP 1972 program and electoral campaign: *Guía para las elecciones 1972;* Luis A. Ferré, "Visión del futuro de Puerto Rico," *Avance,* July 13–19, 1972, p. 60; ibid., July 27–Aug. 3, 1972, pp. 13–17; *El Mundo,* Sept. 25, 1972, p. 14A; Oct. 3, 1972, p. 18A; Oct. 16, 1972, p. 19B; Oct. 30, 1972, p. 9B.

99. *Avance,* Nov. 15, 1972, pp. 8–10; *El Mundo,* Nov. 9, 1972, pp. 1A, 18B; Nov. 16, 1972, p. 4A. For Romero's support of statehood as an electoral issue see ibid., Oct. 12, 1972, p. 10C.

100. "La estadidad no será relegada," p. 9; *El Mundo,* Nov. 9, 1972, p. 7B; Feb. 1, 1973, p. 14A.

101. *El Mundo,* Nov. 13, 1972, p. 1A; Nov. 26, 1972, p. 8A; Dec. 16, 1972, p. 7A; Jan. 30, 1973, p. 3A; Feb. 4, 1973, p. 14A.

102. Ibid., Jan. 11, 1973, p. 5B; Jan. 14, 1973, p. 3A; Jan. 15, 1973, p. 16A.

103. Ibid., Nov. 14, 1972, p. 7A; Jan. 28, 1973, p. 1A.

104. "La estadidad no será relegada," pp. 8–9; *El Mundo,* Dec. 9, 1972, p. 5A, and Jan. 16, 1973, p. 7A.

105. Carlos Yamil Otero, "¿Quién controla el PNP: Ferré o Romero?" *Avance,* Sept. 17, 1973, pp. 10–15; Cerezo, "PNP—Energías de ilusión," p. 9; Dimas Planas, "No hay lucha interna en el PNP," *Avance,* Oct. 1, 1973, pp. 12–13.

106. Bothwell, ed., *Puerto Rico,* vol. 4, p. 579.

107. Data from Comisión Estatal de Elecciones, *Elecciones Generales, 1968, 1972, 1976* (San Juan: Estado Libre Asociado, 1969, 1973, 1977).

108. *Avance,* July 15, 1974, pp. 6–7; July 1, 1974, pp. 12–13.

109. P. Ramos, *Ferré,* pp. 229–30; *Avance,* Dec. 23, 1974, p. 9.

CHAPTER SEVEN

The New Progressive
Party and the Politics
of Equality

Under the leadership of Carlos Romero Barceló the PNP presented a new program and strategy for statehood, which must be understood under what I have
termed the "politics of equality." Believing that statehood is a claim for equality in citizenship, the PNP launched a more aggressive campaign for statehood
in the United States, at a time when sectors there were considering statehood
as an alternative to the crisis of Commonwealth. This political discourse based
on the notion of equality, central to PNP's politics under Romero, argues that
Puerto Ricans have fulfilled their duties as U.S. citizens but have not received
all the benefits of citizenship due to their colonial status. Political equality,
possible only with statehood, is necessary for Puerto Ricans to participate fully
in federal social and economic programs that will assure their material well-
being. The PNP added an "anticolonialist" rhetoric to its statehood strategy,
arguing that Puerto Ricans, as U.S. citizens, can exercise their right to self-
determination by demanding statehood; once Puerto Ricans decide in favor of
statehood, Congress has a duty to accept this demand, as the recognition of
their rights as American citizens.

This statehood strategy provides the framework to understand the economic
policies of the Romero administration. The economic strategy of the Romero
government sought the development of nonmanufacturing activities (finance,
services) to strengthen Puerto Rico's economy and to turn the island into an
economic intermediary of U.S. capital in the Caribbean. This economic strategy, which included a redefinition of the Commonwealth's industrialization

program, was supposed to ease the economic transition to statehood. But Romero's administration, plagued by corruption and abuses of power, was severely criticized in Puerto Rico and the United States. The events after the 1984 elections cast doubt on Romero's leadership in the government and within the party, leading to the first PNP rupture and to the formation of the Puerto Rican Renovation Party (PRP). But the PRP represented also a reaction by sectors of the local bourgeoisie to the socioeconomic and political crisis in Puerto Rico. The loss of the 1984 elections and the PNP's inability to achieve a post-Romero transition have placed big obstacles to the PNP's chances of becoming a governing party once again.

THE STATEHOOD AS EQUALITY DISCOURSE

The Rise of the Statehood Alternative

The PNP's administration and statehood strategy under Romero reflected the growth of pro-statehood forces in Puerto Rico and the rising interest for statehood in the United States. Statehood became a viable alternative for the United States in the 1970s as a result of the economic and political crisis of the Commonwealth at the time. The growing dependence of the Commonwealth's industrialization program on subsidies to American capital (especially, after 1976, the federal subsidies provided under IRS Code Section 936); the decline of real investments in the island; rising unemployment; and marginalization of a growing section of the population called into question the capacity of the Commonwealth to maintain economic and political stability. The political legitimacy of the Commonwealth was also undermined by the federal government's refusal to grant more powers to the island. But U.S. policy toward Puerto Rico has remained one of support for the status quo, until reform becomes absolutely necessary. Opposition to statehood in Puerto Rico and the United States prevented a policy for statehood within the U.S. government.

The crisis of Puerto Rico's "economic model" in the 1970s raised concern in Puerto Rico and the United States about the Commonwealth's economic and political viability. For the last two decades the economy of Puerto Rico has followed the pattern established in the late 1960s: it has been dominated by U.S.-owned manufacturing firms attracted to Puerto Rico by local and federal subsidies. Since the mid-1970s manufacturing has been dominated by high-tech, capital-intensive firms, mostly pharmaceuticals and electronics, which are characterized by large investments but produce few jobs.

To spur American investments on the island, and thus its industrialization program, the Commonwealth has increasingly depended on federal subsidies, mostly those brought by Section 936 of the IRS Code. Section 936, approved by Congress in 1976, established that any U.S. "domestic corporation" could be defined as a "possession corporation" if it derives at least 80 percent of its gross income from sources within a U.S. possession and at least 50 percent of its gross income from the active conduct of trade or business within a U.S. possession; the profits of any possession corporation are tax exempt. IRS Code Section 936 was purposely written for Puerto Rico, the possession that is responsible for 98 percent of all Section 936 transactions. According to the U.S. Treasury, Section 936 funds in Puerto Rico increased from $5.3 billion in 1977 to $10.5 billion in 1982. Section 936 has resulted in great profits for possession corporations. By the late 1970s profits from Section 936 grew at an annual rate of $1.6 billion; the estimated repatriated profits for Section 936 corporations in 1982 were over $2 billion. The pharmaceutical industry alone, according to a 1976 IRS report on possession corporations, accounted for 58.2 percent of the total federal tax exemptions from Section 936. But of all the Section 936 funds in 1977, only 30 percent were available for investments in the island, and most were in short-term deposits, unavailable for long-term investment.[1]

Finance capital has increased its importance in Puerto Rico's economy since the 1970s, spurred by the dramatic growth of Section 936 funds on the island. In 1982 Section 936 funds represented 38.7 percent of all deposits in commercial banks in Puerto Rico; of these, 73 percent ($3 billion) were in American and Canadian banks, representing 57.5 percent of all deposits of foreign banks in Puerto Rico. Section 936 funds in U.S. and Canadian banks represented 28 percent of all deposits in commercial banks in Puerto Rico. In 1982, of the estimated $10.5 billion in Section 936 funds in Puerto Rico, $7 billion were in commercial banks and $1 billion in savings-and-loans banks; another $2.5 billion were in deposits in brokerage firms going to Puerto Rico in the last few years (E. F. Hutton, Becker, Paine Webber, and so on). The unbridled growth of Section 936 funds has been accompanied by a decrease in real investment in Puerto Rico, showing the government's inability to force the use of Section 936 funds for productive investments. The real value of fixed investment in Puerto Rico diminished from $974.8 million in 1972 to $438.6 million in 1982. Real investment in Puerto Rico had a negative relative growth since 1972 (-12.7 percent), falling to -23 percent in 1982; the share of real fixed investment in the total gross product of the island decreased from 30.9 percent in 1972 to 10.9 percent in 1982.[2] In an economic report to the government in the mid-seventies, economist James Tobin concluded that there were some $5 billion in direct investments in Puerto Rico, with an annual rate of increase of $1 billion. The report estimated that 50 percent of these investments were in financial assets.[3]

By the early 1980s the Commonwealth's industrialization program was heavily questioned in Puerto Rico and the United States, as not only was unemployment rising drastically but real investment was declining. The pharmaceutical and electronics industries were making huge profits but providing no jobs or stimulus to the local economy. Section 936 turned Puerto Rico into a financial center but these funds were not used for productive investments on the island. The economic situation became so critical that in 1984 a bipartisan commission of the Puerto Rican bourgeoisie, the so-called Committee for the Economic

Development of Puerto Rico, publicized its findings on the "economic crisis" so that the two main parties would pay attention to the problem.[4]

The economic crisis and political problems of Puerto Rico also raised concern in the United States. A State Department report characterized Puerto Rico as "a problem for the eighties" for the United States; and a Latin American expert included Puerto Rico among one of the "four explosive cases" for U.S. foreign policy in Latin America.[5] But the opposite was also true: the United States became a problem for the Commonwealth. An important element in the crisis of the Commonwealth has been its delegitimation by the American state. The U.S. policy of support for the status quo and changes in U.S. economic policies have undermined the political basis of the Commonwealth.

The U.S. status quo policy toward Puerto Rico has contributed to the Commonwealth's instability by preventing it from adapting, even within the colonial framework, to new economic and political conditions. Since the late 1950s, with the stillborn Fernós-Murray Bill, Puerto Rican autonomists have been trying to reform the Commonwealth structure. By the mid-1970s the PPD administration of Rafael Hernández Colón submitted a new proposal to reform the Commonwealth by widening its local powers and giving it an international presence. The U.S. government's reaction to the PPD's demands was negative; the Department of Interior characterized the newly proposed definition of Commonwealth as "free association" as "impermissible under the U.S. Constitution" and concluded that "Puerto Rico remains a territory of the United States."[6]

The economic and political instability of the Commonwealth during the seventies, together with heightened international criticism, led public and private sectors in the United States to search for a solution to the "Puerto Rican problem." Four main conclusions emerged from the debate within the American government. The first and most general conclusion of the various U.S. government reports dealing with Puerto Rico from 1975 to 1981 was the questioning of Commonwealth status. Since the Commonwealth itself was the problem, no reform or continuation of the status was generally recommended. The Commonwealth government was seen as a federal funds "junkie" and Congress's inclination to continue its funding was doubted. Furthermore, Commonwealth has perpetuated "a quasi colonial status for the island" and has not satisfied the demands for greater political power that come about in a world characterized by "mounting nationalism," which could result in a political conflict harmful to U.S. interests.[7] Finally, the legitimacy of the Commonwealth was questioned on the basis of the decreasing electoral support for that status and the increasing support for statehood in Puerto Rico. This analysis led to the conclusion that statehood, and then independence, have emerged as viable alternatives to the Commonwealth; several reports commissioned by Congress discussed the viability and costs of statehood for Puerto Rico.[8]

The second general conclusion of these reports was that the U.S. government, not the Puerto Ricans, will ultimately decide which alternative is accepted. As a corollary, it follows that the American state should take the lead in the resolution of the political status issue. A 1975 State Department report by Arthur Borg concluded that "we really cannot afford to leave this matter entirely to a process of the Puerto Ricans 'figuring out what they want,' " and concluded that the United States needed "to 'steer' the Puerto Rican political-status question."[9] A later report from the State Department indicated the need for the American government to clearly define the alternatives acceptable to it. It has also been proposed that the U.S. government create a "colonial office" to "coordinate" the resolution of the political question in Puerto Rico.[10]

The third conclusion, closely related to the second, was that the alternative chosen must represent the best interests of the United States, particularly its strategic-military interests in the area. This has been a consideration favoring statehood and militating against independence.[11] Also, Puerto Rico has become a liability for the United States in its relations with the Third World, particularly in Latin America. Furthermore, by resolving the status question, the United States would take away from the Soviet bloc an important issue in their anti-American campaign. It is generally agreed that U.S. economic interests in Puerto Rico must be protected, for the United States has billions invested on the island, and its market is the second largest in the American continent for U.S. goods.[12] As with the strategic issue, economic considerations tended to support statehood as the best alternative for the United States.

The fourth general conclusion of the reports was that whichever status alternative is accepted should represent the least possible "costs" for the United States. Again, statehood was considered the best alternative for the United States once the Commonwealth status is rejected. Independence remains a second-best choice in the event Congress, or the Puerto Ricans, reject statehood.[13] But the costs of statehood are not altogether favorable for the United States or Puerto Rico. The most widely accepted conclusion is that Puerto Rico would benefit from an increase in federal funds under statehood. But this view was challenged by the Kiefer Report of the Library of Congress, which argued that federal taxes would negate any economic benefit from an increase in federal funds.[14] Furthermore, the Kiefer Report concluded that statehood would undermine economic stability on the island by eliminating the main incentive for American capital to invest there, namely, tax exemption. Other reports suggest that the "political stability" created by statehood would induce rising investments by American capital in Puerto Rico.[15]

But statehood also has political costs to be considered. Statehood could lead to political instability, and even a civil war, if the opposition to statehood is fierce. Terrorism, both on the island and in the United States, is a widely anticipated response to this alternative. The cultural issue is also an important variable for the United States in considering statehood. Puerto Rican annexationists demand cultural autonomy and Spanish as an official language under statehood. The acceptance of statehood for Puerto Rico without satisfying these claims, or Puerto Rican support for statehood and the rejection by Congress on these terms, could result in an explosive situation for Washington.[16]

The situation in Puerto Rico has also been the object of study by American private institutions that seek to influence public policy. Their main goal has been to convince U.S. policymakers that Puerto Rico is a very serious problem for the United States that must be solved immediately.[17] The U.S. mass media have also taken an increasing interest in the political and economic situation of Puerto Rico. The statehood issue, in particular, has become part of the public debate in the United States (as with Reagan's 1980 public support for statehood). Some American newspapers, notably the *Wall Street Journal*, have supported unconditional statehood for Puerto Rico, citing the island's strategic value and the right to political equality of U.S. citizens.[18]

For the first time since the United States invaded Puerto Rico in 1898, statehood was seen as a viable alternative by sectors within the United States during the Carter and the first Reagan administrations. Nevertheless, if statehood became an alternative acceptable to the United States, there is still no statehood policy within the U.S. government. That is, there is no consensus among the different institutions of the American state to grant statehood to the island in the immediate future. The policy of the status quo still reigns in Washington.

Statehood Is for the Poor

The rise of the group headed by Romero Barceló represented more than a simple change in the PNP's leadership; it signified a change in the party program. The redemption program of the PNP under Ferré was supplanted by a new program, which I have called the program of equality. This transition was marked by Romero's publication of *La estadidad es para los pobres (Statehood Is for the Poor)* at the end of 1973. The date is important, for it coincided with the approval of the party's new bylaws, a crucial step in Romero's consolidation of power in the PNP.

The importance of Romero's statehood primer is twofold. In the first place, it clearly viewed the constituency of contemporary annexationism. The PNP's appeal to the poor was not new, since it was an important element in Ferré's 1967–68 campaign (it was Ferré who coined the phrase "statehood is for the poor"). But in Ferré's program, the benefits to the poor comprised a part of a wider program of reforms whose purpose was to promote capitalist stability in Puerto Rico. Ferré's program was aimed at the bourgeoisie as well as the poor. By contrast, Romero's rhetoric appealed directly to the poor: since statehood benefits the poor, they should support statehood. Romero's goal was statehood, and social reform or stability were subordinated to statehood. Romero argued that statehood is for the poor precisely because the rich do not want it. In spite of this quasi-populist rhetoric, Romero's program is not populist: poverty is seen as a "fact of life," a social condition to be mitigated.[19] Romero does not want to reform society to eliminate poverty, instead he argues that statehood will benefit the poor (who will nevertheless remain poor). The poor, in Romero's scheme, are the means to achieve the final goal, statehood. Nevertheless, the "statehood is for the poor" slogan was abandoned by the PNP after 1976, because although Romero's rhetoric appealed to the poor, the party also received considerable support from the rich. The PNP rhetoric began then to emphasize the "statehood as equality" discourse.

Secondly, *Statehood Is for the Poor* presented the outline of the program of equality. Romero's argument was as follows: Puerto Ricans comprise a "people" formed under Spanish colonialism, with a particular culture and customs. But Puerto Rico has too many people and few resources; this is the basis for the island's economic problem. Although the Puerto Ricans' standard of living has improved thanks to the social and economic progress brought by the Americans to the island, they continue to be subordinated politically to the United States. Despite social and economic progress, Puerto Ricans have not achieved political equality with their fellow citizens on the mainland. The Commonwealth, a useful institution in a particular historical period, has become a barrier to further progress. The Commonwealth benefits "the businessmen who come to Puerto Rico to get rich by paying low wages and no taxes," and the rich in Puerto Rico that support the PPD. Independence is not viable because it would impede further progress by preventing U.S. capital from coming to the island and thereby hindering its economic development. Under Commonwealth, although Puerto Ricans pay no federal taxes, neither do they receive "the benefits that Puerto Rico would derive from its full participation in federal aid programs"; moreover, they do not benefit from the federal minimum wage and are paid low wages by marginal industries.[20] Statehood is the only alternative for Puerto Rico since it provides the political equality that allows Puerto Ricans to vote for the president, to send representatives to the U.S. Congress, and to get equal treatment in the distribution of federal funds. Federal taxes should not scare the people since the poor do not pay taxes, although they enjoy all the benefits of citizenship, including federal aid. Because of its level of economic development, Puerto Rico will receive more in federal aid than it will pay in federal taxes. Statehood will not hurt the "Puerto Rican personality," since neither the Spanish language nor the Puerto Rican culture are negotiable for the attainment of statehood. Congress has the obligation to grant statehood once the majority of Puerto Ricans demand it.

Romero did not introduce anything new to the statehood discourse. The novelty of Romero's program is that it combined existing elements of the statehood discourse under the strategy of *estadidad ahora* (statehood now), couched in the language of "equality." In contrast to the programs of José Celso Barbosa and Ferré, in which statehood was part of a wider project, statehood is the axis of Romero's program. As Romero's PNP delineated its political and economic strategy, "equality" became central to their program.

Political Equality

The PNP's statehood program under Romero was built around the concept of political equality. It argues that although Puerto Ricans have fulfilled the duties of citizenship (for example, the "blood tax," loyalty), their rights as

American citizens have not been recognized. The statehood movement is simply the expression of the desire of Puerto Ricans to achieve the equality they deserve as U.S. citizens.[21] This argument was not really new, since it had emerged in the forties with the concept of U.S. citizenship as "the gateway to statehood": the mere fact of U.S. citizenship implied that Congress must grant statehood to Puerto Rico. But Romero's PNP argued from a somewhat different perspective: since U.S. citizenship granted Puerto Ricans certain rights that are being violated by the U.S. government, their demand for statehood is a demand for equality in citizenship rights.

The "statehood as equality" discourse had different levels of argument. The ethical argument said that "statehood has become a moral question involving the political and human rights of a community of 3.3 million disenfranchised American citizens."[22] Statehood is not merely a question of dollars and cents; it is a question of dignity. Since it is also an issue of political ideals, the demand for political equality is a demand for democratic rights.[23]

More concretely, the equality discourse argued that U.S. citizenship safeguards the economic and political equality required to assure Puerto Rico's progress; but Puerto Ricans "can achieve that equality only with statehood."[24] Puerto Ricans lack political equality because of the prejudice and discrimination they suffer as a result of their "second-class citizenship." Using an image already presented by Barbosa, Romero characterized the Puerto Ricans as "sharecroppers on the American plantation," who "pay none of the overhead, and none of the property taxes, but we remain entirely at the mercy of the plantation managers."[25] Puerto Rico's colonial status is the basis for the second-class citizenship of Puerto Ricans, and only statehood can provide the political equality to overcome this discrimination.[26] But political equality is important for another reason—it is the basis for economic and social equality within the U.S. federation: "No ethnic, racial or religious group within any nation, has ever in history been able to achieve social and economic equality, until that group has first achieved political equality. . . . And political equality means statehood."[27] The PNP's demand for equality in citizenship is based on the argument that Puerto Ricans have fulfilled their duties but have not received the full benefits of U.S. citizenship.

The Duties and Rights of Citizenship

The demand for political equality presupposes that Puerto Ricans have some rights of citizenship that are being violated or are not recognized by the American state. But the concept of citizenship implies both rights and duties. The PNP's argument is that even though Puerto Ricans are not recognized as full citizens, they have fulfilled their obligations as American citizens: they have paid their "blood tax" by defending U.S. interests in war. The fulfillment of military duty entitles Puerto Ricans "to the fundamental right of equal protection in their own country."[28] It is not surprising then that the Romero administration's propaganda emphasized the participation of Puerto Ricans in the U.S. armed forces and on the battlefield.[29]

The concept of "blood tax" also implies that Puerto Ricans have paid their share of taxes, in blood. The Puerto Ricans do not pay taxes—a fundamental duty of citizenship—because the Commonwealth relationship with the United States so stipulates. But the Puerto Ricans have fulfilled their citizenship duty by having one of the highest rates of participation in the American armed forces and of death in battle. The PNP argues that the blood tax is a sufficient contribution for Puerto Ricans to be recognized as equals in citizenship: "It is a very well known American principle that taxation without representation is tyranny. The American citizens in Puerto Rico can add with dignity that the highest form of taxation is military conscription. In this sense, the Puerto Ricans have paid more than their dues." Although Puerto Rico is not an incorporated territory, it has nevertheless paid its taxes, which qualifies it for statehood. But more important yet for the PNP's strategy, since Puerto Ricans have fulfilled their duties of citizenship, they have the right to receive its full benefits, particularly "equal treatment" in the distribution of federal funds.[30]

Federal funds play a crucial role in the PNP's program under Romero. As discussed earlier, political equality is not important in itself but as a means to provide economic and social equality; "equal treatment" means equal participation in federal social and economic programs.[31] Federal funds have played a crucial role in the PNP's statehood programs, but their strategic role has changed. For Ferré, federal funds served to alleviate social tensions produced by capitalism in Puerto Rico. For Romero, federal funds are needed because "Puerto Rico does not have sufficient material resources to satisfy its own needs. We depend on federal funds to solve our basic problems. . . . This is an unalterable reality."[32] For Ferré social and economic reforms were necessary to provide stability to capitalism; thus federal funds played a secondary role in his social program. For Romero, federal funds *are* the economic and social reform; thus they are central to his economic program for Puerto Rico. According to a U.S. observer, Romero's "economic recovery program is based on the very un-Republican theory that federal spending is the best bootstrap for Puerto Rico."[33] But to Romero, the only "dignified way for Puerto Ricans to solicit federal funds is under conditions of equality with the other states."[34] Furthermore, federal funds promote the structural basis for popular support for statehood. Asked if "the dependency on federal funds is a means of moving towards statehood without the people having made that important decision," Romero responded: "It certainly is."[35]

The Strategy and Requisites for Statehood

The discourse of equality provided the framework for the PNP's new statehood strategy: "Statehood Now" or statehood by *fait accompli*. For Ferré, by contrast, the attainment of statehood is a gradual process; the Commonwealth is moved in stages, toward greater ties of "permanent union" that facilitate statehood (for example, the presidential vote). For Romero, Puerto Rico is already prepared for statehood, but it is necessary to use an adequate strategy to attain it. Nothing is more revealing of the PNP's new strategy for statehood than the new version of the requisites of statehood.

The Status Commission of the mid-1960s enumerated three requisites for statehood: (a) political and economic stability, (b) majority support for statehood among Puerto Ricans, and (c) congressional approval of statehood. Ferré's PNP used these requisites to define their evolutionary strategy for statehood. Romero's faction, however, introduced their own version of the requisites for statehood, molded by the "Statehood Now" strategy:

> The U.S. Constitution sets no conditions for statehood. But Congress has traditionally required that three standards be met for admission:
>
> 1. That residents of a proposed new state be imbued with the principles of democracy as exemplified by the American form of government. . . .
>
> 2. That a majority of a proposed new state's electorate desire statehood. . . .
>
> 3. That population and resources be sufficient to support a new state government and pay a new state's share of costs to the Federal government.[36]

The differences between the Status Commission and Romero's requisites were clear. First, the requisite of economic and political stability has no relationship to the democratic ideals of a population; a population can be "imbued" with democratic ideals and still be economically and politically unstable. Second, the capacity to "share the costs" of the federal government depends on the economic and political stability of the new state. Third, there is no mention in Romero's version of perhaps the most important requisite of all: the acceptance of Puerto Rican statehood by the U.S. Congress.

Romero's faction was aware of the requisites demanded by Congress. For example, Romero attacked those who argued that Puerto Rican statehood would lead to a situation similar to that in Northern Ireland, Quebec, or the Basque region, emphasizing, by contrast, the political stability of Puerto Rico, "where no government has ever been overthrown by internal revolt . . . [and] there is no reason whatsoever to suppose that the advent of statehood would result in any significant upsurge in violence."[37] In contrast to the traditional PNP argument that Puerto Rico was in the throes of economic crisis, under Romero the party praised the economic development brought by industrialization and made possible by the presence of U.S. capital in Puerto Rico.[38]

The omission of the role of Congress in the statehood process was not an oversight but an intrinsic element of the PNP's statehood strategy under Romero. Puerto Rico's admission to the federation requires the support of American public opinion and political institutions. To gain this support, the Romero administration created the Puerto Rico Federal Affairs Administration in Washington, D.C., whose purpose was to sell the idea of Puerto Rican statehood to the American public. But if Romero was conscious of the need for support by the American public and Congress, why did he omit Congress's role from the requisites for statehood? Because it would imply a willingness by Congress to admit Puerto Rico to the federation, a decision Congress has been reluctant to make in the past and is unlikely to make in the immediate future. Instead, the PNP's new strategy was to obtain statehood by a *fait accompli:* for the U.S. citizens of Puerto Rico to demand their constitutional rights, their political equality, from the same political body that granted them citizenship. According to Romero, Puerto Ricans

> have a constitutional, inherent right to have political equality, and you have political equality only with the vote and with representation. So if we were to have a plebiscite in Puerto Rico and the majority of Puerto Ricans were to vote for statehood, that would mean we were asking for that political equality. If Congress were to turn that down, that would be negating democracy itself.[39]

Herein lies the importance of the equality discourse within the PNP's statehood strategy: to embarrass Congress, to damage the United States' image internationally should Congress reject Puerto Rico's demand for statehood.

> How . . . could America preach democracy and human rights anywhere on earth after having flatly denied political equality on its own citizens? Furthermore, in addition to being mocked as massively hypocritical, the United States would under such circumstances almost certainly also be accused of blatant bigotry, since the target of its rejection would have been a people seeking admission as the nation's first and only predominantly Spanish-speaking state.[40]

For Romero, then, the demand by Puerto Ricans for statehood is sufficient for Congress to grant statehood to Puerto Rico; congressional willingness should not be a requisite.

This "immediatist" strategy for statehood was elaborated by a group of young statehooders. They argue that Puerto Rico fulfills the "Jeffersonian guidelines" for admission to the federation as a state: a sufficiently large population, experience in democracy, and a desire for statehood. Puerto Rico should follow the "Tennessee Plan," according to which the territorial population organizes itself politically and demands statehood from Congress. They argue that Puerto Rico, like many other states, has gone through the "colonial experience" and that the only dignified solution is to grant statehood. Furthermore, while only Congress has the power to admit new states, the "Principle of Popular Sovereignty" gives the territorial population the right to self-determination—the right to form a state within the federation. The process of admission to the federation should be initiated once a majority (60 percent) of the population supports statehood. The argument concludes:

> There being no constitutional, legal or historic impediments to Puerto Rico's admission into the Union, the people of the Island can legitimately demand admission as an inalienable right inherent in their American citizenship and in their right to equal protection. Once the petition for admission has been made, statehood will become the only rational, democratic and dignified solution to Puerto Rico's political status problem.[41]

The Statehood Now program represented an attempt to mobilize mass support in order to force Congress to address the issue of Puerto Rican statehood. The strategy of statehood by *fait accompli* reflected the electoral strength of the statehood movement in Puerto Rico; it was a response to attacks on the commonwealth status both in the United States and in Puerto Rico. If the PNP had some success in presenting a legal-ethical argument for statehood, they were less successful in elaborating a viable economic strategy for the transition to statehood.

The PNP's Program of Economic Transition to Statehood

The PNP's political strategy was accompanied by an economic "recuperation" policy that was linked to a program for the economic transition to statehood. Romero's five-point transition plan did not differ in essence from that presented previously by Ferré and Arthur Burns: (1) "equal treatment" in all federal programs, (2) the gradual imposition of federal taxes over a twenty-year period, (3) the concomitant adjustment of Puerto Rico's fiscal structure, (4) reform of the tax-exemption program, (5) a gradual increase in Puerto Rico's delegation to Congress until its due representation is attained.[42] As before, the major problem of the economic transition program was how to convince the United States of Puerto Rico's economic viability as a state, while at the same time presenting a strategy for economic growth.

A major issue for the PNP concerned the tax-exemption-based industrialization program: namely, how to secure investments by American capital in Puerto Rico after the current incentives are terminated. Several alternatives were suggested. PNP Resident Commissioner Corrada del Río proposed that industries currently enjoying tax exemption would continue to do so until their exemption expired, and that any federal tax levied on tax-exempted industries should be returned to the government of Puerto Rico during the twenty-year transition period "to develop an incentive and subsidy program for those industries that had enjoyed tax exempt status."[43] Romero, on the other hand, proposed that the U.S. government should assume Puerto Rico's public debt, arguing that this "would enable Puerto Rico to devote more of its local resources to satisfying the infrastructure requirements of its post-statehood economy."[44] These proposals reflect Romero's transition strategy—to provide new incentives to American capital by means of direct or indirect federal subsidies.

The central problem of the economic transition program was how to keep U.S. capital in Puerto Rico. Two somewhat related proposals were presented: first, attract high-tech companies that could pay the federal minimum wage and for which tax exemption is not the principal incentive for settling in Puerto Rico. Both the Ferré and Romero governments have pursued this economic policy. A second argument was presented in Arthur Burns' report to the Status Commission: to argue that statehood provides the necessary political stability to secure American investments in Puerto Rico.[45] This was Romero's argument to U.S. investors; he argues that some "marginal manufactures" will leave the island with statehood, but the majority will not:

> Why? Because, although the return on investment may be lower under statehood, an investor views potential profit as a direct function of risk, and the political security and stability offered by statehood will automatically reduce the currently existing demand for larger return on Puerto Rico investment, than the return demand on the mainland.[46]

This was the programmatic basis for the Romero administration's economic policy, particularly the attempt to amend the tax-exemption program (the Industrial Incentives Act of 1978) and the emphasis on the promotion of high-technology industries. But this did not solve the problem of how Puerto Rico could compete with states offering U.S. investors the same incentives and the political stability of statehood, or with Third World countries offering lower wages. The solution presented by PNP strategists was to argue that Puerto Rico could offer the best of both worlds: the incentives and political stability offered by the states and a high rate of profits based on lower wages than those in the United States.[47]

Bertram Finn, once chairman of Governor Romero's Finance Committee, most clearly elaborated the economic transition program. Finn built his argument for the economic viability of statehood on the so-called comparative advantages of the island. The first of these advantages is Puerto Rico's "natural and human resources." He argued, for example, that exploitation of Puerto Rico's copper and oil could stimulate new investment of U.S. capital. But "Puerto Rico's greatest comparative advantage" is its "human resources," that is, its labor force. Finn emphasizes that the "surplus supply of labor" will ensure lower wages than on the mainland, even after statehood; and this will be the main incentive for American capital in Puerto Rico.[48] Puerto Rico's second "comparative advantage" is its climate, ideal for tourism and agriculture, geared toward the U.S. market, and its proximity to the Caribbean and Latin American markets. The growth of these areas along with those of manufacturing, construction, services, commerce, and finance will provide the Puerto Rican economy a "structural balance" to make statehood economically viable.

Finally, Finn argues that statehood will stimulate the expansion of commerce, finance, and services by turning Puerto Rico into a center of U.S. economic activity in the Caribbean and Latin America.

However, Finn argues that two areas would require special assistance from the federal government: the integration of Puerto Rico to the U.S. fiscal structure, and the reform of the tax-exemption-based industrialization program. Finn reiterates the need for a twenty-year transition period to adjust Puerto Rico's fiscal structure to that of the United States during which the federal government would recognize current exemptions while allowing them to expire. To alleviate the fiscal condition of the new state, Finn proposes the gradual phasing out of custom duties and excise taxes; the transfer of federal land in Puerto Rico to the new state; and monetary aid to the new state as was done with other states. Other economic aid to Puerto Rico could be in the form of a special statutory treatment (for example, exemption from federal maritime laws) and assigning a standard amount of government contracts to industries in Puerto Rico. Finally, Finn asserts that the federal government should assume responsibility for Puerto Rico's public debt.

The transition to statehood promoted by Romero's PNP would be very expensive for the United States. But this strategy was predicated on the belief that the United States would be willing to pay the price because statehood is the only way to safeguard its economic and strategic interests in the Caribbean and to secure U.S. investments in Puerto Rico.[49] Romero promoted Puerto Rico as the answer to the "Russian threat to the Americas." One way to serve the "cause of freedom" was to send units of the Puerto Rican National Guard in U.S. military expeditions to the Caribbean and Central America. Finally, the PNP argued that having a "Spanish-speaking state" would improve U.S. relations with Latin America and with its own Hispanic population.[50]

Thus, the PNP's statehood strategy under Romero was based on the undeniable fact that the United States has important economic and military interests in Puerto Rico and that it is willing to pay a high price to retain the territory. The Romero administration attempted to implement several measures to facilitate the transition to statehood, mostly during the 1977–1981 term, when the PNP controlled both the executive and legislative branches of the Commonwealth government.

THE ROMERO ADMINISTRATION

A New PNP Government

The 1976 elections showed that Romero's group controlled both the party organization and its program. The party reorganization two years earlier had given Romero total control over the party machinery. Similarly, the PNP's electoral program showed the influence of the new leading group, as concepts like "New Life," "redemption," and "social justice," which were central to the party's program under the leadership of Ferré, were absent. But while the 1976 program promised to advance the struggle for statehood, it emphasized the party's "economic recuperation" program.[51]

The main objective of the PNP's economic recuperation program was to restore the private sector's "faith and trust" in the government so as to stimulate private investment. This was a direct attack on the government intervention that characterized the Hernández Colón administration; it also responded to the notion that the transition to statehood would require the elimination of such measures.[52] The economic recuperation program promised to restore manufacturing, services, tourism, agriculture, construction, and commerce (the "vital" economic areas for statehood, according to Finn). While criticizing the tax-exemption-based industrialization program, the PNP proposed the reform "of the industrial development program to include . . . the promotion of service industries" (defined as commerce, transportation, communications, public utilities, finance, insurance, and real estate), that is, to expand the tax-exemption program to include these areas. Another important proposal was the so-called Fund for the Development of Puerto Rico, whose goal was the promotion of the "internal formation of capital." The fund was to comprise investments from both the private and the public sector; it would receive funds from the retirement programs of the public and private sectors, the sale of government land, government income from copper mines, and Section 936 funds. Its goal was to promote "the development of the economic infrastructure of Puerto Rico."[53] This economic program not only showed the existence of a new party program, but it presented the framework for the economic policy of the Romero administration.

Ironically, the PNP 1976 electoral campaign avoided the issue of statehood, as the party maintained that the "status is not at issue" (that is, that the elections were not to decide the political status of the island). The PNP campaign called attention to the economic misfortunes of the Hernández Colón administration, attributing Puerto Rico's economic problems to his administration. In the 1976 campaign Romero argued for the need to continue with commonwealth status and its industrialization program until a majority of the people supported statehood; nevertheless, he promised that his administration would promote statehood in Puerto Rico and in the United States. A crucial aspect of the PNP campaign was the presentation of Romero as a "man of the people," emphasizing the populist rhetoric of the party and its candidate.[54]

The PNP's electoral triumph in 1976 reflected the increasing support for the party, as it received 158,000 more votes than it had received in the previous election. It won forty mayoralties, the House of Representatives, and the Senate, gaining control of the legislature. The bulk of the PNP's support came from large urban centers, winning most of the major cities, and from the economically stagnant regions of the island (the eastern and central regions). Puerto Rican annexationism had ceased to be merely an urban phenomenon and extended to the whole island.

The PNP reorganization carried out by Romero after 1973 altered the composition of the party leadership. The Romero administration was characterized by a sociopolitical division of labor: administration was entrusted to the "professional politicians," while economic policy was entrusted to the party sector directly linked to banking and finance. A study on the composition of the past four government administrations concluded that the majority of the administrators under the first Romero administration (1977–1981) came from the areas of public administration (44 percent) and the private sector (35 percent); a majority of those coming from outside the private sector came from Romero's administration in San Juan. The study concluded that "the number of professional politicians in the government agencies increased" during the Romero administration.[55] Although this secured Romero's grip over the government structure, it also promoted the widespread corruption that characterized his administration.

The majority of administrators who came to the Romero administration from the private sector were in banking and finance; they were largely responsible for the administration's economic policy in favor of this economic area.[56] This is a crucial element differentiating Ferré's and Romero's administrations, with important consequences also for their statehood programs. The Romero administration's reliance on the banking and finance sector to elaborate its economic program reflects the predominance of this sector in Puerto Rico's economy by the end of the 1970s. The banking and finance sector, and its allied sectors such as "services" (communications, commerce, tourism) became the focus of the administration's economic program. Romero's economic policy (Industrial Incentives Act, the twin-plant program, the new incentives, the International Trade Center) was aimed at getting their support.

The economic transformations in the 1970s that brought American finance capital to the fore of Puerto Rico's economy also strengthened the local financial bourgeoisie within the ranks of the local bourgeoisie. An analysis of local banks shows that the local financial bourgeoisie grew along with finance capital as a whole. Although they are still subordinated to U.S. banks, local banks controlled 54 percent of total assets from 1976 to 1982 and have maintained their share of the Section 936 pie, controlling one-fourth of the Section 936 funds of commercial banks in Puerto Rico.[57]

This process has occurred as the local industrial bourgeoisie's position within local capital has declined and as American capital has gained increasing control over the island's industry. Since the Commonwealth's industrialization program started, the share of EDA-promoted industries of the island's net manufacturing income has increased steadily: in 1970, 81.6 percent of net manufacturing income came from EDA-promoted industries; by 1975 this figure had reached 86.8 percent, and by 1980 it was 92.5 percent. Although the number of EDA-promoted local firms increased during the 1970s, their number and importance are minimal. American capital dominates the most important areas of manufacturing: chemicals and electronics. The bastions of local capital in manufacturing, food, and apparel have declined in economic importance (from 34.8 percent of net manufacturing income in 1970 to 19.5 percent in 1982). Furthermore, even these industries have been increasingly penetrated by American capital. According to a government study, the least productive industries are precisely those of local capital: hides, plastics, bricks, and glass. Between 1980 and 1982, 59 percent of all plant closings were in industries in which local capital is predominant (hides, clothing and textiles, wood, furniture, tobacco, food processing, stone products, and paper).[58] These developments were reflected in the program and politics of the PNP.

The bourgeoisie and intermediate social sectors linked to finance and banking capital held a dominant position in the PNP under Romero. They are located in the economic areas most integrated to American capital; banking, finance, high-tech manufacture, and business services. Their economic and social location is reflected in the statehood program. In Ferré's program, statehood was part of the broader historical project of the local industrial bourgeoisie; it included the goal of securing and strengthening the economic basis of the local bourgeoisie as a mechanism to secure the reproduction of capitalism in Puerto Rico. Statehood is the project of Romero's PNP. Since the bourgeoisie and intermediate sectors are increasingly linked and subordinated to American capital, their project is to secure the presence of American capital in Puerto Rico through policies favoring U.S. capital on the island; statehood is the safest form to achieve this goal.

The Political Economy of Equality I: Incentives, "Like Other States"

The Romero administration faced an economic crisis in Puerto Rico, a crisis with structural underpinnings and not merely conjunctural (1970s oil shocks, recession, and so on). It was based on the weakening of the postwar social, economic, and political structures in Puerto Rico, and changes in the U.S. and world economies.[59] The Romero administration thus has to be understood in terms of how it dealt with the crisis and at the same time presented a program for economic growth, necessary to promote political stability and make statehood attractive in the United States; its economic program was linked to the program for the economic transition to statehood.

An important part of the Romero administration's economic program was the reform of the existing tax-exemption program. Since the beginning, Romero indicated that his administration "will seek alternative incentives that facilitate our economic growth" and that the current incentives would be extended to other areas like the service industries.[60] In his first speech to the Manufacturers' Association in March 1977, Romero reaffirmed his goal of reforming the tax-exemption program and stated that, henceforth, tax exemptions would be granted if a sufficient number of jobs were created at acceptable wages. The governor made it clear that his administration would "move away from the concept of 100 percent industrial tax exemptions."[61]

Despite the strong opposition by important sectors of the bourgeoisie in Puerto Rico (local and American), the Romero administration revised the tax-exemption program with the Industrial Incentives Act of 1978. The preamble of the new law stated that the bill reflected a "new approach to the industrial and economic development of Puerto Rico." The goals of the new law were: to create more jobs, to strengthen the economic infrastructure as an additional incentive to foreign capital, and to share the tax burden equitably among those able to pay (that is, foreign corporations). The law eliminated total tax exemption except for those companies already in the program and the "intangibles" of any company. The new rates of tax exemption were based on the period of exemption, the company's geographical location, the kind of goods manufactured, and, in some cases, the firm's payroll. The law also granted tax exemption (up to 50 percent) to nonmanufacturing industries, the so-called service industries (which included commerce, finance, public relations, advertising, and communications); other industries exempted by the new law included tourism, light industry, and heavy industry (including pharmaceuticals).[62]

The results of the new law were not those expected by the administration. The number of jobs and firms promoted by EDA decreased after the law was passed. The tax burden has not been equitably distributed; according to EDA's director, José Madera, only $164 million in corporate taxes were collected between 1978 and 1982 as the result of the new law. The law also failed to attract service industries to Puerto Rico; since the law's enactment (in 1978) to 1982, only thirty-five new "service companies" came to the island.[63] In July 1983 Romero passed a law reforming his own 1978 act, increasing the tax exemption for service industries to 75 percent and extending the period of exemption. The 1978 act was also amended in 1982 to extend the period of tax exemption for light industry (many of these companies had 100 percent exemptions) in an attempt to counteract the drop in employment.[64] Bertram Finn, one of the masterminds of Romero's economic program, suggested that new incentives, including increased tax exemption, were needed to attract American capital.[65] In 1983 Romero extended tax exemptions to research and development firms in Puerto Rico, in what he characterized as "a logical extension of the revised 936 program," in other words, as compensation to corporations hurt by Congress's reforms of Section 936.[66]

The Romero administration's economic program sought to introduce new incentives for American capital instead of total tax exemption.[67] An important new incentive was the Authority for the Financing of Industrial, Commercial and Environmental Control Facilities (AFICA for its Spanish acronym). AFICA's goal was to provide U.S. corporations with the funds necessary to comply with federal environmental regulations. The new agency was empowered to sell bonds to finance industrial projects (to reduce the investments of corporations complying with federal environmental laws). From 1977 to 1983 the agency issued $935 million in bonds (through financial institutions like A. G. Becker, the great majority of which benefited U.S. corporations.[68] Other new incentives to American capital were the Liquidity Fund and the Development Fund. The Development Fund, supposedly a subsidiary of the Government Development Bank, was to provide loans to the private sector; however, its source of capital was the Liquidity Fund, which obtained its funds from a "tollgate tax" of 7 percent on profits repatriated by Section 936 corporations. That is, Section 936 corporations were allowed to repatriate 75 percent of their profits with a tollgate tax of 7 percent; they had to reinvest 25 percent of their profits in Puerto Rico, which after eight years could be repatriated tax-free. By 1981 the tollgate tax collected from Section 936 corporations amounted to $55.8 million.[69]

The Romero administration's economic policies, such as the 1978 Industrial Incentives Act and the new incentives, were meant to "accustom" American corporations in Puerto Rico to paying taxes and receiving incentives other than total tax exemption. Those corporations willing to pay taxes in exchange for other incentives (lower wages than in the United States, skilled labor force, infrastructure, financial aid from the government) might be able to withstand the economic transition to statehood; under statehood they would have to pay federal taxes, but they would be exempted from local taxes, "like other states." If we also take into account measures such as the reduction of individual income tax and the full application of the federal minimum wage, it is evident that the Romero administration was trying to reconcile the tax and wage structure of Puerto Rico with that of the United States, necessary for a transition to statehood.[70]

The Political Economy of Equality II: Economic Growth and the Caribbeanization of the Puerto Rican Economy

The PNP sought to replace the PPD as the intermediaries of U.S. capital in Puerto Rico. They sought to open new areas of investment in Puerto Rico and to mediate in the expansion of U.S. capital in the Caribbean. PNP strategists argued that the PPD's economic program based on tax exemption to manufacturing firms could not generate a stable economic growth. The PNP's economic strategy was one of "multiple growth," in which other sectors of the economy besides manufacture are subsidized through tax exemption and other incentives. This policy does not exclude manufacturing firms; for example, new incentives were proposed for some high-tech industries (mostly pharmaceutical and electronics).[71] One of the most popular incentives was the training of the labor force for the "new requirements" of capital; that is, to provide the technical training required by advanced production. Romero proposed an "educational trust fund" to finance the technical education of the public school population. Nelson Famadas, one of Romero's main economic advisors, proposed that Puerto Rico be developed into a research center for the United States and the Caribbean, where industrial research funded by the local government would serve as an incentive to attract American capital.[72] The Romero administration also sought more federal contracts for Puerto Rico, particularly by military industries, and this policy showed some positive results. In 1983 the Romero administration and the U.S. Defense Department negotiated to bring the "top nine" defense corporations to the island of Vieques, the area with the greatest tax exemption and the locus of fierce confrontation between the population and the U.S. Navy.[73] Another part of the multiple growth strategy was to turn Puerto Rico into a tourism center for the United States. The Romero administration tried to strengthen the struggling tourism industry with the 1983 Tourism Incentives Act, which extended the length and amount of tax exemptions and granted new tax incentives to most hotels.[74]

Agriculture, too, was an important part of the multiple growth strategy. Agriculture's development based on high-tech industries would provide U.S. capital with another area for investment while enabling Puerto Rico to become an exporter of tropical foods to the U.S. market.[75] According to an agricultural development plan released in 1978, the Romero administration's agricultural strategy was to "produce efficiently most of the food consumed in Puerto Rico using modern, farm-tested techniques." In order to make Puerto Rico an "agricultural exporter" of vegetables and fruits to the American market, farmers were to be given tax exemptions, loans, and other incentives.[76]

The real meaning of this agricultural industrialization program is suggested by the two main agricultural projects of the Romero administration: the production of vegetables and fruits along the southern coast and the production of rice in the north. The vegetables-and-fruits project required the "transfer of modern agricultural technology" to former sugar lands in the south. This technology was provided by an Israeli corporation, which was given loans, subsidies, and land. This program was opposed by local farmers, who derived none of the benefits. The same thing happened with rice in the north. The Romero administration granted the Comet Rice Corporation cheap land and loans and built them a rice mill in exchange for their technology.[77] As Romero stated in his proposal for the creation of the Agricultural Development Administration, agricultural development was to be promoted by means of tax exemption and other subsidies.[78]

Another policy of the Romero administration's economic strategy was what may be called "the Caribbeanization" of the Puerto Rican economy. This strategy was conceived early in Romero's first term, but it was in response to the Reagan administration's Caribbean Basin Initiative (CBI) that it was aggressively promoted.[79] This strategy presented Puerto Rico as the economic power and the model for economic development in the Caribbean. The Romero administration argued that, because of its economic development, Puerto Rico should function as the technological and investment center of the Caribbean, and as the link in the transfer of capital and technology from the United States to the Caribbean. As described by EDA director José Madera, Puerto Rico should be the "technological axis of a Caribbean regional economy interlinked with the United States."[80] This strategy would, on the one hand, open the Caribbean to American investment and the marketing of American goods through Puerto Rico; and, on the other hand, it would open the Caribbean to sectors of Puerto Rican capital, particularly finance and trade. But the strategy also had political implications: only statehood, argued the PNP, would secure Puerto Rico as "a base for the expansion" of American capital in the Caribbean and Latin America.[81] According to Romero:

> As a state, Puerto Rico can aid in the commercial and political relations [of the United States] with the Caribbean region. The possibility that Puerto Rico may increase its involvement with the Caribbean countries does not mean that it will separate from the United States . . . the Nation will benefit from our position in the Caribbean.[82]

The two most important elements of the Caribbean economic policy were the "twin-plant concept" and the export of "Puerto Rican products" to the Caribbean. The Romero administration already supported the twin-plant policy by early 1978.[83] It proposed that raw materials be procured and the initial processing of a product be done in a wage-depressed area of the Caribbean; the product would then be finished in a more advanced economy of the area. That is, the cheap labor of the Caribbean would be used for the initial manufacturing of a product, and its final processing would be done in Puerto Rico with the use of advanced technology, skilled labor, and lower wages than in the United States.[84] By the early 1980s there were several U.S. corporations, mostly electronics firms, working under the Caribbean twin-plant project using Puerto Rico as the final stop in the productive process.[85] Puerto Rico's role in the Caribbean twin-plant program was supported by the Reagan administration, which included it in its CBI proposal, and by sectors of the local bourgeoisie, mainly in finance and trade.[86]

The other element in Romero's Caribbean policy was the transformation of Puerto Rico into a Caribbean trade and finance center. This policy consisted, first, on the marketing of U.S. goods in the Caribbean using Puerto Rico as an intermediary; and, second, on the sale of goods manufactured in Puerto Rico, particularly the high-tech goods produced by U.S. capital on the island. The Romero administration promoted the so-called trade missions, during which representatives of the Puerto Rican government and members of the local banking, trade, and industrial sectors would negotiate commercial agreements with countries in the Caribbean. Romero's government also supported the creation of a World Trade Center in San Juan, to market goods manufactured in Puerto Rico in the Caribbean and in Latin America. In 1979 EDA opened its Department of Services and Industries, "in anticipation of expanding Caribbean and Latin American markets."[87]

Romero's Caribbeanization strategy envisioned closer political ties to Caribbean countries, particularly Jamaica following Edward Seaga's victory there.

In 1983 an accord of mutual cooperation between Jamaica and Puerto Rico was signed. Puerto Rico agreed to provide technical aid for Jamaica's economic, technological, and cultural development, including the implementation of the twin-plant program between the two countries; this was to be financed by the Agency for International Development. Romero's government obtained Seaga's support to make Puerto Rico a member of the Caribbean Development Bank and Caribbean Common Market (CARICOM), which would certainly enhance Puerto Rico's position within the area.[88]

The Campaign for Statehood

The PNP's strategy under Romero included pushing forward economic measures to make the statehood transition economically viable and political measures to advance the statehood process in Puerto Rico. The strategy of presenting statehood to Congress as a *fait accompli* required the support of a majority of Puerto Ricans and of crucial sectors within the United States.

During the first years of the Romero administration, the United States was the principal target of its statehood campaign. The PNP had just won control of the local executive and legislative branches and they were optimistic that their electoral support would continue to grow. They also believed that the presidential primaries in Puerto Rico would create support for statehood. But a major reason the PNP emphasized the statehood campaign in the United States seems to be President Ford's declaration, on December 31, 1976, in support of statehood for Puerto Rico. It was argued that Ford was just repaying a political debt to the local Republicans for their support at the 1976 Republican Convention.[89] In any case, the Ford declaration stimulated debate within the United States of the Puerto Rican statehood issue. Days before the president's departure from office, he submitted a bill laying down the guidelines for statehood for Puerto Rico. The so-called Ford Statehood Bill created a committee to determine the preconditions for and the consequences of statehood. However, the bill was not wholeheartedly supported by the Romero administration; the only logical explanation for this may be a clause stipulating that "Congress, after receiving the Commission Report, would set the terms and conditions of statehood"—in opposition to Romero's statehood strategy. Nevertheless, the Ford Statehood Bill gave Romero the opportunity to present his statehood program in the United States.[90]

According to PNP, its control of the Republican and Democratic parties' local organizations and its participation in the U.S. presidential primaries were the most successful measures in advancing the cause of statehood in the United States. The PNP argued that, "these developments are viewed by statehooders as logical new steps on the path toward statehood."[91] While the local machinery of the National Republican Party was in the hands of the PNP, the Democratic party machinery was still controlled by the PPD in the early 1970s. But in 1976 a group of statehooders penetrated the local Democratic structure and supported a then virtually unknown candidate, Jimmy Carter, for the presidency. Carter's victory tilted the local Democratic machinery to the statehooders and signaled the beginning of an alliance between Romero and Carter. For the first time since the fifties, the Democratic party abandoned its defense of the commonwealth and gave its support to the "right of self-determination" of Puerto Ricans, which culminated with President Carter's 1978 proclamation committing the United States to support whichever alternative the Puerto Ricans chose, including statehood. In the same year, the statehood faction, directly linked to Romero, took control of the local Democratic party machinery.[92] In 1980 the first presidential primaries were held in Puerto Rico; both candidates supported by the PNP, George Bush and Jimmy Carter, were victorious. According to Romero, Carter's triumph over the candidate supported by the PPD was "a clear voice for statehood."[93] These primaries set the pattern for relations between U.S. political leaders and the PNP: any presidential candidate seeking the PNP's support must be committed to statehood.[94]

Romero's statehood strategy changed after the 1980 elections. During the 1980 electoral campaign, statehood was not an issue, aside from Romero's proposal to hold a status plebiscite in 1981. The 1980 PNP electoral program was similar to that of 1976, emphasizing the achievements of the Romero administration, particularly how it had forced the American corporations to pay taxes. Fueling an anticommunism campaign, the PNP accused the PPD of allying with the Socialist party and Cuba against statehood. The PNP campaign stressed that the only guarantee for retaining federal funds was statehood.[95] The results of the elections surprised everyone. The computerized vote counting was stopped with PPD candidate Hernández Colón having a slight advantage; when the count was continued, Romero pulled ahead. Violence erupted between the PPD and the PNP. In July 1981 the State Electoral Commission certified Romero as the governor-elect, with charges of fraud coming from all sectors of the opposition.[96] The PPD won in both houses of the legislature and a majority of the municipalities.

Romero's 1980 electoral victory was a Pyrrhic one. The PPD-controlled legislature started a faultfinder campaign against the Romero administration, focusing on public corruption. In 1981 the Senate approved a bill calling for an investigation of the Cerro Maravilla case, in which two proindependence youths were shot by the police, a case with political overtones and government coverup. By mid-1981 party members, too, began to publicly question Romero's leadership, accusing him of distancing himself from the party and government and of forming a "Carlista" faction that alienated the rest of the PNP leadership from party and government activities. Hernán Padilla, the PNP mayor of San Juan, began to be promoted for the party's presidency and candidate for governor.[97] Confronted by this situation, Romero took up the cry of "Statehood Now" to secure his party leadership and to improve his political image.

Statehood Now

The PNP's Statehood Now campaign began in June 1981 with a statement by PNP Senator Oreste Ramos, Jr., that the party was suffering from "ideological anemia" regarding statehood. Later that month, the Comisión Estadista (Statehood Commission) was formed as an "autonomous" organization whose main purpose was to "educate" people about the advantages of statehood; it was headed by Romero supporters and was part of Romero's party "reorganization." [98] The Statehood Now campaign was formally launched with Romero's Fourth of July speech, in which he declared that the goal of his administration was the attainment of statehood at the earliest moment. This speech reintroduced the attack on colonialism to the PNP's statehood discourse. This anticolonial posture became crucial to Romero's "equality" politics and has dominated the PNP's political rhetoric since then. [99] In January 1982 former Romero aide Antonio Quiñones Calderón began to publish the newspaper *La Democracia,* which during its short life became the main public advocate of statehood and of the Romero administration. In March Romero forced the PNP Legislative Caucus to support a plebiscite on statehood, despite strong opposition by a sector of the party's leadership. Romero also announced that he was to be the PNP candidate for governor in the 1984 elections, getting the support of the party's women, youth, and mayor's organizations. [100]

Romero continued the Statehood Now campaign, under the slogan that the eighties were "the decade of decolonization," with the formation of a commission representing the three main electoral parties whose aim was to present concrete measures to resolve the political status issue. [101] Romero's attempt to set the commission's agenda, and conflicts between the PNP and the PPD, made any agreement impossible. Romero, aiming at the U.S. public, used the occasion of the Southern Governors' Association meeting, held in Puerto Rico in September 1981, to demand support for statehood. In January 1982 PNP representatives headed by Romero met with President Reagan, who reaffirmed his support for statehood. [102]

The reorganization campaign culminated in the PNP Assembly in November 1982, when Romero's group suspended the party's bylaws and named Romero as candidate for governor in 1984. Immediately after the assembly, Padilla and his supporters tried to contest Romero's leadership in the party. Romero responded by sidelining any opposition within the party; he forced the removal of PNP Vice-President Angel Viera Martínez from his position as House Speaker; Viera, in turn, joined Padilla's group. [103]

Publicly, Romero presented his conflict with Padilla as one of different conceptions of statehood. Padilla was opposed to Romero's Statehood Now campaign; he argued that Puerto Rico's socioeconomic problems were more pressing than its political status. But Padilla's main criticism of Romero concerned the latter's control of the PNP, and he demanded a complete "renovation" of the party's leadership and internal structures. [104] In a speech before the PNP

Central Committee in February 1983, Romero reaffirmed that statehood was the ideological and programmatic basis of the PNP, a direct attack on Padilla:

> statehooders should not weaken the struggle for statehood. This has always been our collective goal and we will achieve it if we keep our unity.
> The ideal of Statehood is not an electoral decoy of the New Progressive Party. It is not an ornament. It is the backbone and reason for being of the party. . . . Statehood is the medicine for the evils of colonialism from which Puerto Rico suffers.[105]

The PNP Central Committee adopted a resolution that came to be known as the Loíza Declaration, a very important document of postwar Puerto Rican annexationism, in which the PNP reaffirmed Romero's views on statehood, attacking the "colonial vestiges" of commonwealth status and the political inequality of the U.S. citizens of Puerto Rico. Once again, the critique of colonialism became the ideological axis of Puerto Rican annexationism:

> Statehood is the reason for being of the New Progressive Party. The political condition that we suffer does not satisfy us; we cannot accept, forever, the legitimacy of a federal power that is exercised without our participation; and we do not accept an incomplete citizenship, destitute of all the political and economic rights that are inherent to it. We can neither accept the fragility of our political relationship with the Nation, which affects the economic and social development of Puerto Rico.[106]

After the Loíza meeting, Padilla's group began to organize parallel structures and openly sought support for the mayor's candidacy.[107] In July Padilla and his followers left the PNP and formed the Partido de Renovación Puertorriqueña (PRP—Puerto Rican Renovation Party). Romero then launched an intense campaign for statehood, which became the centerpiece of his political discourse.[108]

The Crisis of Romero's Leadership

Romero has been accurately characterized as an aggressive, astute, and unmerciful politician. Nevertheless, Romero's political behavior cannot be explained solely in terms of his personality, but as part of a political program. This is the attempt to gain control of state and civil institutions in order to promote a political program, and the attempt to destroy all opposition by any means. This is legitimized as necessary to attain statehood.

The PNP under Romero attempted to gain control of several state institutions, particularly such ideological-educational structures as the public school system, the public university, and the Institute of Culture, to further the cause of statehood.[109] This policy also extended to nonideological government institutions such as the Economic Development Administration and the police. It was estimated that the police voted three-to-one in favor of the PNP in the

1980 elections; the association of the members of the police has been closely linked to PNP politics. The federal court in Puerto Rico, whose members customarily have been annexationists, are also linked to the PNP.[110]

Romero's politics were also characterized by the attempt to quiet all opposition, often violently. Nothing is more telling in this respect than the harassment and persecution of Padilla and his followers in the party. The use of force to break the student strike at the University of Puerto Rico in 1981 and to oust squatters from public lands in Villa Sin Miedo in 1982 reflected Romero's refusal to compromise. The attacks on the Puerto Rican Bar Association and the Puerto Rican Supreme Court by PNP members and by the federal court in Puerto Rico followed the same pattern.

Romero's government and party leadership were severely strained by the Senate's investigation of the events at Cerro Maravilla, the federal investigation of government corruption, and the creation of the Puerto Rican Renovation Party. While the Puerto Rican Justice Department and two federal grand juries exonerated the police and the Romero administration, the Senate investigation revealed that the youths were killed in cold blood by the police; that they were entrapped by a police undercover agent; that there was a conspiracy to carry out the action and later to conceal the events by the police and members of the Justice Department; that Romero intervened in the local and federal investigations; and that the federal government was involved in these events, possibly including FBI participation in the events leading to the killings and concealment by the U.S. Justice Department of evidence that could have ''discredited the Government of Puerto Rico.'' Romero reacted to the Senate hearings with his characteristic aggressiveness: he condemned the investigation as part of a ''communist conspiracy'' against his government; he attacked the media; he refused to cooperate with the Senate investigation and in fact tried to stop it; the police and PNP members harassed those involved in the investigation, including several senators; and Romero fired two secretaries of justice who opposed his maneuvers in the affair. After testimony was given linking the police to the youths' assassination, Romero was forced to accept the Senate's proposal for an independent investigation; but his government's actions prevented the continuation of the public hearings, precisely at the stage of the investigation when a conspiracy by the government to conceal the facts might have been proven. In February 1984 ten police officers were charged with perjury before the federal grand juries investigating the case; they were found guilty in 1986. In 1987 they faced criminal charges in Puerto Rican courts.[111] These events were politically devastating for Romero, as public opinion supported the Senate hearings and questioned the governor's obstruction and the government's role in the incidents. By the end of 1983 sectors within the PNP, arguing that the Cerro Maravilla affair would harm the party, campaigned for a new party president and candidate for governor.[112]

The federal housecleaning of local corruption was also very damaging to the Romero administration. Not since the 1930s was Puerto Rico plagued by such a level of government corruption. According to the comptroller of Puerto Rico, at least 10 percent ($600 million) of the government budget of Puerto Rico was lost through corruption (misapplication of funds, unlawful use of funds, and theft); this affected almost every agency of the commonwealth government and a number of municipal governments.[113] There are several reasons for this extensive corruption: the extremely low wages in the public sector; the allocation of government jobs through patronage, giving priority to political loyalty over technical or administrative capability; and finally, the use of the state apparatus to enrich the party in power and its followers. The use of the government to provide political favors to the private sector in exchange for donations to the party created an environment in which it became customary to use the public posts for personal gain as well. Corruption in the Romero administration reached the highest levels, including cabinet members, directors of public agencies, and outstanding members of the PNP leadership.[114]

This "institutionalized corruption," which included the unlawful use and theft of federal funds (for example, the theft of $100 million in food stamps), forced the federal government to intervene. Federal investigations revealed that corruption involved not only federal programs, but the justice system and the police as well; members of the police were charged with drug trafficking, robbery, kidnapping and murder, and operating a death squad.[115] The federal investigation effectively "put the local government in a form of receivership under federal tutelage."[116] In effect, the federal government directly intervened to secure the reproduction of the commonwealth state apparatus given the incapacity of the governing party to do so. The local Justice Department was forced to investigate organized crime and government corruption even though it affected members of the PNP. Romero's political legitimacy was further undermined by the rupture that led to the formation of the PRP.

THE PRP AND THE POLITICS OF REDEMPTION

The Bourgeois Reaction to the Crisis

The formation of the Puerto Rican Renovation Party by PNP dissidents headed by Hernán Padilla transcended the issue of statehood and the internal power struggle in the PNP. The Romero-Padilla conflict and the subsequent rupture in the PNP reflect the revival of the conflict between the two different programs of contemporary annexationism, between the politics of redemption and the politics of equality. The formation of the PRP signified the revival of the politics of redemption.

The formation of the PRP came at a time when there was great concern over the economic and political stability of Puerto Rico, particularly by sectors of the local bourgeoisie. Antonio Luis Ferré, son of the former governor and director of Ferré Enterprises and of the proannexationist newspaper *El Nuevo Día,* was notable in calling attention to the chaotic economic and political situation in Puerto Rico and to the need for a new economic development strategy. Ferré, Jr., criticized the political leadership of Puerto Rico, particularly the Romero administration, for not facing these critical problems: "The governor has lacked the stature to call for a government of Puerto Rican unity, with the best people above any political considerations. . . . There is among the people the sensation that the country is without leadership, without direction."[117] Ferré, Jr., later characterized the current period as the "mud era of Puerto Rican politics," concluding with an appeal to "develop a common action program to solve the social and economic problems that afflict Puerto Rican society."[118] Other sectors of the local bourgeoisie supported the appeal for a "government of unity" to secure political and social stability.[119] In early 1984 the so-called Committee for the Economic Development of Puerto Rico, a bipartisan organization of the local bourgeoisie that included Ferré, Jr., issued a report entitled "The Economic Crisis of Puerto Rico," giving voice to the alarm of the local bourgeoisie over the island's economic situation.[120]

As a corollary to the argument that a government of "national unity" was needed to solve Puerto Rico's pressing social and economic problems, the argument emerged that "status politics" hindered national unity and should be left aside. In late 1981 Abidam Archilla, prominent businessman and PNP founder, published a series of articles proposing the creation of a "No-Status Party." According to Archilla, a group of "status politicians," engaged in a power struggle, use the status issue to attract followers; once in power, they address neither the status question nor the critical social and economic problems of Puerto Rico. The No-Status Party would leave status politics aside and concentrate on providing a good government. "It would devote itself exclusively to the proposition of uniting all our people . . . to activate a planned, energetic frontal attack on our pressing economic and social problems for the good of all our people."[121] This call to form a party and government of national unity to solve Puerto Rico's problems became the political platform of the PRP.

By mid-1982 public opinion polls, particularly those of *El Nuevo Día,* showed that the PNP was losing public support, due mainly to Romero. By 1983 Padilla was ahead of Romero in the polls, and weeks before the formation of the PRP he was leading all candidates. The polls also showed that the most pressing public issue was the solution of social problems and not the status question. These polls showed that the population was pessimistic about the future of Puerto Rico, characterizing the current situation as "sombre."[122]

The conflicts between Romero and Padilla had grown since the beginning of Romero's second term. While the Romero administration criticized the Reagan administration's policies toward Puerto Rico, Padilla supported these policies, including the New Federalism under which the island would receive a block grant for federal funds instead of equal treatment as demanded by Romero. Padilla's "Republican connection" gave him access to the White House and to more federal funds for San Juan, a role traditionally played by the governor.

Padilla also began to criticize Romero's policies, including his relationship with the PPD-controlled legislature, his attack on Puerto Rico's Olympic Committee and Olympic autonomy, his management of the university strike, and even his proposal for a statehood plebiscite.[123] The big confrontation between the two came with Padilla's appointment as special U.S. ambassador to the United Nations. Padilla defended the U.S. position that the U.N. should not intervene in the United States' internal affairs and that the status of Puerto Rico had been decided by the Puerto Ricans. This contradicted Romero's position that Puerto Rico was a U.S. colony and that its status was still unresolved.[124]

Even before Padilla announced his intention to challenge Romero for the PNP leadership, Romero mobilized the party machinery and the government apparatus against Padilla.[125] After Padilla announced his challenge, the PNP Central Committee decided to hold closed primaries (for card-carrying members) rather than open primaries (to include all party followers) as Padilla demanded. After this decision, which restricted the party primaries to the core of Romero's supporters, Padilla and his followers abandoned the PNP. The PRP was formed in August 1983 in Ponce, with Padilla as party president and the PRP's candidate for governor. In a record time of three months, the PRP was officially inscribed as an electoral party.[126]

The PRP and the Program of Redemption

The PRP's program was an attempt to revive Ferré's program of redemption that gave life to the PNP a decade and a half earlier. It argued that the social, economic, and political crises of Puerto Rico could be solved only by a "government of consensus" that would restore faith in political institutions so as to achieve the social and economic stability necessary for the reproduction of the system; the PRP was the harbinger of that government of consensus. Once again, there was a conflict between statehood and the need for stability.

The PRP program resolved this conflict in favor of stability. As in Ferré's statehood program, the PRP proposed a gradual approach to the attainment of statehood. Padilla introduced to the statehood discourse the concept of "statehood by consensus," the most succinct exposition of which is found in Padilla's response to the Loíza Declaration. According to Padilla, "there is no incompatibility between being a statehooder and solving the problems of my people"; the task of a statehood party "consists in convincing and persuading our people to continue on the road to statehood." In a direct attack on Romero's Statehood Now campaign and chaotic administration, Padilla argued that only after the people are convinced and "feel secure that statehooders can provide them with tranquility, security, and progress" will they decide in favor of statehood; he maintained that the statehood movement had stagnated in the last several years because of Romero's administration.[127]

Statehood will be possible only by consensus, which requires the solution of the country's social and economic problems: "Statehood is an instrument of change and social and political reform that needs time, but more than anything else, it requires the consensus of the people. . . . The future of statehood depends on the renovation and change that our people demand to solve their immediate problems.''[128] Padilla's statehood by consensus strategy differs from Romero's statehood by simple majority because, as Padilla explains, ''As long as there is one Puerto Rican who doubts the benefits of statehood, we cannot be tranquil.''[129] Padilla's strategy was a response to the reality that the majority of the population did not support statehood and, more importantly, that statehood as proposed by Romero was opposed by important sectors in the United States, who were afraid to grant statehood in the absence of an overwhelming majority. Padilla opposed Romero's proposal for a ''Statehood, Yes or No'' plebiscite, favoring as the only viable alternative a plebiscite that included all three status alternatives, and where Congress has defined the conditions in which it will accept each alternative.[130] For Padilla the attainment of statehood would require ''a process of gradual mutual agreement,'' emphasizing the need for a greater political integration, which would include both a greater participation by Puerto Ricans in the political affairs of the United States and a better understanding of the values and political system of the United States.[131]

The PRP's statehood strategy was accompanied by a program to solve the crises that affected Puerto Rico. Puerto Rican society is beset by a moral crisis that, according to Padilla, stems from the ''lack of the elements that give us tranquility, stability, and coexistence in harmony with society.''[132] At the political level Padilla pointed to the origins of this crisis in the ''politics of confrontation'' between the PPD and the PNP: ''Political conflicts overshadow all other efforts, and both sides have become increasingly confrontational and unable to work together on economic and social issues which require a minimum level of bipartisanship.''[133] This was the basis for the PRP's argument that the issue of statehood should be delayed in favor of solving the island's social and economic problems. In order to achieve this, it would be necessary to form a government of unity and to forge a consensus among all sectors of society. Thus in order to facilitate a government of unity, the PRP platform stated that the party did not favor any particular status alternative. This would also promote the consensus required to solve the status issue.[134] According to Padilla, the politics of confrontation and the PNP's policy of *continuismo* turned the government into ''an instrument of the New Progressive Party,'' which in turn encouraged the governmental corruption that corroded the moral fiber of the country. The separation of government and party in the PRP's government of unity, along with the recruitment of the most capable public administrators, would secure a responsible government devoted to solving Puerto Rico's problems.[135]

According to the PRP's economic program, Puerto Rico is too dependent on ''foreign investment and trade for its economic development; it is necessary to strengthen its domestic economic base to prevent a social and economic catastrophe. According to Padilla, Puerto Rico has become a ''shopping center for imports," and this has destroyed the local productive capacity aimed at the local market. As a consequence of this and "foreign" control of Puerto Rico's industrial production, Puerto Rico suffers from high unemployment and a lack of capital investment. In order to "assure that Puerto Rico's economic future is in the hands of Puerto Ricans," the PRP proposed a policy of "import substitution" utilizing incentives and protection for the "small entrepreneur" (that is, local capital).[136] Padilla criticized the current tax-exemption program, which favors American capital and discriminates against local capital. He argued that the government should provide subsidies and incentives to the small entrepreneur and should develop those areas in which there is little private investment.[137] The PRP's economic strategy was similar to that proposed earlier by Ferré: the promotion of American capital in areas of high technology, and the promotion of local capital in labor-intensive production for the local market and possibly to expand to the Caribbean.[138] The PRP favored developing local agriculture to satisfy local demand and to export staples, emphasizing that agriculture should be in local hands and that the government should promote agriculture through subsidies and incentives to the local farmer.[139]

The PRP's popular support deteriorated throughout 1983. An October 1983 public opinion poll showed Padilla a distant third behind Romero and Hernández Colón in the race for governor.[140] The PRP also suffered from organizational problems. Their leadership came entirely from the PNP, particularly the middle-class sectors and professionals who occupied middle-level leadership positions in the PNP. They were unable to attract leaders from other parties to legitimize their claim of being a party of national unity, and they had difficulty recruiting effective leadership at the local level.[141]

The PRP's program was a response to the decline of the local bourgeoisie and the advance of American capital, and to the crisis of legitimacy of the political-ideological institutions under Romero and the deepening crisis endangering the reproduction of the system itself. Once again, a sword of Damocles hung over the Puerto Rican annexationist bourgeoisie: to secure their own economic and political reproduction, they sought annexation to the United States; but the increasing integration to the United States undermined their material and political basis. The redemptionist program of the PRP was not a magic solution to their problems, but it provided a breathing space from the economic and political chaos of the Romero administration and an opportunity to elaborate a new statehood strategy.

The PNP, the 1984 Elections, and after

Several days after the November 1984 elections, the pro-statehood *El Nuevo Día* published the results of an electoral opinion exit poll with a front-page headline that read: "Anti-Romero Voting in the Elections." The poll revealed that most of the "undecided-independent" vote went to the PPD candidate, Rafael Hernández Colón, a sign of this voter bloc's antipathy for the PNP's

Carlos Romero Barceló.[142] Hernández Colón became governor, defeating Romero Barceló by a margin of 50,000 votes, with just over 1.7 million votes cast. The PPD also won both houses of the legislature and fifty-nine of seventy-eight municipal governments.[143] The *El Nuevo Día* poll also revealed that two crucial issues in the anti-Romero voting were his administration's corruption and handling of the Cerro Maravilla case, and the emphasis on statehood as the main electoral campaign issue. Nevertheless, Romero received 44 percent of the vote for governor and the PNP retained its hold over some of the major cities, including the capital, San Juan.

The 1984 elections had contradictory results for the PNP. The pro-statehood party still got 44 percent of the votes cast, despite the fact that Romero's only electoral flag was statehood, while the PPD campaign concentrated on the administration's corruption and mismanagement, the Cerro Maravilla case, and the worsening conditions of Puerto Rico's economy. The PPD even campaigned for, and gained, thousands of proindependence votes fearful of another annexationist government. The Renewal Party also attacked Romero's mismanagement of government and party, and was able to detract over 60,000 votes from the PNP. The race was closer than expected; an *El Nuevo Día* poll days before the elections showed Romero ahead by one percent (35 to 34) over Hernández Colón, with a large portion of the voters still undecided. An earlier May poll by the same newspaper showed Romero ahead by 2 percent (30 to 28).[144] Another October poll showed Hernández Colón ahead by 2 percent, with a significant rise in support from the middle-class vote.[145]

The results of the 1984 elections created the conditions for a struggle over the party's leadership. The PNP has been unable to achieve a post-Romero transition, mainly because of Romero himself. The man who responded ''What defeat?'' to reporters' questions about the electoral results has been unwilling to accept a new party leadership. This presents a critical situation to the PNP, because even if San Juan mayor Baltasar Corrada del Río and his group have the party machinery, Romero still has a large chunk of the PNP vote, particularly among the lower-income, less-educated groups, indispensable for any PNP victory.

Immediately after the 1984 elections important sectors of the party, including Ferré and the PNP Mayors' Federation, began to demand changes in the party leadership. After several months of infighting, Romero announced in September 1985 that he was taking a ''political vacation,'' leaving Corrada del Río as acting president. In June 1986 Corrada was elected party president by the PNP Assembly.[146] Apparently tired of vacationing, Romero came back to the political arena in full vigor. In October 1986 he became PNP senator and immediately took command of the party's legislative caucus. Romero also began to campaign heavily for the presidency of the local Democratic party machinery. Partly responding to Romero's threat, the PNP Central Committee approved in January 1987 a resolution supporting Corrada as the party's gubernatorial candidate. In February 1987 Corrada became the official PNP candidate for governor.[147] But Corrada has been unable to strengthen his position in the party. He has shown no great competence in managing the affairs of San Juan and has been caught in local controversies that have undermined his public image. Corrada has been unable to tighten the party's organization or straighten its dismal financial situation; party leaders have complained of apathy among PNP members.

After 1984 the Mayors' Federation has become a new center of authority in the party. Corrada had to win the federation's support to become the party's official candidate. The federation placed one of its own as PNP vice-president. Lacking Romero's charismatic presence, Corrada has not created fervor among the PNP masses and has not made inroads into the party's local structures, heavily controlled by the mayors. The PNP is so disorganized that sectors inside the party clamored for the return of Hernán Padilla to the PNP; both Corrada and Romero made public overtures for Padilla's support. Infighting has extended to other areas of PNP politics as well; for example, the November 1987 assembly of the PNP-controlled U.S. Republican party in Puerto Rico ended in insults and accusations among top party leaders, unable to agree on a common candidate for the primaries. Corrada has achieved support, including that of the Mayors' Federation, more out of these sectors' fear of Romero and his tight control of the party than because of his own leadership. As a consequence, Corrada has been losing support inside and outside the party; two 1987 *El Nuevo Día* polls showed Corrada rapidly losing ground to Governor Hernández Colón. Taking advantage of all this, Romero announced his candidacy for PNP governor in November 1987.[148] Although all sides have promised a friendly primary campaign, the PNP may end up divided and conflict-ridden for the 1988 elections.

As under Romero, Corrada's PNP has campaigned for statehood as the party's "sole ideological basis." In one of his first acts as PNP president, Corrada created the forty-five-member Committee to Achieve Statehood in August 1986. Heavily criticized by some party leaders, the committee finished a year's work with a report recommending a statehood plebiscite if the PNP wins the 1988 elections.[149] Also, the independent Puerto Rican Citizens' Action group has supposedly collected and taken to Congress hundreds of thousands of signatures in favor of statehood; the group pushes for statehood above party lines.[150] Two separate bills calling for a statehood referendum were submitted in Washington by Vice-President Bush and Senator Dole; they were mostly attempts to enhance their presidential candidacies among local Republicans.[151]

Meanwhile, criticizing the party's lack of effort to push for statehood seriously while in government, some PNP Young Turks have called for a "civic insurrection" in favor of statehood if the party wins in 1988 or simply to disband as a statehood party.[152] Others have criticized the use of statehood as a *modus vivendi* for their own personal advancement, forgetting statehood as soon as they win.[153] On the other hand, since 1985 the PNP's rhetoric has focused on the issue of the "associated republic," supposedly a new status being pushed by Washington. The PNP has reacted with a defensive posture, attacking the PPD for secretly pushing Puerto Rico to independence and maintaining that statehood is the only way to retain the permanent union with the United States.[154]

The social forces that today support statehood in Puerto Rico will continue to do so in the near future; thus, whatever its current condition, the statehood movement will certainly play an important role in the island's coming political struggles. However, the 1984 electoral defeat, the party's internal struggle, the inability of the statehood movement to gain a decisive majority, and the continued congressional opposition to statehood have made statehood an uncertain alternative for the island. From the perspective of the U.S. government, the future of Puerto Rico, including statehood, remains "a problem for the eighties." From the perspective of statehooders, statehood is the only means to achieve "the equality of citizenship within the nation whose citizens we are."[155] The solution to this dilemma, and to Puerto Rico's economic and political problems, remains on the agenda for Puerto Ricans and Americans as well.

NOTES

1. Figures from Luis P. Costas Elena, "I.R.C. Section 936 and Fomento Income Tax Exemptions in Puerto Rico," *Revista del Colegio de Abogados de Puerto Rico*, pt. 1, 40, no. 4 (Nov. 1979), pp. 563–64, 566, 577–78, 587, 595; Costas Elena, ibid., pt. 2, 41, no. 4 (Feb. 1981), pp. 113, 125; 1982 figure from *San Juan Star*, Sept. 18, 1983, p. B6.

2. Figures from Junta de Planificación, *Informe económico al Gobernador 1982* (San Juan: Junta de Planificación, 1983), pp. 19, 131, 133–34, 222; and *San Juan Star*, Sept. 18, 1983, p. B6.

3. Comité Para el Estudio de las Finanzas de Puerto Rico, *Informe al Gobernador* (Río Piedras: Editorial Universitaria, 1976), pp. 59–60.

4. Comité Para el Desarrollo Económico de Puerto Rico, *La crisis económica de Puerto Rico: Resumen ejecutivo del diagnóstico y recomendaciones* (mimeo, Jan. 1984).

5. Dolores Wahl, "Puerto Rico's Status: A Problem for the Eighties," Executive Seminar in National and International Affairs, Department of State, April 1980; Alfred Stepan, "The United States and Latin America: Vital Interests and the Instruments of Power," *Foreign Affairs* 58, no. 3 (America and the World, 1979), p. 664.

6. See *Report of the Ad Hoc Advisory Group of Puerto Rico* (Washington, D.C.: Ad Hoc Advisory Group, October 1975), the quote is from Roberta Ann Johnson, "Puerto Rico: The Unsettled Question," in Richard Millet and W. Marvin Will, eds., *The Restless Caribbean: Changing Patterns of International Relations* (New York: Praeger, 1979), p. 109.

7. U.S. Department of State, "The problem of Puerto Rico's Political Status," Case study by C. Arthur Borg (Seventh Session, Senior Seminar in Foreign Policy, Department of State, 1974–75), pp. 6, 14, to be referred to as Borg Report; "Puerto Rico: Commonwealth, Statehood or Independence," Memorandum to the President of the United States, Office of the Assistant Secretary of Defense, July 12, 1977, pp. 1, 6, 9, 12, 14; U.S. Library of Congress, *Puerto Rico: Independence or Statehood?: A Survey of Historical, Political, and Socioeconomic Factors, with Pro and Con Argu-*

ments, Prepared by William Tansill (Washington, D.C.: Congressional Research Service, 1977), p. 38, to be referred to as Tansill Report; U.S. Library of Congress, *Puerto Rico: Commonwealth, Statehood, or Independence?* Prepared by Peter Sheridan (Washington, D.C.: Congressional Research Service, 1978), p. 3, to be referred to as Sheridan Report; General Accounting Office, *Puerto Rico's Political Future: A Divisive Issue with Many Dimensions,* Report to the Congress of the United States by the Comptroller General (Washington, D.C.: General Accounting Office, 1981), pp. i–iii; Wahl, "Puerto Rico's Status," p. 12.

8. Commonwealth is questioned in Memorandum to the President, pp. 6–9; Borg Report, p. 15; Wahl, "Puerto Rico's Status," pp. 1, 12; Tansill Report, pp. 35–36; Sheridan Report, pp. 1–2. Congressional studies on statehood include U.S. Library of Congress, *Treating Puerto Rico as a State Under Federal Tax and Expenditure Programs: A Preliminary Economic Analysis,* Prepared by Donald W. Kiefer (Washington, DC: Congressional Research Service, 1977), to be referred to as the Kiefer Report; the Tansill Report of 1977, the Sheridan Report of 1978, and GAO, *Puerto Rico's Political Future,* all previously cited.

9. Borg Report, pp. 16–17.

10. Wahl, "Puerto Rico's Status," pp. 7, 17. On the need for a colonial office see Borg Report, p. 17; also proposed by José A. Cabranes, "Puerto Rico: Out of the Colonial Closet," *Foreign Policy* (Winter 1978–79), pp. 90–91; and Jeffrey Puryear, director of the Latin American Program of the Ford Foundation, in "Puerto Rico's Waiting," *New York Times,* April 14, 1981, p. A-23.

11. Borg Report, p. 16; Memorandum to the President, p. 10; Sheridan Report, pp. 3–4.

12. Sheridan Report, p. 3; Memorandum to the President, pp. 10–12; Borg Report, p. 16.

13. Independence as the "second best alternative" was proposed by the Borg Report, p. 15; and Wahl, "Puerto Rico's Status," p. 10. Independence as the "best alternative" was supported by Memorandum to the President, p. 24; and from a State Department journal, Eric Svendsen, "Puerto Rico Libre," *Open Forum,* no. 20 (Spring/Summer 1979), pp. 21–27; and from the conservative side, Robert Wesson, "A Different Case for Puerto Rican Independence," *Worldview,* 21, no. 11 (November 1978), pp. 8–10.

14. Kiefer Report, pp. 4, 34, 36; Tansill Report, p. 40; and GAO, *Puerto Rico's Political Future,* pp. 54–56.

15. Kiefer Report, p. 4, 44; GAO, *Puerto Rico's Political Future,* pp. 56–60. The latter view is from Tansill Report, p. 40.

16. Memorandum to the President, p. 27; Wahl, "Puerto Rico's Status," p. 12; Borg Report, p. 16; Sheridan Report, p. 4.

17. *El Nuevo Día,* June 1982, p. 7; and March 18, 1983, p. 4. Results of these conferences were: Jorge Heine, ed., *Time for Decision: The United States and Puerto Rico* (Lanham, MD: North-South Publ., 1983); Richard J. Bloomfield, ed., *Puerto Rico: The Search for a National Policy* (Boulder, CO: Westview, 1985).

18. Ronald Reagan, "Puerto Rico and Statehood," *Wall Street Journal,* Feb. 11, 1980, p. 20; *Forbes,* Aug. 6, 1979, pp. 47–48; *Fortune,* Aug. 13, 1979, pp. 163–76; *New York Times,* Editorial, Aug. 21, 1979, p. A18; Tom Wicker, "An American Colony?" *New York Times,* Aug. 14, 1981, p. A23; *Wall Street Journal,* Feb. 3, 1982, p. 1. In favor of statehood: *Wall Street Journal,* Editorials for Oct. 18, 1979, p. 16, and Aug. 20, 1981, p. 26; *Southeast Missourian,* Editorial, July 18, 1979; Editorial, *Wash-*

ington Times, reproduced in *El Nuevo Día,* July 8, 1982, p. 13. Uncertain about statehood was *New York Times,* Editorial, Jan. 15, 1982.

19. Carlos Romero Barceló, *La estadidad es para los pobres* (San Juan: N.P., 1973), p. 24.

20. Ibid., pp. 42 and 57.

21. Carlos Romero Barceló, "Puerto Rico, U.S.A.: The Case for Statehood," *Foreign Affairs* 59, no. 1 (Fall 1980), p. 75.

22. Puerto Rico Federal Affairs Administration (PRFAA), *Puerto Rico, U.S.A.: A Political History* (Washington, DC: PRFAA, n.d.), pp. 14–15.

23. Carlos Romero Barceló, "Statehood for Puerto Rico," *Vital Speeches* 45 (July 1, 1979), p. 565.

24. Carlos Romero Barceló, Address by the Governor of Puerto Rico Commemorating the 205th Anniversary of the Declaration of Independence of the United States of America, July 4, 1981 (San Juan: Administración de Servicios Generales, n.d.), p. 21.

25. Carlos Romero Barceló, "Statehood for Puerto Rico," (address delivered before the Americas Society Conference on "The Press and the Political Status of Puerto Rico," New York, March 17, 1983, p. 6.

26. Carlos Romero Barceló, speech delivered before the Committee on Decolonization of the United Nations, New York, Aug. 28, 1978, reproduced in *Puerto Rico Business Review* (Special Supplement) 3, no. 9 (Sept. 1978), p. 4. Also, Romero Barceló, "Statehood for Puerto Rico" (1979), p. 567.

27. Romero Barceló, "Statehood for Puerto Rico" (1983), pp. 7–8.

28. Luis R. Dávila Colón, "The Blood Tax: The Puerto Rican Contribution to the United States War Effort," *Revista del Colegio de Abogados de Puerto Rico* 40, no. 4 (Nov. 1979), p. 618.

29. See, e.g., PRFAA, *Puerto Rico, U.S.A.: In Defense of Democracy* (Washington, DC: PRFAA, 1979); and PRFAA *Dateline . . . Puerto Rico, U.S.A.* (May–June 1980), pp. 8–10; (Nov.–Dec. 1980), pp. 8–10; (July–Aug. 1980), pp. 11–14.

30. Quote from Dávila Colón, "The Blood Tax," p. 628; also pp. 616, 618. And Romero Barceló, Address Fourth of July 1981, pp. 23–26.

31. Romero Barceló, Address Fourth of July 1981, p. 28.

32. "CRB se prepara para el '76," *Avance,* May 20, 1974, pp. 13–14. Also *La estadidad es para los pobres,* pp. 19–20.

33. Jonathan Evan Maslow, "Puerto Rico the 51st State?" *New Republic,* July 2, 1977, p. 13.

34. "CRB se prepara para el '76," p. 13.

35. In "Should Puerto Rico be a State?" *US News and World Report,* April 11, 1977, p. 14.

36. PRFAA, *A Political History,* pp. 15–16.

37. Romero Barceló, "The Case for Statehood," p. 69.

38. PRFAA, *Puerto Rico, U.S.A.: Science and Industry* (Washington, D.C.: PRFAA, n.d.), and *Puerto Rico U.S.A.* (Washington, DC: PRFAA, n.d.), pp. 49–63.

39. Romero as quoted in Ronald Walker, "Romero and Statehood," *San Juan Star,* Oct. 11, 1982, p. 17. This is the position elaborated by the Grupo de Investigadores Puertorriqueños, a group of young statehooders interested in providing an intellectual argument for statehood, in the huge but confusing *Breakthrough From Colonialism: An Interdisciplinary Study of Statehood* (Río Piedras: Editorial de la Universidad de Puerto Rico, 1984), particularly part 5 in vol. 2.

40. Romero Barceló, "The Case for Statehood," p. 67.

41. Nélida Jímenez Velázquez and Luis R. Dávila Colón, "The American Statehood Process and Its Relevance to Puerto Rico's Colonial Reality," in Heine, ed., *Time for Decision*, p. 260. Argument elaborated more extensively in *Breakthrough From Colonialism*, particularly vol. 2, ch. 4, pt. 4.

42. "Exención contributiva: Una polémica que se traduce en 5 puntos para traer la estadidad por filtración," *Avance*, Nov. 18, 1974, pp. 6–7.

43. Baltasar Corrada del Río, U.S. Congress. House, "Puerto Ricans Celebrate Adoption of Constitution," *Congressional Record*, 95th Cong., 1st Sess., vol. 123, no. 20, July 25, 1977, p. 24837.

44. Romero Barceló, "The Case for Statehood," p. 79.

45. "Presentation by Dr. Arthur Burns, Liaison Consultant on Behalf of Statehood for Puerto Rico," in United States–Puerto Rico Commission on the Status of Puerto Rico, *Status of Puerto Rico: Hearings*, vol. 3 (Washington, D.C.: U.S. Government Printing Office, 1966), pp. 623–35.

46. Romero Barceló, "Statehood for Puerto Rico" (1983), p. 5. Also "The Case for Statehood," p. 79; "Should Puerto Rico be a State?" p. 47; and *La estadidad es para los pobres*, pp. 59–61.

47. Romero Barceló, "The Case for Statehood," p. 79. See also *Puerto Rico Business Review* 5, no. 3 (March 1980), p. 2.

48. Bertram Finn, "The Economic Implications of Statehood," in Heine, ed., *Time for Decision*, pp. 185, 188, 198, 207–8. Finn's argument is elaborated further in *Breakthrough From Colonialism*, ch. 2, pt. 4, vol. 2.

49. Carlos Romero Barceló, "The Russian Threat to the Americas," *Vital Speeches*, no. 45 (May 15, 1981), pp. 457–58. Also, Carlos Romero Barceló, *Forjando el futuro*, edited by Antonio Quiñones Calderón (Hato Rey: Ramallo Bros., 1978), pp. 211–12; and *San Juan Star*, May 12, 1982, p. 20.

50. On the anticommunist theme: Romero Barceló, "The Russian Threat to the Americas," p. 457; *San Juan Star*, Feb. 1, 1982, p. 6. On the use of the NG: Romero Barceló, "The Case for Statehood," pp. 72–75, 67; *El Nuevo Día*, Aug. 17, 1983, p. 5. On Puerto Rico's links with Latin America: Romero Barceló, "Statehood for Puerto Rico," p. 6.

51. 1976 PNP Program in Reece B. Bothwell, ed., *Puerto Rico: Cien años de lucha política* (Río Piedras: Editorial Universitaria, 1979), vol. 1, pt. 2, p. 1293.

52. Romero Barceló, "The Case for Statehood," p. 77.

53. 1976 PNP Program in Bothwell, *Puerto Rico*, vol. 1, pt. 2, pp. 1300–7.

54. *El Mundo*, Oct. 13, 1976, p. 1A, 12C; Oct. 20, 1976, pp. 10–11A; Oct. 23, 1976, p. 10C; Oct. 18, 1976, p. 1A. Romero's populist image was presented in Comité Carlos '76, *Carlos Romero Barceló . . . el hombre, el amigo, el político* (n.p.: Comité Campaña Carlos '76, 1976).

55. Juan A. Ríos Vélez, "Análisis del diseño de la rama ejecutiva para determinar el tipo de gobierno que se quiere implantar" (Master's Thesis, Sch. Pub. Admin., UPR, 1981), pp. 47 and 52.

56. Romero's first EDA director, Manuel H. Dubón, was a tax law specialist for corporations, and his successor, José R. Madera, came from the banking sector (Citibank); Secretary of the Treasury Carmen A. Culpeper also came from the banking sector (Citibank), as well as PRIDCO's first president under Romero, Enrique Rodríguez-Negrón (Bank of America, Banco Popular, Swiss Bank) and his successor Eugenio H.

Fontanes (Citibank, Banco Crédito y Ahorro Ponceño). Also from the banking sector were Mariano Mier, former president of the Government Development Bank (Banco Popular); Luis S. Montañez, director of the Bureau of the Budget (Banco de San Juan); Ivar Pietri, special assistant to Romero and later Vice-president of the GDB (Citibank); and Neil Montilla, president of PRIDCO (Citibank). Nelson Famadas, chairman of the Governor's Economic Advisory Council, was a partner in a financial consultant firm; his predecessor, Bertram Finn, previously with EDA, became vice-president of A. G. Becker of Puerto Rico.

57. "Análisis de la banca comercial de Puerto Rico," *El Mundo*, Feb. 5, 1982, p. SC8; *Informe Económico al Gobernador, 1982*, p. 133.

58. Data from Junta de Planificación, *Estadísticas socioeconómicas 1980* (San Juan: División de Análisis Económico, 1980), pp. 3–4; *Informe Económico al Gobernador 1983* (San Juan: Junta de Planificación, 1984), p. A7; and *Informe Económico al Gobernador 1982*, p. 69. Also, Oficina del Gobernador, Consejo Asesor Sobre Política Laboral, *Plan de acción para aumentar la productividad en la economía de Puerto Rico: Diagnóstico y recomendaciones* (San Juan: Consejo Asesor, 1979), p. 37.

59. See Emilio Pantojas, "La crisis del modelo desarrollista y la restructuración capitalista en Puerto Rico," (mimeo: CEREP, 1984); and Edwin Meléndez, "Accumulation and Crisis in the Postwar Puerto Rican Economy" (Ph.D. diss., Dept. of Economy, Univ. of Massachusetts, 1985), ch. 6.

60. Carlos Romero Barceló, "Mensaje del Honorable Gobernador de Puerto Rico a la Octava Asamblea Legislativa en su Primera Sesión Ordinaria," Feb. 24, 1977. (San Juan, Administración de Servicios Generales, 1977), pp. 25–26.

61. *Forjando el futuro*, pp. 123–33; and Carlos Romero Barceló, speech delivered before the Puerto Rico Manufacturers' Association, Oct. 22, 1977, p. 3.

62. "'Ley de Incentivos Industriales de 1978," *Leyes de Puerto Rico 1978* (Octava Asamblea Legislativa) (Hato Rey: Equity de Puerto Rico, 1979), p. 59. Also, "The 1978 Industrial Incentives Program," in *Puerto Rico Business Review* (Special Supplement—Feb. 1979).

63. New EDA-promoted firms have declined from 196 to 170 between 1977–78 to 1980–81; "nonlocal" firms have declined from 116 to 70 during the same period. See *El Nuevo Día*, Jan. 31, 1982, p. 4. Figure for corporate taxes from *San Juan Star*, Nov. 5, 1982, p. 6. Service industries discussed by Fred H. Martínez, in ibid., May 16 and 23, 1982, p. B3 and B5, respectively.

64. *San Juan Star*, July 12, 1983, p. 16; *El Nuevo Día*, Dec. 4, 1982, p. 27.

65. *San Juan Star*, Nov. 23, 1981, pp. 1 and 14. Arguments by Finn appear in ibid., Sept. 6, 1981, p. B3; June 6, 1982, p. B6; and Oct. 23, 1983, p. B3.

66. Ibid., Feb. 20, 1983, p. 1.

67. Romero, *Forjando el futuro*, pp. 148–56; and *Puerto Rico Business Review* 2 no. 5 (May 20, 1977), pp. 1–3.

68. 1983 figure from *Puerto Rico Business Review* 8, nos. 7–8 (July–Aug. 1983), p. 38. The corporations benefiting the most from this program are the pharmaceuticals and petrochemicals, like Abbot, Squibb, PPG, Bristol, Cyanamid, Merck, Sharp and Dome, Pfizer, Upjohn, and Union Carbide; also the electronics industries, like Prime Computers, Wang, Weinthrop Labs, and Sykes Datatronics. See ibid., 6, no. 6 (June 1981), pp. 1 and 9; 5, no. 3 (March 1980), pp. 1 and 15; *San Juan Star*, June 16 and 17, 1982, p. 26 and 36, respectively; Nov. 24, 1982, p. 22; and *El Nuevo Día*, March 31, 1982, p. 72, and July 9, 1982, p. 50.

69. *Informe económico al Gobernador 1982*, p. A26.

70. *Dateline . . . Puerto Rico, U.S.A.* (March–April 1981), p. 6.

71. See the articles by Bertram Finn in *San Juan Star*, Aug. 7, 1982, p. S2; and May 15, 1983, p. B3. Also that of José Madera in ibid., Sept. 29, 1983, p. S30; Madera's statements in ibid., Aug. 28, 1983, p. B1; and the views of Nelson Famadas in *El Nuevo Día*, June 11, 1983, p. 9.

72. Comments by Madera in *El Nuevo Día*, May 25, 1983, p. 74; *San Juan Star*, July 5, 1983, p. 1; and interview with Famadas in ibid., Sept. 18, 1983, p. B2.

73. Puerto Rico received $200 million in military contracts during 1982; *San Juan Star*, Nov. 5, 1982, p. 20; Oct. 23, 1983, p. B1; and Nov. 3, 1983, p. 23; *El Nuevo Día*, June 22, 1983, p. 4.

74. *San Juan Star*, Oct. 29, 1981, p. 21; Sept. 19, 1982, p. B1; and June 5, 1983, pp. B1, 8.

75. Romero Barceló, "Mensaje del Honorable Gobernador," p. 30; Romero Barceló, *Forjando el futuro*, pp. 59–76; *El Mundo*, April 9, 1977, p. 14A; "Should Puerto Rico Be a State?" pp. 47–48; and Romero Barceló, "The Case for Statehood," p. 80. Also *Dateline . . . Puerto Rico, U.S.A.* (Sept.–Oct. 1980), pp. 27–28.

76. *Puerto Rico Business Review* (Feb. 1978—Special Supplement), p. 1; *San Juan Star*, Nov. 5, 1981, p. 6; Aug. 18, 1982, p. 10; Sept. 25, 1983, p. B8; *El Nuevo Día*, Jan. 19, 1983, p. 11; and *Dateline . . . Puerto Rico, U.S.A.* (Sept.–Oct. 1980), pp. 27–28.

77. *San Juan Star*, Oct. 17, 1982, p. B1; April 18, 1982, p. B1; March 10, 1983, p. 3; July 23, 1983, p. 2; Sept. 14, 1981, p. 1; Jan. 9, 1983, p. 1; March 11, 1983, p. 3.

78. *El Nuevo Día*, Jan. 19, 1983, p. 11.

79. *El Mundo*, March 16, 1982, p. 1A, and April 18, 1982, p. 1; also the article by Finn in *San Juan Star*, March 7, 1982, p. B7.

80. *San Juan Star*, July 22, 1983, p. 32. Also *El Nuevo Día*, Oct. 4, 1981, p. 2; March 4, 1982, p. 72; and April 12, 1983, p. 23.

81. *El Nuevo Día*, March 4, 1982, p. 72.

82. Ibid., March 28, 1982, p. 2.

83. Speech by Carlos Romero Barceló before the Caribbean Business, Trade, and Development Conference in Miami, reproduced in *Puerto Rico Business Review* 3, no. 1 (Jan. 1978), p. 1.

84. *San Juan Star*, Oct. 4, 1981, p. 16; Feb. 27, 1983, pp. B1, 6; Aug. 28, 1983, p. B3; and Aug. 21, 1983, p. B1; *El Nuevo Día*, March 17, 1983, p. 118.

85. Among others, Qume, Digital, Power Parts Sigma, Dwyer Instruments, GTE Sylvania, Masco, and Wellmach in Haiti; Inter and Playtex in Barbados; Bristol in the Dominican Republic; General Electric, Honeywell, and Applied Magnetics in the Eastern Caribbean islands; and several others in Jamaica. See *San Juan Star*, Feb. 27, 1983, pp. B1, 6, and Aug. 21, 1983, p. B1.

86. Ibid., Sept. 11, 1982, p. 21, and Dec. 8, 1981, p. 27; *El Nuevo Día*, May 24, 1983, p. 54.

87. *El Mundo*, Sept. 2, 1980, p. 16A, and March 27, 1981, p. 3A; *El Nuevo Día*, June 5, 1981, p. 24; Sept. 25, 1983, p. 44; and Aug. 25, 1982, p. 72; *San Juan Star*, May 22, 1983, p. B1, and Aug. 11, 1983, p. 3. EDA quoted from *Puerto Rico Business Review* 6, no. 9 (Sept. 1981), pp. 17–18.

88. *San Juan Star,* Oct. 31, 1981, p. 3; Feb. 6, 1982, p. 6; May 31, 1983, p. 3; and Aug. 11, 1983, p. 36; *El Nuevo Día,* June 17, 1982, p. 16, and July 4, 1983, p. 19.

89. *The Nation,* Jan. 15, 1977, p. 36; *The New Republic,* July 21, 1977, pp. 12–14.

90. Quote from U.S. Congress, House of Representatives, Puerto Rico Statehood Act of 1977: Communication From the President of the United States Transmitting a Draft of Proposed Legislation to Enable the People of Puerto Rico to Form a Constitution and State Government, to be Admitted into the Union, and for other purposes. 95th Cong., 1st Sess., House Document no. 95–49. See Romero, *Forjando el futuro,* pp. 148–231, for the several speeches in favor of statehood during 1977, aimed primarily at the American public.

91. *Puerto Rico, U.S.A.: A Political History,* p. 22.

92. See Juan M. García-Passalacqua, "Ideological Links Between Puerto Rican and U.S. Political Parties," in Heine, ed., *Time for Decision,* pp. 213–34.

93. Quoted in *New York Times,* March 17, 1980, p. A1; see also ibid., Feb. 19, 1980, p. A16.

94. Ronald Reagan, "Puerto Rico and Statehood," p. 20; *San Juan Star,* Sept. 28, 1981, p. 1; June 30, 1982, p. 6; Feb. 11, 1983, p. 3; Oct. 31, 1983, p. 3.

95. *El Mundo,* Oct. 14, 1980, p. 1A; Oct. 24, 1980, p. 15A; Aug. 27, 1980, p. 10C; Sept. 10, 1980, p. 1A; July 22, 1980, p. 10C. For the 1980 PNP program see Partido Nuevo Progresista, *Programa del Partido Nuevo Progresista para el cuatrenio 1981–84* (Hato Rey: Ramallo Bros., 1980). An analysis of the 1980 elections appears in Harold Lidin, "Puerto Rico's 1980 Elections: The Voters Seek the Center," *Caribbean Review* 10, no. 2 (Spring 1981), pp. 28–31; and Alines Frambes Buxeda, "Economía, publicidad y comicios de 1980 en Puerto Rico," *Homines* 5, nos. 1–2 (Jan.–Dec. 1981), pp. 67–101.

96. See Lidin, "Puerto Rico's 1980 Elections"; and Frambes, "Economía, publicidad y comicios de 1980."

97. *San Juan Star,* July 28, 1981, p. 1; *El Mundo,* Feb. 15, 1982, p. 7A; *El Nuevo Día,* May 3, 1981, p. 4.

98. *El Nuevo Día,* June 9, 1981, p. 6; July 1, 1981, p. 32; *San Juan Star,* July 4, 1982, p. 1, and July 12, 1982, p. 6; *El Mundo,* Jan. 20, 1983, p. 6A.

99. *El Nuevo Día,* July 5, 1981, p. 4; Oct. 1, 1981, p. 39; Nov. 4, 1981, p. 37; and July 7, 1982, p. 3; *San Juan Star,* Aug. 4, 1982, p. 18.

100. *San Juan Star,* March 22, 1982, p. 3; Aug. 2, 1981, p. 1; Oct. 13, 1981, p. 3; and Oct. 26, 1981, p. 12; *El Nuevo Día,* May 7, 1981, p. 5, and March 28, 1982, p. 3.

101. *San Juan Star,* Sept. 4, 1981, p. 1.

102. Ibid., Sept. 30, 1981, p. 3, and Jan. 13, 1982, p. 1.

103. Ibid., Nov. 14 and 15, 1982, pp. 3 and 1, respectively; Nov. 19, 1982, p. 1; Feb. 28, 1983, p. 3; and Jan. 30, 1983, p. 2; *El Nuevo Día,* Feb. 1, 1983, p. 4.

104. *San Juan Star,* Nov. 18, 1983, p. 2; *El Nuevo Día,* Sept. 6, 1983, p. 3.

105. Carlos Romero Barceló, "Por el bien de nuestra causa y el bien de Puerto Rico," in *El Nuevo Día,* Feb. 21, 1983, pp. 8–9.

106. Partido Nuevo Progresista, "Declaración de Loíza," in *El Nuevo Día,* March 11, 1983, p. 23.

107. Ibid., March 21, 1983, pp. 2–3; *San Juan Star,* April 29, 1983, p. 34.

108. *El Nuevo Día,* March 14, 1983, p. 28; April 19, 1983, p. 13; May 4, 1983, p. 3; June 11, 1983, p. 5; July 28, 1983, p. 5; and Aug. 8, 1983, p. 2; *El Mundo,* Sept. 26, 1983, p. 30; *San Juan Star,* Nov. 4, 1983, p. 3; Nov. 22, 1983, p. 3.

109. See the article by Fernando Picó in *San Juan Star*, June 28, 1982, p. 18; and ibid., Nov. 22, 1982, p. 3.

110. See the articles by Harry Friedman in *San Juan Star*, Jan. 17, 18, and 19, 1982, p. 1, respectively. Also, Lidin, "Puerto Rico's 1980 Elections," p. 28; *San Juan Star*, Sept. 21, 1981, p. 3; March 11, 1982, p. 3; July 14, 1983, p. 3.

111. The best analysis and summary of the Cerro Maravilla case is by Manny Suárez, *Requiem on Cerro Maravilla: The Police Murders in Puerto Rico and the U.S. Government Coverup* (Maplewood, NJ: Waterfront Press, 1987). Also, Anne Nelson, *Murder Under Two Flags: The U.S., Puerto Rico, and the Cerro Maravilla Cover-up* (New York: Ticknor & Fields, 1986).

112. *El Nuevo Día*, Oct. 26, 1983, pp. 4–5, and Nov. 27, 1983, p. 5.

113. *San Juan Star*, Jan. 13, 1983, p. 6; *El Nuevo Día*, Oct. 16, 1983, p. 3.

114. *San Juan Star*, Feb. 28, 1983, p. 1; March 17, 1982, p. 1; July 8, 1983, p. 1. See also the article by Juan M. García-Passalacqua in ibid., April 25, 1983, p. 31.

115. Ibid., March 19, 1982, p. 1; and *El Nuevo Día*, April 29, 1983, p. 6; Jan. 8, 1983, p. 2; July 23, 1983, p. 2; Sept. 18, 1983, p. 3.

116. J. M. García-Passalacqua, "The Issue of Corruption," *San Juan Star*, Jan. 27, 1983, p. 31.

117. Quote from "El país en el limbo," Editorial, *El Nuevo Día*, March 8, 1981, p. 2. Also by Ferré, Jr., "En camino hacia la recuperación," ibid., May 30, 1982, p. 7.

118. "Un alto en el camino," ibid., Dec. 10, 1981, p. 46. Also, Antonio L. Ferré, "Pan, paz y palabra," ibid., Oct. 26, 1983, pp. 6–7.

119. *El Mundo*, Jan. 12, 1982, p. 8B; *San Juan Star*, Sept. 24, 1982, pp. 5–6; *El Nuevo Día*, July 17, 1983, p. 73, and Sept. 25, 1982, p. 20.

120. Comité para el Desarrollo Económico de Puerto Rico, *La crisis económica de Puerto Rico*.

121. "The No-Status Party," *San Juan Star*, Oct. 6, 1981, p. 15. Also from Archilla, "The Status Syndrome," ibid., Dec. 19, 1981, p. 2.

122. Ibid., Aug. 19, 1982, p. 3; Oct. 2, 1982, p. 3; Nov. 15, 1982, p. 3; and March 12, 1983, p. 1. *El Nuevo Día*, June 1, 1983, pp. 2–4; Oct. 27, 1983, p. 5.

123. *El Mundo*, Nov. 23, 1981, p. 10C; *San Juan Star*, Feb. 8, 1982, p. 6; Oct. 4, 1981, p. 7; Oct. 28, 1982, p. 22; March 11, 1982, p. 3; Jan. 30, 1982, p. 2.

124. *San Juan Star*, Sept. 3, 1982, p. 1.

125. Ibid., March 11, 1982, p. 3; Jan. 30, 1982, p. 2; Sept. 25, 1982, p. 1.

126. *El Nuevo Día*, May 15, 1983, pp. 2–3; *San Juan Star*, July 3, 1983, p. 3; July 15, 1983, p. 1; and Oct. 17, 1983, p. 10.

127. Hernán Padilla, "Voto Explicativo del Doctor Hernán Padilla sobre la Declaración de Loíza," *El Nuevo Día*, Feb. 28, 1983, p. 15; also ibid., June 19, 1983, pp. 10–11.

128. "Voto explicativo," ibid.

129. *San Juan Star*, March 2, 1982, p. 3.

130. Ibid., June 19, 1983, p. 5, and May 5, 1983, p. 1.

131. Talk by Dr. Hernán Padilla, School of General Studies, University of Puerto Rico, Oct. 21, 1983.

132. *El Nuevo Día*, Oct. 3, 1983, p. 4. Also, Partido de Renovación Puertorriqueña, *Plataforma política* (San Juan: PRP, 1983), p. 1.

133. Hernán Padilla, "Hernán Padilla Explains His Objectives," *San Juan Star*, Sept. 6, 1983, p. 16. Also Hernán Padilla, speech before the Association of Food Whole-

salers, Importers, and Retailers of Puerto Rico, Aug. 25, 1983, pp. 2–4; and PRP, *Plataforma política*, p. 1.

134. *El Nuevo Día*, March 24, 1983, p. 12; *San Juan Star*, July 19, 1983, p. 2. Also PRP, *Plataforma política*, pp. 1–2.

135. Padilla, Talk at UPR. Also *San Juan Star*, Oct. 1, 1983, p. 14; and *El Nuevo Día*, Sept. 8, 1983, p. 31.

136. *San Juan Star*, Oct. 19, 1981, p. 3. Padilla, "Padilla Explains His Objectives"; Hernán Padilla, speech before the Association of Public Accountants of Puerto Rico, Sept. 10, 1983, pp. 11–13; and PRP, *Plataforma política*, p. 3.

137. *El Nuevo Día*, March 28, 1983, p. 18; *San Juan Star*, Oct. 26, 1983, p. 14.

138. *El Nuevo Día*, Aug. 26, 1983, p. 6; and PRP, *Plataforma política*, p. 11.

139. *El Mundo*, June 27, 1983, p. 7A; PRP, *Plataforma política*, pp. 27–33; Hernán Padilla, speech before the Puerto Rican Teachers' Association, December 27, 1983.

140. *El Nuevo Día*, Oct. 25, 1983, pp. 2–3.

141. *El Nuevo Día*, March 4, 1983, p. 10; Oct. 27, 1983, p. 49; *San Juan Star*, May 30, 1983, p. 3; July 30, 1983, p. 14; Aug. 19, 1983, p. 3; Sept. 15, 1983, p. 18.

142. *El Nuevo Día*, Nov. 11, 1984, pp. 1–3.

143. Comisión Estatal de Elecciones, *Informe Estadístico Elecciones Generales 1984* (San Juan: Comisión Estatal, n.d.).

144. *El Nuevo Día*, Oct. 30, 1987, pp. 2–3; May 27, 1987, p. 2.

145. *El Reportero*, Oct. 2, 1987, p. 3.

146. *El Nuevo Día*, Nov. 17, 1984, p. 3; June 23, 1986, p. 4; *San Juan Star*, Sept. 15, 1985, p. 2.

147. *El Nuevo Día*, Oct. 5, 1986, p. 8; Feb. 6, 1987, p. 6.

148. Ibid., Nov. 1, 1987, pp. 4, 8; Nov. 2, 1987, p. 7; and Nov. 4, 1987, p. 4.

149. *San Juan Star*, Aug. 1, 1986, p. 12; *El Nuevo Día*, June 4, 1987, p. 16.

150. *San Juan Star*, April 4, 1985, p. 3; Aug. 8, 1986, p. 31.

151. Ibid., May 18, 1987, p. 14; *El Nuevo Día*, May 13, 1987, p. 7.

152. See the article by Oreste Ramos, Jr., in *El Nuevo Día*, March 10, 1987, p. 43.

153. See the article by Antonio Quiñones Calderón in ibid., Sept. 4, 1986, p. 69.

154. See, e.g., ibid., Nov. 3, 1986, p. 51; Nov. 13, 1986, p. 4; and May 31, 1987, p. 8.

155. Words by Romero in ibid., Dec. 29, 1984, p. 2.

Selected Bibliography on the Statehood Movement

Anderson, Robert W. *Gobierno y partidos políticos en Puerto Rico*. Madrid: Editorial Tecnos, 1970.

Barbosa, José Celso. *Orientando al Pueblo, 1900–1921*. Edited by Pilar Barbosa. San Juan: Imprenta Venezuela, 1939.

————. *Problema de razas*. Edited by Pilar Barbosa. San Juan: Imprenta Venezuela, 1937.

Barbosa de Rosario, Pilar. *Manuel F. Rossy y Calderón: Ciudadano cabal*. San Juan: Editorial La obra de José C. Barbosa, 1981.

————. *De Baldorioty a Barbosa: Historia del autonomismo puertorriqueño, 1887–1896*. San Juan: Editorial La Obra de José Celso Barbosa, 1974.

————. *La Comisión Autonomista de 1896*. San Juan: Imprenta Venezuela, 1957.

Bothwell, Reece B. "Puerto Rico en la Federación Americana." *El Estado* 3, no. 18 (April–May 1949): 9, 11.

————. ed. *Puerto Rico: Cien años de lucha política*, 4 vols. Río Piedras: Editorial Universitaria, 1979.

Cebollero, Pedro A. "Statehood for Puerto Rico, Too Late to Go Back on It." *El Estado* 2, no. 7 (Nov.–Dec. 1946): 29–41.

Ciudadanos Pro Estado 51. *La Estadidad: Ideal en marcha*. Pamphlet, 1967.

Colombán Rosario, J. "Statehood: Fifty Years of Struggle: 1898–1948." *El Estado* 3, no. 15 (July–Aug. 1948): 27–29.

Colón, Ramiro L. "Puerto Rico tiene necesidad de resolver el problema de soberanía." *El Estado* 4, no. 27 (Nov.–Dec. 1951): 18–24.

Córdova Díaz, Enrique. "Modern Republicanism and the Statehood Party of Puerto Rico." *El Estado* no. 51 (Nov.–Dec. 1956): 15, 17–18.

Córdova Díaz, Jorge L. "The 1956 Election and Statehood." *El Estado* no. 51 (Nov.–Dec. 1956): 14.

Dávila Colón, Luis R. "The Blood Tax: The Puerto Rican Contribution to the United States War Effort," *Revista del Colegio de Abogados de Puerto Rico* 40, no. 4 (Nov. 1979): 603–39.

Degetau, Federico. *Pequeño resumen de sus obras en favor de la ciudadanía y el estado para Puerto Rico.* Edited by Ana Degetau. Madrid: n.p. 1916.

del Toro Cuebas, Emilio. *Puerto Rico: Nuevo estado de la Unión.* San Juan: APPE, 1943.

Estadistas Unidos. *El ABC de la Estadidad.* Pamphlet, published in May 1967.

Ferré, Luis A. *El propósito humano.* Edited by Antonio Quiñones Calderón. San Juan: Ediciones Nuevas de Puerto Rico, 1972.

———. "Ferré afirma Ley 600 deja indefenso a Puerto Rico en el orden económico." *El Estado* 4, no. 27 (Nov.–Dec. 1951): 25–27.

———. "The Puerto Rican Constitution." *El Estado* 4, no. 22 (Sept.–Oct. 1950): 25, 27.

Figueroa Díaz, Wilfredo. *El movimiento estadista en Puerto Rico.* Hato Rey: Editorial Cultural, 1979.

Finn, Bertram P. "The Economic Implications of Statehood for Puerto Rico: A Preliminary Analysis." In Jorge Heine, ed., *Time for Decision: The United States and Puerto Rico* (Lanham, Maryland: North-South Publ., 1983).

García Calderón, Jose M. "La reacción se ha apoderado del Partido Republicano," *El Mundo,* Oct. 29, 1960, 18–19.

Geigel, Fernando J. *El ideal de un pueblo y los partidos políticos.* San Juan: Tipografía Cantero Fernández, 1940.

Grupo de Investigadores Puertorriqueños. *Breakthrough From Colonialism.* 2 vols. Río Piedras: Editorial de la Universidad de Puerto Rico, 1984.

Gutiérrez, Arsenio. *Estadidad de izquierda.* Hato Rey: Ramallo Bros., n.d.

Informe de los delegados del Partido Republicano de Puerto Rico ante la Convención Nacional Republicana celebrada en Chicago, 21 de junio de 1904. San Juan: Tipografía "El País," 1904.

Iriarte, Celestino. "La Ley 600 del Congreso no ha hecho a Puerto Rico libre de su dependencia Congresional." *El Estado* 4, no. 27 (Nov.–Dec. 1951): 11, 15.

Lugo Silva, Enrique. "Roosevelt's Contribution to Puerto Rican Self-Government." *El Estado* 4, no. 19 (June–July 1949): 11, 15.

Maldonado, Teófilo. *Hombres de primera plana.* San Juan: Puerto Rico: Editorial Campos, 1958.

———. *Rafael Martínez Nadal: Su vida.* San Juan: Imprenta Venezuela, 1937.

Martínez Fernández, Luis. *El Partido Nuevo Progresista.* Río Piedras: Editorial Edil, 1986.

Martínez Saldaña, Ruth. "Anatomía de un partido político en su lucha por llegar al poder: El caso del Partido Nuevo Progresista." Master's Thesis, Sch. of Pub. Admin., UPR, 1972.

Medina González, Julio. *El escándalo.* Mayaguez: Tipografía La Voz de la Patria, 1904.

Mergad, Angel M. *Federico Degetau: Un orientador de su pueblo.* New York: Hispanic Institute, 1944.

Mirabal, Antonio. "Ponce y los partidos políticos de Puerto Rico." *El Día* (Ponce), Dec. 18, 1949, 27, 31–32.

Negrón Portillo, Mariano. "El liderato anexionista antes y después del cambio de soberanía." *Revista del Colegio de Abogados de Puerto Rico* (October 1972): 369–91.

Padilla, Hernán. "Padilla Explains His Objectives." *San Juan Star,* Sept. 6, 1983, 16.

————. "Voto explicativo del Doctor Hernán Padilla sobre la Declaración de Loíza." *El Nuevo Día,* Feb. 28, 1983.

Pagán, Bolívar. *Historia de los partidos políticos puertorriqueños.* 2 vols. San Juan: M. Pareja, 1972.

Partido Estadista Puertorriqueño. "Programas políticos." *El Mundo,* Oct. 31, 1948, 12.

Partido Nuevo Progresista. "Declaración de Loíza." *El Nuevo Día,* March 11, 1983, 23.

————. *Programa del Partido Nuevo Progresista para el cuatrenio 1981–84.* Hato Rey: Ramallo Bros., 1980.

————. "Programa 1972." *Guía para las elecciones 1972: programas oficiales.* San Juan: Banco Popular, 1972.

Partido de Renovación Puertorriqueña. *Plataforma política.* N.p., 1983.

Partido Republicano Puertorriqueño. *Constitución y plataforma, 1923.* San Juan: Tipografía Germán Díaz, 1923.

————. *Asamblea Republicana celebrada en San Juan, 1 y 2 de julio de 1899.* San Juan: Imprenta de "El País," 1899.

Partido Revolucionario Cubano. *Memoria de los trabajos realizados por la Sección Puerto Rico del Partido Revolucionario Cubano, 1895 a 1898.* New York: A. W. Howes, n.d.

Pedreira, Antonio. *Un hombre del pueblo: José Celso Barbosa.* San Juan: Instituto de Cultura Puertorriqueña, 1965.

Pietrantoni, Julio. "Statehood, Our Supreme Anxiety." *El Estado* 3, no. 15 (July–August 1948): 35–37.

Ponsa Feliú, Francisco. "United States Citizenship: The Gateway to Statehood." *El Estado* 1, no. 3 (Jan.–Feb. 1946): 11, 27, 29.

Quintero-Rivera, A. G. *Conflictos de clase y política en Puerto Rico.* Río Piedras: Ediciones Huracán, 1976.

Quiñones Calderón, Antonio. *Del plebiscito a La Fortaleza.* Hato Rey: Ramallo Bros., 1982.

————. *Que el record hable: La obra de Carlos Romero Barceló.* Hato Rey: Ramallo Bros., 1980.

————. *La obra de Luis A. Ferré en La Fortaleza.* Santurce: Servicios Editoriales, 1975.

Ramírez, Rafael L. *El arrabal y la política.* Río Piedras: Editorial Universitaria, 1977.

Ramos, Aarón G., ed. *Las ideas anexionistas en Puerto Rico bajo la dominación norteamericana.* Río Piedras: Ediciones Huracán, 1987.

Ramos, Pepe. *Ferré: Autobiografía dialogada.* San Juan: Panavox Multimedia, 1976.

Ramos de Santiago, Carmen. *El gobierno de Puerto Rico.* Río Piedras: Editorial Universitaria, 1970.

Rivera Santiago, Rafael. *Comprensión y análisis.* San Juan: Imprenta Venezuela, 1938.

Romero Barceló, Carlos. "Por el bien de nuestra causa y el bien de Puerto Rico." *El Nuevo Día,* Feb. 21, 1983, 8–9.

————. "Puerto Rico, U.S.A.: The Case for Statehood." *Foreign Affairs* 59, no. 1 (Fall 1980): 60–81.

———. *Forjando el futuro*. Edited by Antonio Quiñones Calderón. Hato Rey: Ramallo Bros., 1978.

———. "Should Puerto Rico Be a State?" *U.S. News and World Report* 82 (April 11, 1977): 47–48.

———. "Exención contributiva: Una polémica que se traduce en 5 puntos para traer la estadidad por filtración." *Avance*, November 18, 1974, 6–7.

———. *La estadidad es para los pobres*. San Juan: n.p., 1973.

———. "La estadidad no será relegada." *Avance*, November 25, 1972, 8–10.

Sánchez Morales, Luis. *De antes y de ahora*. Madrid: Centro Editorial Rubén Darío, 1936.

Suárez, Manny. *Requiem on Cerro Maravilla*. Maplewood, New Jersey: Waterfront Press, 1987.

Todd, Roberto H. *Patriotas puertorriqueños*. Madrid: Ediciones Iberoamericanas, 1965.

———. *La invasión americana: Como surgió la idea de traer la guerra a Puerto Rico*. San Juan: Cantero Fernández, 1938.

———. *José Julio Henna, 1848–1924*. San Juan: Cantero Fernández, 1930.

Torregrosa, Angel M. *Miguel Angel García Méndez*. Puerto Rico: n.p., 1939.

U.S. Department of State. *Puerto Rico's Status: A Problem for the Eighties*. Report prepared by Dolores Wahl for the Executive Seminar in National and International Affairs, Department of State, April 1980.

———. *The Problem of Puerto Rico's Political Status*. Case study by C. Arthur Borg. Seventeenth Session, Senior Seminar in Foreign Policy, Department of State, 1974–75.

U.S. General Accounting Office. *Puerto Rico's Political Future: A Divisive Issue with Many Dimensions*. Washington, D.C.: GAO, 1981.

U.S. Library of Congress. Congressional Research Service. *Puerto Rico: Commonwealth, Statehood, or Independence?* Prepared by Peter Sheridan. Washington, D.C.: Congressional Research Service, 1978.

———. *Treating Puerto Rico as a State Under Federal Tax and Expenditure Programs: A Preliminary Economic Analysis*. Prepared by Donald W. Kiefer. Washington, D.C.: Congressional Research Service, 1977.

———. *Puerto Rico: Independence or Statehood?: A Survey of Historical, Political, and Socioeconomic Factors, with Pro and Con Arguments*. Prepared by William R. Tansill. Washington, D.C.: Congressional Research Service, 1977.

United States-Puerto Rico Commission on the Status of Puerto Rico. *Status of Puerto Rico*. 4 vols. Washington, D.C.: U.S. Government Printing Office, 1966.

Villar Martínez, Ilya, and Haroldo Dilla Alfonso. "Las tendencias anexionistas en el proceso político puertorriqueño." *El Caribe Contemporáneo* no. 6 (June 1982): 70–91.

Index

About the Author

EDGARDO MELÉNDEZ is an assistant professor of Political Science at the University of Puerto Rico, Río Piedras Campus.